Walter Hill

Also by Wayne Byrne

*Welcome to Elm Street: Inside the Film
and Television Nightmares* (McFarland, 2022)

Burt Reynolds on Screen (McFarland, 2020)

By Wayne Byrne and Nick McLean

*Nick McLean Behind the Camera: The Life and Works
of a Hollywood Cinematographer* (McFarland, 2020)

Walter Hill

The Cinema of a Hollywood Maverick

WAYNE BYRNE

Foreword by Allan Graf

McFarland & Company, Inc., Publishers
Jefferson, North Carolina

ISBN (print) 978-1-4766-8810-7
ISBN (ebook) 978-1-4766-4887-3

LIBRARY OF CONGRESS AND BRITISH LIBRARY
CATALOGUING DATA ARE AVAILABLE

Library of Congress Control Number 2022044349

© 2022 Wayne Byrne. All rights reserved

No part of this book may be reproduced or transmitted in any form or by any means, electronic or mechanical, including photocopying or recording, or by any information storage and retrieval system, without permission in writing from the publisher.

Front cover image: director Walter Hill
on the set of *Johnny Handsome* (1989)

Printed in the United States of America

*McFarland & Company, Inc., Publishers
Box 611, Jefferson, North Carolina 28640
www.mcfarlandpub.com*

To the memory of C. James "Jimmy" Lewis

Acknowledgments

I would like to thank the following people for their contributions: Lloyd Ahern, Alessandro Camon, Neil Canton, Ken Friedman, John Fusco, Bob Gale, Gina Gershon, Maggie Greenwald, Larry Gordon, Larry Gross, Nicholas Guest, Bobby LaBonge, Matthew Leonetti, William Malone, David Mansfield, Dan Moore, Michael D. O'Shea, Michael Paré, Van Dyke Parks, Craig Raiche, William Sadler, Jack Sholder, and Herschel Weingrod.

Special thanks to Allan Graf for a beautiful foreword of great personal insight and emotion.

To Walter Hill, life and cinema are all the richer for you and your films. Thank you for taking part in this celebration of your art.

Sincere gratitude to Jeff Sanderson of Chasen PR for connecting me with Walter Hill and for your help in arranging those crucial conversations. To Paul Farren for conducting fascinating, in-depth interviews with three important contributors to this project (Camon, Friedman, and Gross), you gathered some truly essential, insightful information. To Layla Milholen and all at McFarland, thank you deeply.

Much love to my parents Angela and Pat Byrne. To Jenny Byrne for your warm support and understanding as I became consumed by the considerable work involved in creating this book. And to Amanda Kramer, for our friendship and your always heartening encouragement; your words have buoyed me through many long days and late nights of writing.

Table of Contents

Acknowledgments vi
Foreword by Allan Graf 1
Introduction 5

One—Walter: Writer 7
Two—Hard Times, Harder Men 17
Three—Tonight Is What It Means to Be Young 68
Four—"Blow something up!" 96
Five—Tales for Television and Way Out West 127
Six—Same Director, Different Hollywood 176
Seven—"It's a collaboration": A Celebration of Walter Hill 198

Interviewees and Dates 205
Index 207

Foreword
by Allan Graf

Walter Hill changed my career and my life. That's a fact. How that happened goes all the way back to 1977. Back then, stunt people could walk around the studio backlots and speak to stunt coordinators, trying to get work by handing out résumés and pictures. One day I happened to be walking around on the Fox lot looking for employment when I heard someone yell out, "Hey, Allan!" This was Pat Kehoe, an assistant director I had worked with before on my very first movie, *Gus*. Pat asked me what I was doing and I told him I was trying to get some work, and I asked him what he was up to. He said, "I'm working on a film called *The Driver*. I want you to meet the director; he is a die-hard USC fan. Do you want to come and meet him?'" And I said, "Sure! Who is the director?" and Pat said, "It's Walter Hill!" I had never heard of Walter Hill before, didn't know him from anybody. So I walk in and sitting there are Larry Gordon, Frank Marshall, and Walter Hill. Pat begins making introductions: "Walter, I'd like you to meet this guy," and Walter says, "He looks familiar to me. What's his name?" Pat says, "This is Allan Graf," and Walter is stunned. "Allan Graf! Number 61, USC Trojans offensive guard. Holy smokes!" I said, "Yeah, that's me! How are you doing, Walter?" And we hit it off immediately. Walter was such a Trojans fanatic that he knew all about my life as a football player. We sat down for a half hour in front of Larry and Frank just talking USC football, and they all got into it as well. Then Walter said, "I've got a part for you in this movie. You can play a cop." And I just said, "Okay, that's awesome!" So I ended up playing this cop and I got to say a couple of lines with the famous French actress Isabelle Adjani. In that moment, my very long friendship with Walter began. Something about him and me just clicked in that moment. I know a lot of it had to do with football—he loved the sport so much and I played on one of the best teams in college football history, the 1972 National Championship team. So that was a big deal.

After *The Driver*, Walter went off to make *The Warriors*. However, he told me he couldn't use me on that movie, and then I started thinking to myself, "Well, that's the end of that! Loyalty only goes so far." But I was dead wrong. Walter soon called me up and said, "Hey, I want you to come and work on this movie I'm doing called *The Long Riders*. I want you to play a part in the movie and you can do the stunts." I said, "Great! I'm with you." Then I spent eight weeks working on *The Long Riders*.

It was on that movie where our relationship started to get really strong. We became buddies on that show. Walter and I would throw a tennis ball around in between shots, and we also started our thumb wrestling gags then. Of course, I always let him beat me, but he would always have to brag that he won. He didn't really, but I let him have his moment. I think our friendship broke the monotony for him. I was someone he could talk to where the conversation didn't have to be about the script. We could talk about anything: sports, world events, family. It got us briefly away from the movie. I like to think that helped him. I'm sure it didn't, but it may have. From that movie on, I always wanted to perform the biggest stunt that I could for him. I wanted him to know that whatever I said I could do, I would do it. I always give 110 percent for Walter, and he could see that from early on and I think he liked that kind of attitude. He knew that the work ethic and skill that I brought to him as a stuntman I would also bring to him as a second unit director and as a stunt coordinator. And we ended up working together ever since.

One of the greatest things about my career working alongside Walter is that every time we make a movie I learn more about the process, about myself as a filmmaker, and about Walter. Going from *The Driver* all the way up to *Dead for a Dollar* has been the greatest learning experience about the art and craft of moviemaking. It has given me a great career and I wouldn't have that without Walter bringing me along with him and affording me such opportunities to step up and prove myself. My work with Walter has been the greatest education and the best life experience I could ever have received.

How much can one say about a man who changed another man's stars entirely? How much can I say about Walter Hill? You just never know what is going to turn your life around. In this case, one person comes into your life and changes the course forever. If I hadn't seen Pat Kehoe that day on the 20th Century–Fox lot, I would never have been introduced to Walter Hill. My life could have been different. In fact, I know it would have been different. But God had a plan and I guess He wanted me and Walter to get together. And for Walter to meet me in that office and know who I was, "Allan Graf, number 61," and talk about me the way he did in front of those big-time producers, it just blew my mind. And then to say, "I've got a part for you." Well, that just changed everything for me. He was so kind to give me these opportunities and I'm just thankful that I came through for him and that he appreciated what I did. I don't know if I'll ever be able to repay him. Perhaps the only way I can show my gratitude is that whenever he works I will be there for him. I will work with Walter anytime. Whenever he needs me, I'm here for him. I'm blessed to know Walter, and my family is blessed to know him, because being able to work like that and to have made the living that I did has given my family so much. I get to say that I worked with one of the greatest directors in Hollywood, but I also get to say that he is my friend and my brother, and that means a lot. It is very emotional for me to write about Walter, because we have been friends for 40 years and the impact he has had on my life is immeasurable.

There are not enough words to say about Walter Hill, but Wayne Byrne has plenty of words to say about him in this book. Amazingly, Wayne takes us through every one of Walter's movies and we hear from many people who respect

Walter, having collaborated with him many times over the years. Wayne has done a really good job. He digs deep into each and every one of Walter's movies, bringing back great memories and providing keen insights into what makes them so special. Walter Hill deserves to be celebrated this way, and I'm honored to be part of it.

Allan Graf on the set of Walter Hill's *Last Man Standing* (courtesy Allan Graf).

Allan Graf is an actor, stunt coordinator, and second unit director who has worked with Walter Hill on films such as The Driver, The Long Riders, Streets of Fire, Brewster's Millions, Crossroads, Extreme Prejudice, Red Heat, Johnny Handsome, Another 48 Hrs., Trespass, Geronimo: An American Legend, Wild Bill, Last Man Standing, *and* Dead for a Dollar. *Throughout his prolific career, Graf has appeared in many television and motion picture productions, including* T.J. Hooker, The A-Team, Tales from the Crypt, Robocop, Universal Soldier, L.A. Confidential, Boogie Nights, Deadwood, *and many more.*

Introduction

"Never trust the artist. Trust the art. The artist is deceptive and unreliable."
—Walter Hill

If one is to subscribe to the Auteur Theory as espoused by the young French filmmakers and critics of Cahiers du Cinéma circa the mid-20th century, Walter Hill must be a classic example of a film director who befits that revered status of *auteur*. These artists are celebrated for being recognizably consistent in their themes and aesthetics, for leaving a distinct artistic flavor across their work, and for exerting a level of control over the final product despite the usual commercial pressures and bureaucratic dictates of Hollywood studios. Hill's own heroes of the form are those who were considered by François Truffaut, Jean-Luc Godard, and the rest of the French New Wavers to be the pioneering auteurs of American cinema: Howard Hawks, Raoul Walsh, John Ford. These directors worked most prolifically and successfully within cinema's Golden Age, when Hollywood conducted business with a factory mentality. Directors and stars were contracted to studios to provide product and had to work within the constraints of tighter censorship and production codes, in a culture that hadn't yet approbated the director as a visionary and celebrity whose name carried more cultural weight than the studios they worked for. There were exceptions, of course—D.W. Griffith, with his signature literally adorning the intertitles of his silent epics, is perhaps the first director to draw attention to himself as the ultimate authority of his art and was duly celebrated as a pioneering artist, but this was before the studio system established itself and its corporate business model, when directors weren't considered uniquely innovative artists in the vein of Griffith but journeymen moviemakers. But the studio craftsmen Hill greatly admired and were later identified as supreme artists dealt with themes that Hill himself would parlay into his stories across the ensuing decades—themes of strong survivors of tough environs, of hard men dealing with intimacy and emotion, within grand evocations of the American West, whether the milieu was urban or rural; it was the cinema of John Ford, Howard Hawks, and Raoul Walsh. Those directors, along with other notables, were able to bring an unmistakable sense of mastery to their work, long before the New Hollywood movement of the late sixties took hold and executives willingly conferred more artistic authority to their visionary filmmakers. Like those giants, Hill is a genre chameleon whose stamp is both unmistakable and indelible, his work appealing to casual mainstream audiences and impassioned film enthusiasts alike. In contradiction to auteur anointment, Hill is transparently collaborative, as quick to hail the input and ideas of those he surrounds himself with as he is to take responsibility for his vision being the driving force of the end result. The following document of Hill's life in cinema is one that celebrates not just the director himself, but the joint effort of many artists and technicians whose collaborative effort brought to the screen a work that is credited as "A Walter Hill Film." This book, aided as it is by the words of Hill and many of those who worked alongside him over the last five decades, is a journey through several decades of Hollywood filmmaking and an investigation into what makes Hill's such a brilliant, bold, and bravura body of work.

ONE

Walter: Writer

It is worth noting that Hill's entry into Hollywood came at the aforementioned moment in movie history when directors were gaining momentum as artists of singular vision and appeared to wield more authorial control over the final product than ever before. I'm referring to the New Hollywood era, that period that could be said to have been instigated in the mid-sixties with groundbreaking, youth-oriented films that captured the attention of the baby boomers as they came of age. Striking films such as *Mickey One, Seconds, Bonnie and Clyde, The Graduate, Night of the Living Dead, Easy Rider,* and *Five Easy Pieces* wooed a new generation of film critics and viewers with their unique style, social conscience, and political relevance. And while these films beguiled the emerging audiences with experimental, artistic use of film grammar, other films used more classical filmmaking modes but carried with them a greater sense of realism and, with the breakdown of the Motion Picture Production Code and shifting cultural mores, an increase in on-screen sex and violence. Filmmakers like Sam Peckinpah, Don Siegel, and William Friedkin were now able to take American Cinema to darker, grittier places with works like *The Wild Bunch, Dirty Harry,* and *The French Connection*. And working in the background of this heady, revolutionary milieu was Walter Hill. The future director's first foray into the world of filmmaking was working as second assistant director on notable New Hollywood films such as Peter Yates's *Bullitt* (1968) and Woody Allen's *Take the Money and Run* (1969).

"We were all just trying to make a living at the time," Hill says. "There is a reverence for the '70s, which is very comprehensible, but for us the studio system still seemed to be the power. It was clear that old parts of the studio system was falling apart but it wasn't so clear that it was breaking up entirely. There was a moment where all the executives wore dark, well-tailored suits and then suddenly in 1970, after *Easy Rider* came out, they all started wearing buckskin coats and blue jeans. And that casual style has prevailed since. That was a big changeover from the old days when they wanted to look like bankers, to be worthy of trust."

For Hill, the position of second A.D. was an education on the politics of filmmaking as much as it was practice for running the logistical elements of a movie set. But filling out time cards was not what Hill had in mind for himself. His ambitions were far more literary.

"I always imagined that I could make a living for myself as a writer," Hill says. "This is both in high school and college, once I had retired my athletic ambitions … or should I say, my athletic ambitions had been retired. I used to draw a bit, but I realized that wasn't going to be the calling. I really had this idea that I could make some kind of living as a writer. Whether or not I was going to write plays or novels, I'm not sure, but I was very interested in movies and the idea of screenplay writing did fascinate me. I finished school and got drafted but flunked my physical, so they made me what they call '1-Y.' I was in perfect health, but I had childhood asthma, so they didn't want me, and they put me in that reserve category called '1-Y.' So, suddenly I had to make a living. I had been considering going to New York and trying to get into journalism and then I got a call out of nowhere which led me to doing some library research for an outfit that used to make documentaries, which were actually little dramatic films for a subcontractor of *Encyclopaedia Britannica*. I had met these people at a party where we were drinking and talking, and I had been a history major and lit minor in school, and they got a contract to do some films and needed somebody to do some research for them. It was the only job on offer, and it paid almost nothing. So, I came up to what I call 'East Hollywood' and suddenly I was just in it, and I knew, sink or swim, I was going to make a living at this. After around three or four days hanging around these people, I offered to write a script for them and a few days after that I announced I could direct one, neither of which happened. There's that famous Samuel Johnson quote: 'We enter the arena uncalled to seek our fortune and hazard disgrace.' So, I decided I would hazard disgrace. Of course, I had to make a living, I had to have some income, so I did production work, which led me into being an assistant director. But I always thought of myself as a writer. I was always writing at night, which was tough to do because working in production, the hours were long. That went on for about three or four years. I would save my money and take some time off, because I couldn't work and write at the same time. But the biggest problem was I wouldn't finish. I must have started six or seven scripts over those years, maybe more. I would write half and then abandon. After working on *Take the Money and Run*, I thought, 'If you think you're a writer, you better finish something,' and once I started finishing scripts I was able to sell and make a living rather rapidly. I sold a western and I wrote *Hickey & Boggs*, and then I did a rewrite on a comedy for which I ended up getting sole credit, or sole blame."

Hickey & Boggs was Hill's first script to go into production and was released by United Artists in 1972. The film is an intriguing crime caper starring Robert Culp and Bill Cosby, directed by the former, and unleashed at a time when the genre was experiencing a renaissance. Prior to the New Hollywood movement bringing back crime stories and in a far more unflinching fashion than ever before, the underworld film wasn't quite the major Hollywood product it once was; the headline-ripping storylines of the thirties and forties police procedurals and gangster melodramas were largely replaced with musical and historical spectacles of the fifties and early sixties. But the new wave of American filmmaking injected new life into the genre, largely thanks to the relaxing of what was acceptable on the screen after the censorious Motion Picture Production Code came to an end in 1966. Arthur Penn's *Bonnie and Clyde* and John Boorman's *Point Blank* were artistically far removed from the traditional crime film of yore, but they brought with them an intensity and grittiness not seen in American Cinema since Edward G. Robinson and James Cagney were roaming the Warner Bros. backlot resplendent in tommy gun and tilted fedora. These new American films were infused with an idiosyncratic auteur resolve and artistic freedom, the kind that could be seen in interesting work that followed in the genre, with films such as Leonard Kastle's *The Honeymoon Killers*, Roger Corman's *Bloody Mama*, and Peter Bogdanovich's *Targets*, while the so-called blaxploitation movement reinvigorated with the likes of *Shaft*, *Across 110th Street*, and *Superfly*. Around the same time there were superior crime films coming from further afield, including Seijun Suzuki's *Branded to Kill*, Jean-Pierre Melville's *Le Samourai*, Elia Petri's *Investigation of a Citizen Under Suspicion*, and Mike Hodges's *Get Carter*.

Hickey & Boggs suffered commercially, although its influence can be felt in the crime pictures to come in the ensuing decades. The film tells the story of the titular duo of private eyes tracking down a missing woman with connections to a crime syndicate operating out of Los Angeles. It opens interestingly with a juxtaposition of the male physique, from Lester Fletcher's slight and dandy queer fence, Rice, grotesquely glistening as he sunbathes next to a children's playground, to Matt Bennett's hulking henchman, Fatboy, equally as oiled but in the more mechanical confines of the gym. In contrast, both Hickey and Boggs are sluggish, unkempt, and as poor in diet as they are in wealth. Cynical and bickering, the pair are hard-bitten by their work navigating the criminal underworld for little financial reward. A contemporary viewing of *Hickey & Boggs* can't help but make one feel as if the film is setting the template for the entire buddy-cop subgenre to come in the ensuing decades, with many traces of it to be found in the future clichés of Richard Donner's *Lethal Weapon*, the film that would cement certain stereotypical tropes for the casual viewing public in 1987. Donner's hit replays several scenarios from Culp's film: the distraught Hickey phoning in his estranged wife's murder from the scene of the crime is reminiscent of Detective Murtaugh calling bereaved father Michael Hunsaker to tell him that his daughter Amanda has been killed; Michael Moriarty's icy blond, Ballard, Mr. Brill's second-in-command lieutenant, seems a progenitor of Gary Busey's golden-haired mercenary, Mr. Joshua, and similarly appears as a helicopter sniper ambushing the film's heroes over a dust-swarmed shootout. Another allusion to Culp's film is the demise of the villain, who is hemmed in and struggling to escape an upside-down petroleum-leaking vehicle before it blows up spectacularly, an explosive fate also suffered by Mitchell Ryan's General McAllister in Donner's picture. As with *Hickey & Boggs*, *Lethal Weapon* suggests a corrupt offshoot of the Vietnam War is assisting in the illicit proceedings, with ex-soldiers using their skills in the criminal underworld. While *Lethal Weapon* went on to spawn its own hugely successful franchise and influence a raft of imitators, *Hickey & Boggs* has become largely forgotten within the cinematic consciousness. However, the film is worthy of reinvestigation, if not to enjoy its seedy underworld environs as one navigates its intricate plot, then to note Hill making his first mark on the film industry in forming the structure of an entire subgenre that would become a Hollywood mainstay ever since, and one which he would further refine and define in 1982 with *48 Hrs*.

In the same year that *Hickey & Boggs* failed, another film written by Hill succeeded. *The Getaway* is a taut action thriller based on Jim Thompson's 1958 novel

Robert Culp (left) and Bill Cosby star as *Hickey & Boggs* (1972).

of the same name. Thompson adapted his book into a screenplay, which was to be directed by Peter Bogdanovich after his acclaimed film *The Last Picture Show* got the attention of film star Steve McQueen and producer David Foster. Bogdanovich hired Hill to rewrite Thompson's draft, but then Bogdanovich would also be relieved of his directorial duties and be replaced by Sam Peckinpah. If the material seemed an unusual choice for Bogdanovich, it was ideal for Peckinpah, who was coming off the raging controversy of *Straw Dogs*. Here the maverick filmmaker returns to his recurrent themes and depictions of outlaws who belong to the wilder West of a bygone America, who live by their own criminal code of honor while envisioning a new way of life if they can just live past the next gunfight. *The Getaway* is the story of Carter "Doc" McCoy (Steve McQueen) and his wife, Carol McCoy (Ali McGraw), who are manipulated into a bank heist that goes desperately wrong. Doc is four years into a 10-year stretch at a Texas prison when he is suddenly granted early parole thanks to conniving businessman Jack Beynon (Ben Johnson), who wants Doc to take part in a daring bank heist along with his traitorous henchmen, Frank (Bo Hopkins) and Rudy (Al Lettieri). This setup involves multiple double crosses, as Carol and Jack had originally planned for her to kill Doc, but she decides to kill Jack instead. Meanwhile, Rudy blasts Frank and plans on doing the same to Doc, who is wise to Rudy's kind and anticipates the impending betrayal. What Doc didn't predict was that Carol would set him up.

Much has been made of Hill's connection to Sam Peckinpah over the years, with many critics and fans noting shared themes and even aesthetic similarities between these two giants of action cinema. For Hill, this professional association meant the opportunity for a personal insight into the mind of a filmmaker who is spoken about in the same kind of reverence as other masters of cinema. "I am a tremendous admirer of Sam's, particularly of the quality of his best work. He did three or four movies which are quite wonderful and which are in the league of Kurosawa,

Ali McGraw and Steve McQueen making their getaway in Sam Peckinpah's explosive action thriller *The Getaway* (1972), written by Walter Hill.

real masterworks of achievement. Sam and I were friends. He wasn't the Minotaur that people sometimes ascribed in my relationship with him, it really wasn't true. We got along quite well and I liked him enormously. He was certainly a troubled fellow; he was alcoholic, he was very controversial, he was also very sensitive. In the years after we worked together, I'd run into him once in a while, and there was always something vivid when you dealt with him, in a positive way. The simple truth of it is that the very large commercial success of *The Getaway* is what got me a chance to direct."

"Walter liked Peckinpah a lot," says screenwriter and future Hill collaborator Larry Gross, "but he certainly had mixed feelings about him. He described that Peckinpah could be difficult to deal with as a human being, which is something Walter would not approve of, but he remained a great admirer of Peckinpah's art and was influenced by it. He is profoundly indebted to him because writing for Peckinpah was instrumental in getting his career going. I wasn't around to observe their relationship but what I know of it is that there was something of a father-son relationship about it, but I don't think Peckinpah had the presence of mind to be anybody's father, and that's just my intuition."

Interestingly, Hill's script for *The Getaway* opens with a dedication to the great Old Hollywood director Raoul Walsh. After giving John Wayne his debut leading role in *The Big Trail* (1930), Walsh went on to make some of the best hard-boiled crime dramas of the Golden Age, including *The Roaring Twenties* (1939), *They Drive by Night* (1940), and *White Heat* (1949), as well as a couple of pictures that would evidently provide inspiration for *The Getaway*, namely *High Sierra* (1941) and its western remake, *Colorado Territory* (1949). The former film opens just as Peckinpah's film does, with career criminal Roy Earle (Humphrey Bogart) leaving behind his life in prison to start afresh. But this premature release is orchestrated by corrupt officials and aging gangster Big Mac, who conspire to enlist Earle to pull off a major heist along with a dubious pair of dishonorable thieves. Affairs of the heart vie for Earle's attention, as the simple life he yearns for can never truly be embraced as long as he is loyal to the life of crime.

"My script deviated from the novel to a fair amount," Hill says, "and as it did it became much more like a genre film back in the forties, something like *High Sierra*, which I always found to be a very admirable movie, as was Walsh's western remake with Joel McCrea, *Colorado Territory*, which is wondrous. It's probably better than the original. So I put a dedication to Raoul Walsh on the script, a nice gesture. I had a friend who said, 'You dumb son of a bitch, Raoul isn't on the distribution list, but he's still alive, so get his address and send it to him. He'd probably be very pleased.' I thought that was a good idea, so I got his address, wrote him a note, and sent him the script. He wrote a letter back, which I thought I had lost and I actually found it a couple of weeks ago, but out of that we had a phone call and he told me to go visit him. He lived out in Simi Valley; it was a very open country back then but it's all tract houses now. He was quite old at this point, way into his eighties and almost totally blind; he had the patch over one eye and he was wearing these dark prescription glasses and part of the glasses were taped off too. His wife really helped him as he was so vision impaired and he was having a hard time. We had this pleasant conversation for an hour or so and Raoul said, 'Save your money!' I thought it was a very Ben Franklin thing of 'hang on to what you've got' but I later realized that there was a much deeper thing that he was trying to tell me, and that was financial independence is the only hedge you have against working for 'them' rather than yourself. It gives you freedom, if you are not worried about making your house payment or sending your kid to school. You don't have to be stinking rich, but if you can get to where you have freedom and independence as a filmmaker, you can choose the jobs you want, you don't have to take something just because someone called you up and said, 'There's a start date and a salary.'"

Walsh's advice was sound and inspiring, but it would be another three years before Hill would step behind the camera on his directorial debut. In the meantime, Hill continued writing scripts, including a comedy that Hill was hired to rewrite called *The Thief Who Came to Dinner*, originally written by Oliver Hailey. This old-fashioned caper tells the tale of bored computer programmer Webster McGee (Ryan O'Neal), who takes up jewel thievery as a new way of life, targeting Texan high society and liberating them of their stones as they wine and dine among their bourgeois inner circle. Webster's way into this world is through Gene Henderling (Charles Cioffi), a businessman with a few skeletons in his closet that he would like to keep there. McGee robs and blackmails Henderling into introducing him to this elite social circle as a prospective entrepreneur. McGee is also aided by Laura Keaton (Jacqueline Bisset), a beautiful socialite who falls for his cheeky charms. However, their seemingly flawless plan faces disruption by weary insurance investigator Dave Reilly (Warren Oates), who is hot on McGee's heels on behalf of Texas Mutual Insurance.

"You know, Wayne, you are one of the few people who has ever asked me about *The Thief Who Came to Dinner* and one of the few people who has seen it. I ended up getting sole screen credit for it, which I probably don't deserve. Oliver Hailey was the original writer but for some reason they just credited me. It's a very old-fashioned movie, like something from the forties or fifties, or even the thirties. It was made out of time and it did not find an audience. As far as I can tell it is an entirely lost film.

People mention *Hickey & Boggs* to me now and then and I can't say they rush over to me in restaurants to ask me about it, but there are some people who know it and occasionally it comes up in conversation. But I don't think anybody has ever mentioned *The Thief Who Came to Dinner* to me."

All the ingredients for a hit are here: beautiful stars with good chemistry in O'Neal and Bisset; supporting players of considerable charm and talent, including Warren Oates, Ned Beatty, John Hillerman, and a regrettably underused Jill Clayburgh. But despite such audience-pleasing pedigree, something went wrong. The film was made by the legendary television partnership of Bud Yorkin and Norman Lear, who together operated Tandem Productions, which produced a number of successful sitcoms. The duo had dabbled in feature films with the satirical *Never Too Late* (1965) and *Divorce American Style* (1967), with Yorkin directing and Lear producing. Coming soon after his star-making turn in Peter Bogdanovich's *What's Up, Doc?* the role of Webster McGee seemed to be tailor-made for a romantic rogue such as Ryan O'Neal. The film trades on a jovial atmosphere that moves along at a brisk pace, and perfectly scoring such shenanigans is Henry Mancini. The composer supplies the film with a nimble, groovy soundtrack with congas, keyboards, and big brass providing the soundtrack to McGee's burglary endeavors. As a light caper with a dash of romance it really should have been sufficient to satisfy the Ryan O'Neal constituency, but while the actor's throwback to Hollywood screwball comedies, *What's Up, Doc?*, proved a massive hit with audiences and critics (accruing a massive $66 million at the box office), the star's commercial allure did not carry over into the similarly toned *The Thief Who Came to Dinner*. The film tanked without a trace and remains virtually unseen.

"The problem is that the movie got messed up in postproduction quite a bit and some things got cut," Hill admits. "I ended up becoming friends with Warren Oates on it. I loved Warren, and he had much more to do in the version that I wrote, but in the old tradition they just cut to the leads. Warren always said it was one of his favorite parts and I wish more of his material had been used. I thought Jill Clayburgh's scene was quite good. She is only in that one scene, but what she did was great. I knew Jackie a bit because I had been second assistant director on *Bullitt* and she, of course, was the female lead; she is very pleasant but I never really knew her that well. *The Thief Who Came to Dinner* was right in Ryan's wheelhouse. The first time I met him was on the set of *What's Up, Doc?* when I was up in San Francisco writing *The Getaway*. It was on that set where I first met Frank Marshall and Neil Canton, who were also working on the movie and who I would go on to work with a lot. I'm still friends with both."

The next two films to be produced bearing Walter Hill's name as writer or cowriter were star vehicles for Paul Newman: *The Mackintosh Man*, directed by the legendary John Huston, and *The Drowning Pool*, directed by Stuart Rosenberg. Neither film was a passion project for Hill; in fact, *The Mackintosh Man* was a reluctant job of work for the writer as his involvement in the production arose from a contract dispute with Warner Bros., who were threatening him with a lawsuit that stemmed from the script sale of *Hickey & Boggs*.

"I wrote *Hickey & Boggs* as an original screenplay for Warner Bros. and they

Warren Oates (left) and Ryan O'Neal play cat and mouse in *The Thief Who Came to Dinner* (1973).

sold it to United Artists for quite a bit more money than they had paid me. I had thought in the spirit of the beehive that we could share the bounty a bit, rather than the penurious amount that I had been paid to write the thing. And at the same time I was under contract for them to write another original script, a western, but I just said, 'Fuck that!' I wasn't going to write any more for them. I didn't understand the studio to be a medium of exchange to other studios. They're not a bank. I thought we were supposed to be making movies. But I had certainly made a deal to do this western and there was a lot of argy-bargy. My agent got in there and said, 'Look, you guys have got some projects, send him a few books, he'll figure one out that he'll adapt.'"

Warner Bros. duly sent Hill a selection of books that they owned and he soon came across one called *The Freedom Trap*, written by English novelist Desmond Bagley and which was, by Hill's admission, not good to begin with. However, adapting the book into what would become *The Mackintosh Man* was enough to help Hill out of the legal wrangle he found himself in with the studio.

"The book was kind of a mess, and so was the script. I did a workmanlike job on it to get out of a lawsuit. And then I couldn't believe it when I found out that John Huston and Paul Newman were coming in to do the movie. So I ended up traveling to England and Ireland to work on it with Huston. John was a grand character, I loved being around him, and obviously he was very fond of Ireland, so I liked all that part of it. I got to spend a couple of very pleasant months in Galway, I was there at the time of the Oyster Festival. While I was there I spent a week in Dublin and then I got to drive through Connemara and go south to the Cliffs of Moher and all the way down to Cork. I was living on Warner Bros.' money, on their expense account. And Huston was great to have lunch or dinner with, but truth be told, I did not like

Paul Newman stars alongside Dominique Sanda in *The Mackintosh Man* (1973).

working with him that much. Nor did he like working with me that much. We didn't hate each other or anything like that, we just disagreed. I was in this position as the writer, but who the fuck was I? This was the great John Huston! He kept wanting to stick with the book and I kept saying, 'I don't think it's going to work, let's come up with some original material here.' Not long after that I was told that my services were no longer required and I went home. It was only toward the end of the process that he said, 'The book is no damn good! I can see that it is no damn good. We've tried to make this work, but it's just no damn good.' I've never seen the movie. I was a little disgruntled about the whole process. But I did read what they shot, and I would say that I wrote a very large percentage of the first half of the movie and very little of the second half, which Huston rewrote with someone else. But he wisely ducked out on receiving screen credit for it."

Following his Irish sojourn with Huston, Hill returned home and, at the request of *The Getaway* producer David Foster and his partner Larry Turman, he began work on adapting Ross McDonald's 1950 book *The Drowning Pool*. As a sequel to the 1966 film noir *Harper*, this would be another star vehicle for Paul Newman, of whom Hill was quite fond. "I liked Newman," Hill admits. "He was a very friendly and engaging kind of guy. He had that actor thing in that he wanted everybody to love him, and that makes it sound like his friendliness was a calculation but that's not what I mean at all. He was a genuinely friendly person with a sweet nature. He wasn't a difficult personality, he was gregarious, liked to tell stories and liked to have a lot of laughs. Now, there were people that he didn't particularly care for, though I won't mention any names, but Paul was a generous and good man."

The version of *The Drowning Pool* that was produced contains little of Hill's draft of the script, as it was rewritten firstly by Lorenzo Semple, Jr., and secondly by Tracy Keenan Wynn. Save for the excellent cinematography of Gordon Willis and

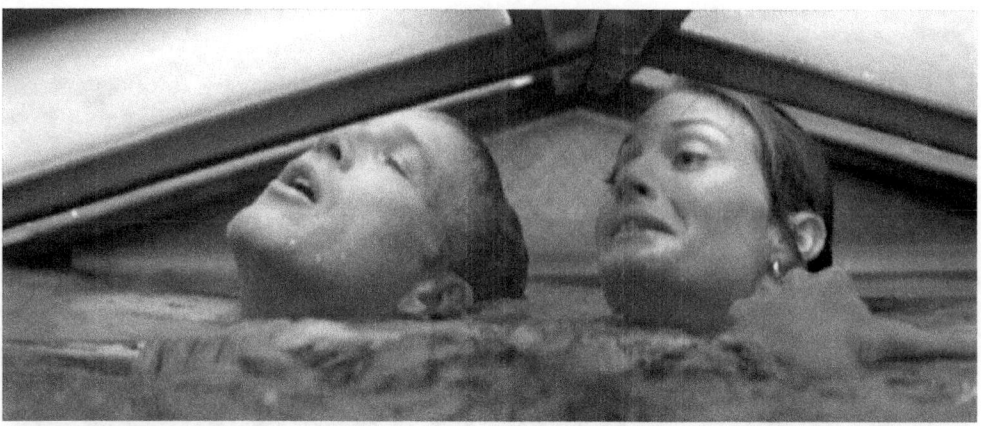

Private investigator Lew Harper (Paul Newman) and mystery woman Mavis (Gail Strickland) experience *The Drowning Pool* **(1975).**

one spectacularly tense scene involving the titular pool, the film is saddled with a muddled plot and sluggish pacing. But things were soon to turn around for Hill, as after five scripts produced to varying degrees of quality, the writer would take a crucial step in advancing his career to become a director. "The simple truth of it," Hill says, "is that the very large commercial success of *The Getaway* is what got me a chance to direct."

Two

Hard Times, Harder Men

In the age of the Old Hollywood implosion, when the classical modes of cinema were no longer commercially viable and the young auteurs influenced by the European tendencies of the French New Wave and Italian neorealism emerged, Walter Hill appeared an anomaly. In the same year that saw *Shampoo* celebrate the sexual revolution, *Nashville* made country music temporarily hip, and *The Rocky Horror Picture Show* brought fetishism to the midnight masses, Hill's directorial debut, *Hard Times*, appeared out of time. The film opens in 1933 with the evocative image of a freight train rolling past the camera as a laconic drifter named Chaney (Charles Bronson) squints out at his new environs and smells fleeting opportunity. It's the Great Depression and desperate men are street fighting to earn a few bucks to live another day. Upon defeating a young opponent and earning six dollars after betting on himself to win, Chaney is approached by Spencer "Speed" Weed (James Coburn), a bare-knuckle boxing promoter who envisions big wins for his tough new acquaintance.

Speed takes Chaney to New Orleans and sets up a bout in Cajun country, but the losing hitter accuses Speed and Chaney of hustling them and refuses to pay up. This raises Chaney's ire and he thrashes a local hostelry in return, showing in no uncertain terms that he is not a man to be messed with. And so as Chaney's reputation as a fierce fighter spreads, Speed finds that the stakes are raised higher than regular entry to a bout, thus leading him to the coffers of local gangster Doty (Bruce Glover). Meanwhile, Speed finds himself in hot water with Chick Gandil (Michael McGuire), the sponsor of Chaney's most recently defeated opponent and who is demanding a fight between Chaney and a Chicago pugilist named Street (Nick Dimitri). If Chaney refuses to fight, Speed will be killed. Despite his protestations against the bout, Chaney steps up to save his friend, defeating his Midwestern opponent after a taxing contest.

The film ends with the reluctant business partners and even more reluctant friends saying farewell. In a fashion typical of Hill's stoic, masculine heroes, theirs is a quiet goodbye with far more said in their exchange of glances than could ever be verbally extrapolated. "Chaney, you ought to say something," pleads Speed, as Chaney gracefully walks away. It's not that there is a lack of emotion present in the scene, it is the kind of emotion that expresses itself in the simple act of companionship; that Chaney and Speed even spent enough time together to hustle and end up grudgingly respecting each other says all that needs to be said about their feelings for

Chaney (Charles Bronson) rides the rails into New Orleans in Hill's directorial debut, *Hard Times* **(1975).**

each other. In Chaney and Speed we have the beginning of the archetypal male relationship of the Hill oeuvre: the loquacious, fast-talking antihero coupled with the stoic, reserved hero. It serves up the kind of relationship dynamic that would inform the pairing of Nick Nolte and Eddie Murphy in *48 Hrs.* and that can be observed in Hill films as diverse as *Crossroads* (with Ralph Macchio and Joe Seneca) and *Red Heat* (with Arnold Schwarzenegger and James Belushi).

After Sam Peckinpah's *The Getaway* became one of the top 10 box office hits of 1972, Hill's name now carried some commercial weight and a new price tag to reflect his newfound bankability. Indeed, it was his work on that Steve McQueen smash that drew the attention of an old acquaintance of Hill's: Larry Gordon, a former production executive for American International Pictures. Gordon helped bring John Milius's *Dillinger* to the screen in 1973 and now had a production deal at the ailing Columbia Pictures—a deal that required him to bring in some potentially lucrative genre films on a low budget. One of those he was keen to make was the story of illegal warehouse boxing called *The Streetfighter*, written by Brian Gindoff and Bruce Henstell. Seeking to develop the script further with an esteemed, established screenwriter, Gordon set his sights on Hill; the only problem being that Hill's fee was beyond the remit of the low-budget production unit that Gordon was overseeing for the studio, so the producer tempted Hill with an offer he couldn't refuse: a minimum fee but with the opportunity to write and direct the film. Regardless of how thrifty or perhaps penny-pinching that may have sounded, for Hill it was an acceptable way into his directing debut. Gordon recalls, "I bought this script which was about a streetfighter when I was at Columbia Pictures. I had been keeping up with the top young screenwriters of the time and Walter Hill was at the top of my list of someone I wanted to work with. But I couldn't afford him. He had written *The Getaway*, which was directed by Sam Peckinpah, and was a big success, so how I approached him was I decided I would let him direct the film as well. So that is how we made the deal."

Hill confirms, "The reason I got a chance to direct is because I had written several movies and one of them was a big, big hit and that's the kind of thing that puts you in there. Larry was starting out as a producer and he was trying to take his experience from American International Pictures over to Columbia, where he had made a deal to make several low-budget action pictures. Larry had a script based on a newspaper article about these guys down in San Pedro that fought in warehouses and places like that, really out-of-the-way illegal fighting. Larry and I knew each other slightly back in those days, and Larry is a very straightforward fellow, and being that I was somewhat in demand as a writer he said, 'If you write the script for scale and direct the picture for scale, then I'll give you a shot. At least I might get a good script out of it, and you can't be any worse than the directors I've been working with.' He wasn't talking about Milius, by the way."

"Walter had been an assistant director, so I knew that he would know what to do and how the set works," Gordon says. "I also heard he was a great guy, a very reasonable guy, so I brought him in and we made our first deal, and that was how he ended up directing his first movie."

One of the elements of the script that attracted Hill's attention was the story's similarity to the experiences of his grandfather, who had worked as an oil driller in the 1920s. The Hill elder had regaled his grandson with tales of life in the fields, where roughneck men from various camps would work hard and play harder. One particular tale of a mysterious transient man riding from town to town and offering his physical strength in return for food and shelter proved particularly evocative, as Hill recalls: "I really think that my grandfather deserves some of the screen credit because he told me this story when I was a kid about something that happened in his life. This was my grandfather on my father's side; he was a wildcat oil driller back in the 1920s, up in the Taft area of California, and he used to go out into the middle of nowhere drilling for oil with these gangs of men. It was like goldmining. A wildcat atmosphere, they had camps where there was a big bunkhouse for everybody to sleep in and had their own cook. It was like being a cowboy. But there were rivalries amongst the various camps of workers and on Sundays they would have games with each other, they would run races, or wrestle, or fight for money. These were rough guys and my grandfather would hold his own with them. They would work six days a week, and it was murderous work, but good money for those times. A working fella could make good money doing this and so they would go out there for six weeks and then go back home to their families. But one Sunday they are having one of their fight-for-money matches when a truck goes rolling by and this guy jumps off the back of the truck and he watches what's going on and says, 'Tell you what, you feed me and give me a place to sleep, then I'll win fights for you and we'll split the money.' So these guys are going 'Okay!' This guy was a strong-looking fella, but he was very quiet and only ever gave his first name. So they set up a series of fights with the other camps and he won four straight fights and made some money, and then one morning they all woke up and he was gone. My grandfather always thought he was somebody on the run from the law, which I would say is a pretty good assumption. My grandfather was very impressed with the mystery of the story and the fact that this guy just totally knocked the shit out of anybody they put up against him. I'd never forgotten this story."

To retain a level of authenticity in depicting the milieu of hard times that these men went through, Hill envisioned the production as a period piece, though this would require further financial frugality when it came to filming. "I thought the film would be better in a period setting," Hill says. "Those events with my grandfather happened back in the 1920s, in relatively flush times, and Larry was happy to make it a period piece if we could hold it to a low budget level. He had just experienced success with *Dillinger*, Milius's movie, which, of course, was period. Most producers would say, 'No way, you can't do a period film on a low budget!' But Larry thought we could get away with it and he asked if I would set it in New Orleans because he knew the town well and had a lot of friends there. So I wrote the script that I wanted to write and I wrote it in a way for me to direct, not the usual kind of blueprint; it was the beginning of, shall we say, my haiku style." And that style is something Gordon has come to value as having the editorial nous and economy of words that offers producers and studio executives a clear vision of what the final product will resemble, to the letter. "Walter is my favorite writer of all time because he doesn't waste any words," the producer says. "He is very terse, he is very to the point, there isn't any flowery description; he has his own style, which I love. In the sixty years I have been doing this I would say that Walter's scripts are by far the easiest screenplays to read."

With the screenplay in place and Hill committed to direct, Gordon's next move was to secure a star to sell the film. For the lead role of the wandering Chaney, he and Hill settled upon a bankable but truculent actor whose tough-guy persona made box office hits out of hard-edged material such as *The Mechanic* (1972), *Mr. Majestyk* (1974), and *Death Wish* (1974). "People liked the script," Hill recalls, "so they said, 'Let's get a movie star!' and they sent it to a couple of people who turned it down, and then they sent it to Bronson, who had it for one day before calling back to say yes after reading it that night; he was a very hot actor at the time. So we thought that when Charlie would come in then our budget would go up … it didn't. They refused to raise the budget and said, 'No, we're just going to pay Charlie out of the budget.' So out of a $3 million budget we paid him a million. I didn't really want Bronson because I thought he was too old and that he wouldn't be any good in the movie, it was written for a younger guy. But I was entirely wrong because Bronson is very, very good in the film. I'm eternally grateful to him for his star presence and the fact that he is so good in the movie, because it really gave me a career. The movie was well-received on the whole."

"We cast Charlie Bronson in the lead role, he was a big star at the time, but he was not easy in any way, shape, or form," Gordon admits. "It wasn't easy for me and it wasn't easy for Walter, but we got through it alive. He was difficult but he was great in the part, perfect for the role."

While Bronson's casting came with the required commercial clout, it also came with its own caveat: accepting the role would mean that his wife, Jill Ireland, had to be cast as love interest Lucy Simpson. It was not unusual for Ireland to appear in her husband's films, as she did in *Villa Rides* (1968), *Cold Sweat* (1970), *Chino* (1972), and many more following *Hard Times*, though it wasn't always entirely welcome. "Charlie was a curious guy," Hill says. "He insisted that his wife play the other part, to which I put up token resistance, but they take you into a small room and say, 'Do you want to be a director or not?' and so we cast her. She wasn't a horrible actress but it wasn't exactly an open competition." Just as Bronson brought his own brooding sense of authority to the production, the casting of James Coburn—with whom Bronson previously costarred in John Sturges's *The Magnificent Seven* (1960) and *The Great Escape* (1963)—meant for additional tension on the set. "Bronson and Coburn didn't get along very well. They had done some movies together but they weren't particularly friendly. I had written the part for Warren Oates and Coburn didn't like that, and he was number two on the call sheet for a Charlie Bronson movie. He didn't like that either. Bronson had a reputation for being a very tough guy on directors and being not a lot of fun to work with, and I couldn't tell you he was a lot of fun to work with, but I got along fine with him; whereas Coburn was one of those guys that everybody liked but I didn't get along with him. He and I just didn't hit it off. So, it was kind of weird that everything somehow got reversed. But then we fell out with Charlie in post because we had cut a lot of his wife's scenes out and she turned on the waterworks. Charlie was devoted to his wife, and he was angry that we had cut the movie down too much. The one thing I know for sure is you can't let other people edit your movie. When you take the job, you are committed to having to make decisions, some of which will be difficult; it would have been easy to keep Charlie happy but ... and I have to say that Larry, unlike most producers, who would have sided with Charlie, had this kid director who had never done a movie and he had one of the biggest movie stars in the business, but Larry stuck by me, he knew what was best for the movie and that really cemented our relationship. He was and is a wonderful producer and a real character."

A more pleasant inclusion to the cast was that of Peckinpah perennial Strother Martin in the difficult part of opium-addicted cut man Poe. After many actors tried and failed in reading for the genteel-though-disheveled medical man, time was running out for Hill and Gordon to cast the part. Hill recalls the moment he chose to take a chance on the interested actor: "I had written the character of Poe—whose name I obviously took from the great Edgar Allan—into the middle of this tough-guy action kind of environment; I wanted something a little off-center. I

Chaney (Charles Bronson, left) and Speed (James Coburn) concoct a plan in *Hard Times* (1975).

thought of this well-educated guy who didn't really fit into this world but who has been forced into it. I wrote a rather stylized part, if you could call it that, and Larry and I read actor after actor but it eluded them. Larry and I were just thinking about what the hell we were going to do when we ran out of time. It got to the first day of shooting in New Orleans and someone had shown the script to Strother Martin, and he called to say, 'I'd like to play this!' We were looking for someone younger, but Larry ran over to the set and asked me if I would accept Strother Martin for the part of Poe. Now, we were both scared to death because we had heard so many people read the part badly that we got ourselves into a position where we didn't want to hire anybody unless we heard them read it and had some confidence in them. But we were totally out of time. So, I said, 'Shit, we know he's good. I like the idea, so let's hire him and get him down here. And if he can't do it the way it is written, then I will just rewrite it. I'll sit there with him and we'll figure it out.'"

The actor turned up the next day exquisitely evoking a Southern legend that he had prepared to use as a model in his delightfully exaggerated rendering of Poe. Hill continues, "So Strother flies in the next day and he comes over to me and the first thing he says is, 'I know how to play this. I want to play it like I'm Tennessee Williams! I want to talk like that, and I want to wear one of those little suits.' And one thing about being a director is to be smart enough to not get in the way, and I don't think that, other than blocking and the occasional line, I ever really directed him. We just talked a bit and he played it, he did it exactly the way he said he would, and he was terrific. I liked him, he was a very gentle man, but I never got a chance to work with him again."

Hard Times earned rave reviews and garnered the kind of financial success that allowed Hill to be recognized as a filmmaker of note, someone who could turn in a star vehicle on a modest budget and with mainstream appeal. "The studio was happy with it," Gordon says, "even though I'm not sure they knew what they had because when they released it we didn't have the greatest marketing campaign. However, because Charlie was as big a star as he was, it attracted audiences and so the movie was a success. It was Walter's first directing success and it was the first movie that I produced too, so it was very good for both of our careers."

Hard Times is an astoundingly accomplished work for a debut filmmaker, announcing the arrival of a fully developed artist right out of the gate. With such a unique authorial stamp heralding Hill's auspicious debut, other writers and filmmakers of the time would sit up and take notice. Hill's future *Johnny Handsome* collaborator, screenwriter Ken Friedman, was on the Columbia Pictures backlot when *Hard Times* and his own *White Line Fever* were both in production. Having read the script and then seen the finished film, Friedman realized that Hill was just as formidable a filmmaker as he was a writer. "Walter's script for *Hard Times* and the way he wrote it made you feel like you had seen the movie," Friedman says. "It was the kind of script you could read in an hour. And then I saw the film and it blew me away. I don't know another director whose first film is as good as that. He was working with people like James Coburn and Charles Bronson on his debut, and Bronson was a very difficult guy, but Walter had their respect right away because he had a confidence about what he was doing."

Another future screenwriting collaborator of Hill's, Alessandro Camon (*Bullet to the Head*), sees parallels in the arrival of Bronson's Chaney and the emergence of a major American film artist: "The opening shot of *Hard Times* is the stranger arriving by train, and to me that stranger is Walter arriving with his first movie. It is the train that he is going to ride through every American film genre for the next 50 years. It also sets out a great recurring motif in Walter's movies: that of the stranger coming to town, whether by train, by car, or by horse." *The Long Riders* actor Nicholas Guest commends the film as "an amazing debut, it is like Walter arrived fully formed as a filmmaker. Only a few directors are like that, but Walter really knows film. He is a great historian of cinema and you can feel that coming off the screen in *Hard Times*. He is channeling the old masters while announcing his own distinctive style."

"I love the movie," Gordon exclaims. "It is one of my favorites. I thought the whole cast was great and we had a fantastic time in New Orleans. I'm from Mississippi and I went to Tulane University in New Orleans, so I knew the South very well. Let's just say I took Walter down South. It was fun and from there Walter and I would go on to make seven movies together."

Indeed, it wasn't long before Hill and Gordon would reunite for another film. This time, however, it would be something entirely different. Hill followed his debut with *The Driver*, a dark neo-noir thriller in which a duo of mononymous characters, including skilled getaway man "Driver" (Ryan O'Neal) and the hard-bitten "Detective" (Bruce Dern), play a game of cat and mouse throughout the Los Angeles criminal underworld. After his accomplices almost fumble a casino heist, The Driver is witnessed leaving the scene by a woman known only as "The Player" (Isabelle Adjani), after which he offers her payment for an alibi; meanwhile The Detective seeks her assistance in identifying the elusive transporter. When she accepts Driver's bribe and refuses to confirm his involvement, the obsessive cop invokes her mysterious criminal background: "You sure have been around the track a few times, honey." But The Detective is so aggressive in his attempts to collar his man that he goes so far as to orchestrate a bank heist using a trio of criminals whom he promises to pardon if they hire The Driver and lead him to his capture. This illegal sting could cost The Detective his badge as it is a controversial concept that won't be easily sold to his superiors downtown, but that doesn't matter, as he notes, "I sold it to myself, that's enough. I want the cowboy." The Driver is initially skeptical when middle-woman "The Connection" (Ronee Blakley) formalizes the heist. He tells her he doesn't like working with guns, and these guys are known shooters. But in meeting the trio, The Driver quite literally takes them on a crash course to display his prowess behind the wheel and to justify his $10,000 up-front price tag and 15 percent of the takings, a rate which is doubled to 30 percent when The Driver realizes just how bad these "second-raters" want his expertise. Predictably, the heist goes wrong and The Driver ends up breaking his own code regarding arms, as he soon blasts his way out of a sticky situation and must sell the hot money for a quarter of its value.

For Hill, the three years between wrapping *Hard Times* and going into production on *The Driver* felt interminable. Having been justly celebrated for his impressive debut, the director was eager to ride that wave and get his next film rolling, but

The Detective (Bruce Dern, left foreground) confronts the Driver (Ryan O'Neal, right, with back to camera) in the climactic scene of *The Driver* (1978).

he soon found out that even after delivering a successful product for Columbia Pictures, the collective memory of the executive elite is a short one. "I got some offers in the immediate aftermath of *Hard Times*," Hill says, "but I got a quick lesson in finding out that you're hot for about three weeks. The phone rings, and then it doesn't. But I wanted to do my own script and then Larry and I decided to do *The Driver*, which took a long time to get going."

The story came from producer Larry Gordon's desire to craft a plot around a professional who had never been the central character of a film before: "I was thinking about what kinds of stories hadn't yet been made into movies and I realized that I hadn't seen a film about a getaway driver. I called Walter and told him about this idea I had for a movie about a getaway driver, and I started by saying 'Steve McQueen gets out of prison.' That's how I started to tell him the story. Steve McQueen gets out of prison and the guard says to him, 'You'll be back!' Then he starts walking down the street when a Rolls-Royce pulls up with a chauffeur who says, 'Hey, Driver, get in!' So, he gets in the back and meets a gangster who wants him to do a job, and the wise guy driving the car says, 'You've been inside for three years, how do we know you still got it?' So the character walks around to the front and says, 'Get out!' He gets in and drives the Rolls-Royce down the street and wedges it between two cars so nobody can get out but him and he says, 'You know my deal. Call me!' That's the idea as I told it to Walter, and of course that scene ended up in the film, it's the one in the underground garage where Ryan O'Neal takes these hoods for a drive. Walter loved the idea, went away, and came back with a script. I knew Walter would be perfect to write and direct it. But it came from this sparse idea, a springboard, which Walter turned into a great script that became this cult movie that people love. There was a big video game which stole from it and then Ryan Gosling did a film called *Drive*, which is the same exact movie."

Hill's script for *The Driver* has drawn much acclaim for its economical style that cuts straight to the core essence of each scene and eschews the exacting format of the typical film noir heist picture structure. Hill eliminates the processes and attention to detail that are usually part of the tediously rigorous criminal endeavors of these kinds of films. Take, for example, the bank heist at the center of the narrative, orchestrated as a sting operation by The Detective to capture The Driver once and for all—the scene cuts straight to the heart of the action, mid-heist, refusing to take us through the rote campaign of planning and scheming that is usually involved in scenes preceding the action of the heist itself. Rather, Hill takes us right to the violent climax of the robbery, the crucial moment of the double cross among the thieves, denying us its execution and feeling no need to lead up to the act itself. Hill's terse style has been noted by several collaborators, including property master Craig Raiche, who applauds Hill's bare-bones approach to description and detail: "The first thing that caught my attention was Walter's distinctive writing style. His script for *The Driver* offered no superfluous detail. He mentioned nothing about any type of camera movement. He offered no insight as to the inner thoughts of his characters. To that point, they were completely nameless. He identified them only by their specific roles in his story. It was as stripped down/bare bones a script as I would ever read, and I found that very intriguing. Soon enough, it was apparent that stripped down and bare bones was also his style of directing. He offered instruction to his actors quite sparingly. He offered as much freedom to create and express their characters as any actor could hope for. Only rarely would he suggest that an actor play a scene with a mindset other than what they'd just expressed."

The Driver would go into production with British company EMI, headed by Michael Deeley and Barry Spikings, whose business plan was to join with major Hollywood studios to split the cost in making easily marketable genre films on American soil but with a focus on international distribution. This initial output of co-financed productions included Sam Peckinpah's *Convoy*, Michael Cimino's *The Deer Hunter*, and *The Driver*. Unfortunately for Hill, the film would get caught in limbo as the search for a star ensued. "I remember being disappointed that it took so long because I wanted to shoot six months after *Hard Times* came out," Hill recalls, "but it's hard getting the money and I kept writing these things where you had to get a star because the studio system demanded an action lead, or somebody who resembled an action lead." The quest for the star who would play the titular taciturn driver took some unexpected turns, as Hill and Gordon were considering everything from bona fide action heroes to international icons of cool to romantic leading men. "When we started we went after a lot of big stars like Steve McQueen and Clint Eastwood to be in it," Gordon recalls, "and Alain Delon was another one of the guys Walter wanted. So Ryan O'Neal wasn't close to our first choice, but we ended up going to Ryan and he did a great job. It was not the kind of movie or the kind of role you would expect Ryan O'Neal to be in but he did as good as he could do, he gave it 100 percent."

O'Neal's mannered performance is unusual for the normally high-spirited actor, having shown deft comedic skill and an ability to charm with incredible ease in the likes of *What's Up, Doc?* (1972), *Paper Moon* (1973), and *Nickelodeon* (1976).

Ryan O'Neal stars as the titular Driver.

In those films he allowed himself to look foolish and even inept, but here he harnesses all the quiet cool and confidence of Jean-Pierre Melville's antiheroes in rendering The Driver as an effortlessly enigmatic and laconic man of mystery. "This was an unusual kind of role for Ryan O'Neal," Hill admits. "We had sent the script to a number of people and they all turned it down and then the idea of Ryan came up, but he had never been seen in a different persona than what was the general perception of him. He had never been in a genre picture like *The Driver* and they don't get more purely genre than *The Driver*. But Ryan wanted to try it and I thought he did a really good job. I was very pleased with his performance. And Bruce, he is always good, especially if you turn him loose on his 'quest.' I've worked with Bruce any number of times and, lord, he is a lot of fun."

"At that time, Ryan O'Neal was as fine and fit a male human being as there was in all of SAG," says Raiche. "He was blessed with extraordinary hand/eye coordination. Many are unaware of his record as an amateur boxer before turning actor. And, yet, in the sequence that took place in an underground parking garage where, bumper by bumper, side-view mirror by side-view mirror, and door by door, he surgically reduces a Mercedes to a worthless hunk of metal. He prematurely destroyed one by driving it into a concrete pillar. Ryan was replaced for that scene's next take by stuntman Everett Creach, who drove and destroyed a second, matching, Mercedes right into that same concrete pillar."

The most celebrated element of *The Driver* is its numerous car chase sequences. Hill had been the second assistant director on Hollywood's most famous car chase picture, *Bullitt*, a film that took the bold choice to shoot much of the action from within the confines of the cars, rather than strictly external shots of the speeding vehicles, and Hill does something similar here. As well as being additionally claustrophobic due to the nighttime setting, the close-quarter framing gives the sequences a sense of intimacy and excitement rarely found in the more elaborately staged chase scenes of American mainstream action films. Raiche recalls the technically challenging construction of the memorable chase scenes:

"Originally, *The Driver* script had a lot of daytime action. But because the film was nearly nonstop car racing, and because Walter's choice of locations was downtown Los Angeles, we soon realized that we'd be shooting almost the entire picture at night. If we tried to do all those driving stunts in daytime, we'd have taken the worst rush-hour traffic in all the US and made it truly impossible for anyone to escape absolute gridlock ... including us. The car speeds occasionally neared 100 mph, and the insert 'camera car' was right there with them. More than a couple of the usual crew people declined to sit atop that vehicle for more than a couple of takes. All speeding-car stunts and crashes have an element of danger, but with expert planning by professional stunt people and experienced effects persons—with helpful assistance from off-duty LA policemen—that danger was truly minimized.

"Key to both our crew and car safety were two retired LA police officers, Jerry Ray and Bob Sizer. They both took an immediate liking to me and semi-secretly put me under their employ. At that time ('77) and at each intersection, the red/yellow/green traffic lights were mounted on top of metal poles on the corners of all sidewalks. Two of the four poles had a locked metal box. Once opened, each box contained a miniature likeness of the full-sized traffic lights complete with red, yellow, and green push buttons. If there was ever some kind of a problem with those traffic lights, one could continue to regulate the flow of traffic by simply pushing the appropriately colored buttons. Those cops gave me the sole responsibility of making sure that the main intersection where stunts took place always had the proper color light for that take. They trusted me so much, in fact, I still have the key that opened those boxes! I vividly remember my first, and last, lesson on proper handling of those buttons. Officer Sizer demonstrated to me the proper grip and then he hit the 'override' switch on the handheld device. With a keen eye he then observed the busy flow of downtown traffic and then he said, 'Now, listen ... this is very important. Don't ever do this!' With that, a bus is some 50 yards away and closing in on our intersection. At just the right time, but without changing the light from green to yellow, he went from green to red! Well, the bus driver managed a short but deftly controlled skid just before his front bumper went past the crosswalk line. 'Will do,' I said."

In comparison with the more classical stylings of *Hard Times*, *The Driver* is a relatively uncommercial piece of filmmaking. It is a stark minimalist affair more in line with the prevailing trends of New Hollywood crime pictures replicating, or at least reflecting, the arthouse aesthetics of international film masters like John Boorman, Robert Bresson, Jean-Pierre Melville, and Seijun Suzuki, successfully evoking the existentialist mood so identifiable in the works of those filmmakers, though Melville's is the most obvious influence on the tone and style of the piece. If there is one film that *The Driver* owes a debt to, it is Melville's 1967 neo-noir classic, *Le Samourai*, in which Alain Delon's silent assassin of modest means moves through the coldly lit Parisian underworld with similar impassivity to O'Neal's getaway man; the normally amiable actor reins in the gregarious personality he displayed in earlier pictures in order to channel the stoicism of Delon. Hill admits to being an admirer of

Melville and his most celebrated film, but he details that it is not an explicit influence, rather the natural progression and development of filmmakers within this relatively new art form of cinema, where what is successful—commercially or aesthetically—will surely impact and shape successive films.

"There was certainly an influence of *Point Blank* in there, but the Melville thing is something I've been linked to a number of times, and I'm always amused by it. I was at a function in France once and they asked me about the influence of Melville and I said, 'Yes, I very much admired *Le Samourai*, I think it's a wonderful movie. But I think something you have to say about Melville, and *Le Samourai* may be the best example of this, is he uses constant tropes from American movies. The Alain Delon character is based on the Alan Ladd character in *This Gun for Hire*. They didn't even change the wardrobe. He wears the same coat.' When people talk about influence, I like to say that we're all connected. We're storytellers, and hopefully we have a personal touch of our own, some unique thing that we want to get into the picture, but there is nobody that stands apart from what came before you, be it in literature, in cinema, in poetry, in music, whatever. I used to demonstrate this point when I was a young director: people said I was influenced by Peckinpah, which was probably true to some degree. Nowadays they tend to say I'm more influenced by Hawks, and I would like to think there was some connection there because I love Hawks. Who doesn't? But you cannot look at Peckinpah's movies and not see the influence of Kurosawa. You cannot look at Kurosawa's movies and not see the influence of John Ford. You cannot look at John Ford's movies and not see the influence of D.W. Griffith. And you cannot look at D.W. Griffith's films without seeing the influence of Charles Dickens. We're all connected. For better or worse, richer or stronger or weaker, we're connected. Jean-Luc Godard once said, 'No critic should ever write a review without mentioning D.W. Griffith.' His influence was that great on what became the modern cinema. That's one of those truths that nobody wants to talk about anymore. To live in the modern world and not have a sense of history is to be half-blind; the idea that nothing happened before you were born and it's all about what's correct now is ridiculous. Think of Faulkner's line: 'The past is never dead. It's not even past.' History is still part of what we're doing."

The Driver is shot with a distinct style by Philip Lathrop, returning to collaborate with Hill after his stunning work on *Hard Times*. Lathrop's icy, cool palette is illuminated by the harsh artificial lighting of downtown Los Angeles, a reflection of The Driver himself: cold, clinical, steely. Lathrop captures this world of endless identikit streets, underground carparks, wrecking yards, abandoned industrial spaces, and featureless apartments with the kind of detachment that befits the milieu inhabited by such aloof antihero protagonists. Many of Lathrop's shots use reflective surfaces within the frame, often shooting through windows, with the glass adding further separation between spectator and subject. This is not a gritty Los Angeles representing a genuine depiction of the criminal underworld, it is a hyper-stylized neo-noir world that updates the high-contrast chiaroscuro of the postwar noir pictures of the 1940s. Hill's minimal use of music also heightens the clinical atmospherics, relying on the ambient sound of the urban environment as it reacts with the automobiles; when the music is cued it almost feels out of place. There are moments where Hill's surface illusion of reality and linearity are tempered with jarring moments of smash-editing, such as the memorable underground carpark scene in which The Driver shows off his skill in automotive destruction. Tina Hirsch and Robert K. Lambert's cutting makes montage out of carnage, reflecting one of the few moments where Driver loses his cool. Hirsch and Lambert's exemplary assembly of footage is at its most dynamic in the film's several car chases, their cuts keeping the energy high in the absence of a driving musical score.

For a film with strong roots in the film noir tradition, including that of the tight-lipped antihero, a visually dark mise-en-scène with stylized lighting, and characters of ambiguous moral fiber, Hill does subvert the conventions of the genre with his contemporary femme fatale. Isabelle Adjani and Ronee Blakley's characters are smart and cunning without the more lurid qualities often assigned the femme fatale. They are a noteworthy rendering of the clichéd character model in this era of Hollywood when filmmakers were freer to depict sex, violence, and all manner of immorality than the previous generation of film noir storytellers could. In the films of the forties and fifties, the femme fatale was defined by her sexual allure; they were playful, teasing, and manipulative. And while The Player and The Connection are clearly attractive women, Hill does not cheapen them to use their sexuality to play the men to their advantage here; their involvement is purely business and intelligence is their power. The fatality of these femmes is that they bring Driver into contact with unscrupulous thieves, which results in him ultimately losing his money. And with names like The Player and The Connection, these women take chances for a living, though it is the latter who pays for such with her life after making a fatal connection.

Both The Driver and The Detective are men of significant ego, and this is what fuels their absolute devotion to outwitting each other. In The Driver, The Detective sees a criminal parallel to his professional lawman and both consider themselves the best at what they do; for one to outdo the other would keep that ego intact. "I'm much better at this game than you are," says The Detective to The Driver, and that line says a lot to how he sees this investigation. Catching The Driver, someone at the top of his profession, would be the ultimate trophy for The Detective, to the point where he is willing to risk his career and pension on an illegal sting operation to get his man; the thrill of the chase is made more exciting by the skill with which both men operate.

The Driver could have been one of the great underrated films of Walter Hill's career, having delivered a lackluster performance at the box office in Western markets, but the film's influence has cast a long shadow over Hollywood; thus contemporary consideration of the film places it among his most highly regarded works. Elements of *The Driver* are evident in a host of major films over the last 40 years, from Michael Mann's *Thief* (1981) and James Cameron's *The Terminator* (1984) to Nicolas Winding Refn's *Drive* (2011) and Edgar Wright's *Baby Driver* (2017). It has inspired articles and think pieces not afforded Hill's greater successes. All things considered, not bad for a film deemed a failure upon release.

"*The Driver* should have been a big hit," Gordon says, "but it wasn't really a commercial movie. I think Walter was influenced by European cinema and also film noir because it has that kind of look to it, it has a lot of darkness and a lot of it was shot at night, which meant it was a very hard movie to shoot. If we had McQueen it would have been a different movie. I don't know if it would have been better or worse, but it certainly would have been different. With Ryan it was immediately less commercial. Frank Marshall came into our lives at that point. He ended up being the line producer and executive producer on the movie and we ended up working together more than once."

That fateful connection made with Frank Marshall on *The Driver* would indeed result in further collaborations, perhaps most notably on what would become Hill's most celebrated film of all: *The Warriors*. Produced and released in 1979, this gritty urban fantasy charts the fallout between rival New York gangs after a summit at Van Cortlandt Park in the Bronx is called upon by Cyrus (Roger Hill), the head of the Gramercy Riffs. Cyrus proposes a truce between the city's gangs in order to band together in becoming a single force to exert control over the five boroughs. "You're standing right now with nine delegates from a hundred gangs," Cyrus announces, "and there's over a hundred more. That's 20,000 hard-core members. Forty thousand counting affiliates, and 20,000 more, not organized but ready to fight. Sixty thousand soldiers. Now, there ain't but 20,000 police in the whole town. Can you dig it?" While basking in the uproarious applause and wild approval of the assembled tribes, Cyrus is assassinated by the deranged and diminutive Luther (David Patrick Kelly) of the Rogues gang. Luther announces that a member of Coney Island gang the Warriors pulled the trigger, and a melee ensues. The Warriors escape, but not without having raised the ire of the Gramercy Riffs, who want blood for their fallen leader. The Warriors are led by "war chief" Swan (Michael Beck) and include Ajax (James Remar), Cleon (Dorsey Wright), Cochise (David Harris), Cowboy (Tom McKitterick), and Fox (Thomas G. Waites). This lost tribe must make it back to the beach while navigating various enemy territories and eluding the gangs who control that turf, a deadly journey that includes some close encounters with the Orphans, the Baseball Furies, and the deceptively seductive all-female Lizzies. The Warriors finally reach Coney Island by dawn, but they are confronted on their home patch by the Rogues. A final sunrise confrontation between Swan and Luther ensues just as the Gramercy Riffs arrive to apprehend the real culprits behind the killing of their messiah.

The film opens with an iconic symbol: the Wonder Wheel at Deno's Wonder Wheel Amusement Park in Coney Island. This image should conjure notions of innocence, of children laughing and youthful merriment, but here it stands ominously, shrouded in darkness, illuminated only in garish purple neon lighting. The shot is accompanied by Barry De Vorzon's eerie, minimalist electronic score, suggesting that this monolith of amusement has a much more sinister meaning than is traditionally associated with it. Then De Vorzon's music comes alive with a mixture of rock and disco elements to score the opening credit sequence, which introduces us to the myriad gangs as they descend upon Van Cortlandt Park. This opening montage is one of several used throughout the film with skillful narrative economy in tracing the Warriors as they traverse the inner-city landscape on their trek back to Coney Island while evading the numerous gangs mobilized to seize them. The device that Hill uses to keep the audience aware of it all is radio personality D.J., whom the

One of the Baseball Furies (Jery Hewitt, left) meets Ajax (James Remar) in *The Warriors* (1979).

Gramercy Riffs use to broadcast the hit put out on the Warriors. Played by Lynne Thigpen (strictly from nose to chin), D.J. interjects with commentary upon the action using witty sports news analogies. Her inclusion is both functional and aesthetic, keeping her diegetic listenership as well as the film's audience abreast of the Warriors' progression and whereabouts in relation to their destination. In dramatic terms, her role is not unlike that of a Greek chorus, reacting to the proceedings as they play out before us and reiterating the kind of emotions the viewer is expected to be feeling. As day breaks, a shot of the searing rising sun transitions to a shot of the Wonder Wheel, appearing once again but no longer shrouded in darkness. Rather it is standing tall in the morning light, symbolizing the Warriors' return to their home patch of Coney Island.

The Warriors is based on Sol Yurick's 1965 novel of the same name and which was later optioned by producer Larry Gordon. The project would become the second collaboration between Gordon and Hill when a previously planned project fell through at the last minute. The pair were set to make their second picture for EMI Films following *The Driver*, a western called *The Last Gun*, but out of that failure arose the opportunity to make a film that has become a touchstone in the careers of both its producer and director. "*The Warriors* came about as a project after I had bought the original book in a used bookstore," Gordon recalls. "Walter and I didn't start on that movie together. The first draft of the script was written by a writer named David Shaber and I brought that script to Walter to rewrite it. That's when Walter came on board."

"Larry Gordon had optioned the book and he was certainly the only producer who understood that this could be made into a movie," Hill says, "because it doesn't have the usual kind of ideas in it, and it doesn't lend itself to star casting, as it's not a

Swan (Michael Beck, right), supported by Mercy (Deborah Van Valkenburgh, middle) and Rembrandt (Marcelino Sánchez, left), makes it back to his home turf of Coney Island for a final showdown with Luther of the Rogues in *The Warriors* (1979).

traditional story. It is, in a sense, all incidents and various situations, it's not a complex narrative that's being worked out. And I thought this was part of his old AIP days, that he was able to see things in a different way than the usual studio producers. That's the other thing about Larry, he is a lot smarter. However, the novel is very different to the movie; the premise that the gang goes to the Bronx and has to fight their way back is the same, but the book is much more of a sociological essay. When Larry brought the book to me I read it and I told him that it would make a terrific film but they'll never let us make it. So, I declined to get involved at that time, but he went out and had a script written. We were going to do a western that I had written, and we were very close to making it and then the financing collapsed six weeks before the shoot. Then when Larry was moving his company from Columbia to Paramount he called me and said, 'Are you still interested in that book, *The Warriors*? I was talking to Paramount about it, and I think I can get them to go for it.' I said, 'If they want to make it, I'm ready!' Within a day or so Frank Marshall and I were in New York starting to look around for locations and I started rewriting the script in the hotel room at night, so the movie got going. It was a terrific producer moment for Larry, to have one movie shot out from under us to having another set up almost instantly."

Prior to becoming a successful Hollywood producer making major blockbusters such as the *Back to the Future* trilogy and *The Witches of Eastwick*, Neil Canton worked the dark and dangerous streets of New York City as Hill's assistant on *The Warriors*. For the future powerhouse producer, this humble beginning meant trailing the director around with the script, accompanying him to and from the set, and eating lunch together. Canton recalls:

"I was just there to help him in any way that I could. It was my version of film school. We spent a lot of time talking about the film and its story. I grew up in New York City and we shot it on location there, so I had some value to add as far as that goes. He would always ask me questions and I would give him honest answers. It was all part of being an assistant, you do whatever is needed. After shooting I would go with him to the editing room, and we would talk about that process. It was a really great relationship, and I probably got more out of it than he did, because that experience really helped me in the long run to understand telling a story and why you would shoot something one way as opposed to the other way. He would ask me questions like, 'When do you think I should use the close-up in this scene?' and he knew exactly when he was going to use it but he wanted to make sure that I understood it also. I would say, 'You should use it right here,' and he would ask me why and I would tell him and he would say, 'That's right, that's exactly how it's going to be.' For me it was a real education in making movies. I had worked with Peter Bogdanovich before and his style of shooting was very different than Walter's; Peter's style was very old-fashioned in that he didn't shoot a lot of coverage, he only used a master to a certain point and then he would shoot the close-up, which meant you could only edit it one way. With Walter there was a bit more flexibility. He shot more because he knew we might need some flexibility in the editing room."

The ensemble nature of the casting means there is no one star or lead character as the head of the picture, though in Michael Beck as Swan we have the most charismatic of the Warriors and someone to provide a romantic interest for Deborah Van Valkenburgh's Mercy. He is the de facto "hero" of the piece. But it was the casting of unknowns that lent the film the sense of suspense and danger that it harbors so well; in casting fresh, unfamiliar faces, the audience never quite knows who is going to be killed off or taken out of the story at any moment. Initially, Hill didn't think that a major studio would let him cast the film without name actors, but once Gordon set the film up at Paramount they soon found out that they had license in filling out the roles with who they saw fit to do so, with one exception.

"One of the things that I was pleased about doing *The Warriors* was that it didn't lend itself to star casting," Hill affirms. "That makes a big difference, especially when it comes to putting movies together timewise. We had free reign in casting the film. I told the studio that I wanted to do a movie with an all-black cast, but they would not go for that, and I think in the end they were right because the film becomes more universalized, more timeless, and a more magical world in that you have gangs who don't look like what real gangs did. But at the same time there is a hint of social reality, so there's a mix of social reality and fantasy. I think the interracial casting helped that. We were finding the movie."

With no shortage of unknown actors for the filmmakers to consider, for Hill it was about finding a cast that would not only prove interesting on-screen but who could weather the long nights of physical work in what would prove to be hostile environments. The inner- and outer-city locations used in *The Warriors* present a contemporary yet stylishly dystopian vision of New York. The daylight scenes on Coney Island do not represent the beguiling amusement world so attractive to tourists, but a barren seascape in which the idle gang members idly dwell. The film manages to be gritty without making overt gestures to hardy urban realism and the

Walter Hill directs various Warriors Dorsey Wright (left), Michael Beck (center), and James Remar (right) on location in 1979's *The Warriors* (Photofest).

social issues that breed the kind of gang lifestyle depicted. And while the film keeps the threats of such settings within the safe realm of fictional adventure, the cast and crew experienced the full brunt of working these locations under the darkness of night.

"It ended up being a rough movie to make," Gordon says. "It was terrible. We had all kinds of problems filming on location. We had to negotiate with real gangs, we had logistical issues to deal with, the nights were shorter than we anticipated, we had rainfall, we had every problem you could imagine making that film. The streets of New York are not too nice at two o'clock in the morning, and then there were some unfortunate issues with its release."

Canton concurs: "It was a very rough shoot. There was a threat of danger all around us, which definitely added to the authenticity of the experience. First of all, it was mostly at night, and that went on for 60 nights. Shooting for 60 nights becomes a strange thing. We found ourselves in a couple of neighborhoods that were particularly dangerous and there was one Friday night when we had a location and the police couldn't control the crowd. We had to pack up the trucks and move to a backup location that was blocks away because of the imminent threat of danger. And there was one or two neighborhoods that had local gangs and even though they were okay with us making a movie about gangs they made it clear that the actors playing the Warriors couldn't wear their colors when they were walking to the set; they would tell us, 'You can't be wearing those colors in our neighborhood.' So, they had to wait until they were on the set to put them on. Then, once the shot was completed, they had to take them off again. So we had some tense moments like that. And at the big conclave scene where all the gangs are present there were some arrests made because some of the extras actually had weapons on them and the police had to confiscate that stuff. We had to have private security, so we had people with us all the time. When you are making a movie you sort of forget that there's a real world outside the set and I remember one time Frank [Marshall] and I took a walk off the set and we turned around and we saw the security guys trailing behind, and we asked them, 'How come you guys are with us?' and they said, 'Because you guys are in a really bad neighborhood right now!' And they said we should turn around and come back towards the set."

If the making of the film had been a hairy experience, the release of *The Warriors* would prove just as precarious. After a promising opening weekend, it would end up mired in controversy after several instances of violence broke out in movie theaters screening the film, leading to the media engaging in a scaremongering and scapegoating campaign that would turn the public away. For anyone looking for some semblance of real life in the film, it could be found in the gritty presentation of a dystopian New York City, a milieu not unusual in the bleak dramas of the 1970s. The squalor of certain parts of the city was the perfect setting for films such as *Death Wish* (Michael Winner, 1974), *Taxi Driver* (Martin Scorsese, 1976), and *Cruising* (William Friedkin, 1980), though *The Warriors* was perhaps the first to use the city's dark and dangerous streets as a playground for the youth to act upon the tensions between rival gangs. But for anyone approaching the film without an agenda to suppress it, they will see that it is far from an irresponsible and inflammatory piece of sensationalism. With its cartoonish assembly of colorful gangs, there is no mistaking that Hill's film is a dramatic fantasy adventure and not some call to arms for real-life rival street gangs. "We had one sneak preview before we opened the movie and it was a disaster," recalls Gordon. "We sneaked in front of an older crowd and they didn't like it at all. Paramount almost didn't release it. Then when they did release it we had a lot of violence in the theaters and the resulting controversy meant *The Warriors* only played for two weekends in the States. Paramount pulled it out of distribution even though it sold out every show across the country for those two weeks, but they just couldn't take the heat so they withdrew the film. We did a lot of business foreign, so all the money Paramount made from it came from abroad. No one understands that, how a film played only two weekends in America and yet it is known so well."

Another person who was aggrieved with the final result, though for different reasons, was the story's author, whose more politically informed sociological discourse is largely absent from the irreverent film version. Yurick was the product of parents with communist sympathies and active union participation, and so his original story delves into the social contexts of underclass street culture and the systemic failures that leads the youth of poverty to find meaning and community in the structure of street gangs. "Yurick didn't like the end result," Hill confirms. "He thought we deviated and changed too much. But writers are often not happy with the movie versions of their work. I only met him a couple of times and then very briefly. He came to the set, and we shook hands, but I never had a creative discussion with him."

After such an inauspicious release, the film's subsequent discovery by successive generations of audiences in the ensuing years has led to *The Warriors* being repackaged across a variety of formats and media as the arbiters of pop culture make sure that it remains relevant. Who would ever have guessed that this tough, streetwise cult film, unloved and abandoned by its studio upon controversial release, would one day become a video game, be referenced by mainstream hip-hop acts, and even be rereleased by said studio in a brand-new edition? Paramount offered Hill the opportunity to amend the film for a 2005 rerelease billed on home video as the "Ultimate Director's Cut" and which featured the kind of comic book paneling and illustrated scene transitions that Hill had originally planned to be part of the aesthetic in the initial theatrical version. However, the director doesn't consider it such a cut at all.

"The rerelease was really not a director's cut," Hill states. "I don't believe in doing those things and I don't like doing those commentary interviews. I've generally avoided all of that. *The Warriors* had a very tough postproduction schedule. We had to go very fast because they had given us a release date, so we had to have an accelerated post. We had gone over budget and they were furious at that; I didn't get along with Mr. Eisner and some of the people there at Paramount. I was angry because there was an agreement that I was going to use comic book art as part of the film to help set that fantasy world up. Orson Welles was going to do the brief intro narration—which Orson had agreed to do—but then suddenly the studio said, 'No, we're not going to go for that, you can't have that.' So, years later they came to me and proposed that I do a version close to what I had wanted to do back then. The cutting of the movie was fine, it was just these additional moments with the comic book panels and the intro. So, I was interested in that idea but unfortunately Welles had passed away by this point and so they wanted me to do the little intro thing, and I did, and which is, needless to say, a poor substitute for Orson's voice."

The Welles opening narration would have detailed the Greek historical inspiration for the film, and as it exists now in the revised edition Hill takes us back to 401 BC and the Battle of Cunaxa, during which "an army of Greek soldiers found themselves isolated in the middle of the Persian Empire. One thousand miles from safety. One thousand miles from the sea. One thousand miles with enemies on all sides. Theirs was a story of a desperate forced march. Theirs was a story of courage. This too is a story of courage."

This contextualizing of the story makes Hill's allusions to its historical origins all the more noticeable; the Greek soldiers are now updated to a Coney Island gang evading the armies that hound and surround them as they desperately flee the hostile territories to get back to their homeland by the sea. And given that it is based on the revolt of Cyrus the Younger, the Persian prince and general who engaged in battle with his older brother, the emperor Artaxerxes II, the handle of Cyrus given to the aspiring modern-day emperor and leader of the Gramercy Riffs is an obvious reference. Similarly, the name of the Warriors' fallen leader, Cleon, sounds like a play on Clearchus, the Spartan general who served under Cyrus the Younger and was later executed upon being caught by the Persian soldier Tissaphernes. It is Cleon who leads the delegation of Warriors to the Bronx summit, only to be fingered as the shooter of Cyrus and thus wrongfully killed by the baying mob out for blood.

Another immediate change to the opening is one that heralds the overall aesthetic of the new version: in an alteration of the opening shot, the illuminated Wonder Wheel is framed as though in comic book panel, frozen in a hand-drawn illustration under the caption that sets the film "Sometime in the future…." While *The Warriors* already worked in a realm of alternate reality, with its heightened colors, distinctly fashioned characters, the immediacy with which it places them in danger, and the urgency to resolve their jeopardy, it was still rooted in a gritty urban milieu with all the menace that accompanies such. However, the later version of the film literally illustrates the comic book aesthetic for anyone not clued in to Hill's pop-literary approach to the material. With the addition of Hill's thematic prologue and this new reframing of the opening, the film is set up with a distinctly different tone and feel, and it incorporates this comic book aesthetic to transition some key narrative moments using paneling and captioning. While it may not be precisely as Hill would have rendered it in 1979 had he gotten his way, it is as close as fans will get to the director's initial intentions.

"The comic book stuff is certainly in the spirit of what I had in mind," Hill states, "but it wasn't the same artist and it wasn't the same style, so it didn't turn out exactly what I had in mind. So, the version that you call the 'Director's Cut' is really 'A Cut of What the Movie Would Have Been Like Had the Director Had His Way in 1979.' We cleaned up some of the print and sized it up better but there were many people who preferred the original version for reasons that are both artistic and sentimental, and I have no problem with that. All I say is the newer version is more like what the original version might have been. If the later version is of any historical interest, it's because of that, it's not that I wanted to recut the movie. I had no problem with the original cut."

Canton says, "*The Warriors* was one of the first comic-book-type movies, but the business was so different when it was first released, no one wanted to make a comic book movie, whereas now that's all that people want to make. So Walter was able to go back to it a few years ago with his 'Director's Cut' and put more of those comic book things in it. But when the movie first came out the art form wasn't there, so the movie was really ahead of its time, even with the subject matter that it dealt with and with the Greek mythology elements. It was quite cutting edge for its day."

Future Hill collaborator and screenwriter Larry Gross says, "The idea of revising a film as he is going along is a process that Walter has explored in great detail. He has said that in the course of making every film he has learned things about the cast and about the material that he didn't know before he started shooting and that has led him to make shifts in emphasis in the writing, in the rewriting, in the design of the film, and in the conception of the film. I think *The Warriors* is the most obvious and spectacular example. Michael Beck is the lead of the Warriors in the film but his role was absolutely not the lead, he was not the main character in the script; another actor, whose name I will not mention and who is in the movie, was meant to be the lead, but after a couple of weeks Walter decided that guy ain't going to be the lead, rather it will be Michael Beck. And so the other actor's character got killed early. Walter derived a huge lesson from that, which is 'you've got to follow the movie.' The movie is going to tell you something that you thought you knew, but the movie is going to evolve. A lot of *The Warriors* was improvised, it was a movie that changed significantly during the course of its making in very fundamental ways."

Of all the films in Hill's catalog of work, *The Warriors* is the one that has cast the widest net of cultural influence. *48 Hrs.* may be the biggest financial success and *The Driver* is the one cited as importantly influential by contemporary critics and filmmakers, but this film is the one that has reached facets of society beyond those of a cinematic context. *The Warriors* has become a classic of the American Cinema thanks to retrospective festival screenings, home video rereleases, and ancillary merchandise such as action figures, video games, and all manner of pop-cultural ephemera celebrating the film. Therefore, it is no wonder that those who made it are reminded of its legacy wherever they roam. "There are people who know every word of it and the love for it spans all ages," Gordon confirms. "My own sons, who are 50 and 48, still consider it their favorite movie. Lin-Manuel Miranda said recently that it was one of the first films that he saw and he loved it, which is the kind of thing I hear a lot. All of these big rappers sample the movie—Jay-Z, Puff Daddy, Dr. Dre. It is a giant cult film here [in America]. I have a big one-sheet poster of the movie hanging in my office and when people come in that is the one thing they pay attention to; they scan over all the other movies but they always stop to talk about *The Warriors*. There is a very famous basketball player named LeBron James, he is the king, the number one basketball player in the NBA and I met him at a dinner not long ago and when his partner introduced us, he said, 'Mr. Gordon has made a lot of movies,' and LeBron said, 'Oh, would I know any of your movies, Mr. Gordon?' I said, 'Well, LeBron, I'll take a chance that you'll know one of them: *The Warriors*,' and here is what he did: this 6'9" and 270-pound man just broke out in a huge grin and mimicked David Patrick Kelly clanking the bottles and he says 'Warriors, come out to play-ay!' Everybody knows *The Warriors*, believe me. I try to think why it has lasted this long and had such a huge impact but I honestly don't know the answer; but I do know this: in a big theater with a packed audience it is as exciting as a heavyweight championship fight."

"*The Warriors* was considered kind of lurid and low," Canton admits, "so you never thought it would go on to be embraced in the way that it has. When it opened there were some incidents that happened in movie theaters here in the United States where some people ended up getting shot and the movie sort of got pulled, so we never thought it would be still playing 40 years later and people would still be celebrating it the way they do. The film has really gone on to take on a life of its own. We were just making a movie and happy for the opportunity. You don't think that your movie is going to have that kind of shelf life; it's like *Back to the Future*, you work really hard on making this movie you really like but you can never anticipate the kind of cultural impact it is going to make. I'll get an email from Walter or Frank every now and then and it will be like, 'Boys, it's been 40 years since we made *The*

Warriors and look at this photo, it's playing at this festival!' It's great that it has gone on to become this cult phenomenon."

Walter Hill was born to make westerns, and if proof were ever required for such a statement, then his first foray into the genre is exhibit A. *The Long Riders* was produced at a time when the western was on a downward spiral from its heyday as the go-to genre for postwar audiences. In terms of commercial and cultural interest, the western had reached its lowest ebb in 1980 with the debacle that was the making of Michael Cimino's *Heaven's Gate*, which was simultaneously produced by United Artists as they were funding *The Long Riders*. Forty years later, it could be said that the genre is still reeling from the industrial fallout of the disastrous production and release of *Heaven's Gate*. Cimino's grandiose film is stately in form and function, a beautiful epic of the art, though a testament to the kind of egomania and self-indulgence afforded some of the more autocratic filmmakers during the New Hollywood era. *The Long Riders* works in complete contrast: it is lean, nimble, and entirely unpretentious. Hill has often said that all of his films are westerns, and the themes, tone, and structure of his nonwestern work certainly reflect those of the genre, but in looking back at his first western proper, we can see not only a devotion to and keen understanding of the genre, but a deviation and subversion of it too.

"I've always said that *The Long Riders* is a Midwestern," Hill says. "Their activities took place in Missouri, and the Northfield thing is in Minnesota. In fact, the film is very green, whereas most westerns are brown. We only have one scene in Texas, which is entirely fictional, when Cole Younger goes there while he's on the run, but there's no real evidence that Cole Younger ever went to Texas. They were men of Missouri, Kentucky, Arkansas, and those areas, and they made the foray up to Minnesota with disastrous results. It has been my fate so far to do theatrical westerns in which I was very much bound by the history of the real-life characters. Finally, Jesse James is going to get shot by the Ford brothers while hanging a picture; Wild Bill must go down to the Number Ten Saloon and get shot in the back of the head by Jack McCall; and Geronimo is going to be put on a train and sent to Florida. These are things you cannot alter. The only time I did a fictional western was *Broken Trail*."

The Long Riders tells the tale of three sets of siblings who comprise the James-Younger Gang and their outlaw activities across the American Midwest. The film opens with a failed bank robbery in which the volatile Ed Miller (Dennis Quaid) kills a bank clerk, which instigates a shootout that leads to Jesse James (James Keach) being wounded. Unhappy with Ed's disregard for human life and for professionalism, Jesse dismisses him from the gang, though the other Miller brother, Clell (Randy Quaid), remains. The rest of the unit consists of Jesse's brother Frank (Stacy Keach) and the Younger boys: Cole (David Carradine), Jim (Keith Carradine), and Bob (Robert Carradine). In this post–Civil War time, the gang are targeting banks and trains throughout the Midwest and in doing so have captured the attention of Pinkerton detective Mr. Rixley (James Whitmore, Jr.), who leads a posse hot on their trail. However, Rixley and his men soon incur the wrath of the James brothers when two innocent members of their family—a cousin and their youngest sibling—are recklessly killed by the agency. Vengeance is theirs. Rixley backs off while the James-Younger gang poorly plot a great raid in Northfield, Minnesota, but by the time the thieves ride north the Pinkertons have already spread the word. What ensues is a cataclysmic event that also sets the scene for one of Hill's most brilliantly executed sequences in his career. The bank's timed vault cannot be opened and with tensions fraught it's not long before all hell breaks loose. A cashier and a citizen are killed, then the locals fight back, leading to much bloodshed in the streets. The Younger brothers are riddled with bullets and Frank is hit in the arm; while they survive, Clell is fatally wounded. Jesse is determined to move on and leave the injured brothers behind, much to their chagrin. Frank naturally joins him as they make their way back to Missouri. The Youngers are inevitably caught by Rixley's posse, though they refuse to cooperate in leading the law to Jesse. The same can't be said for the devious Ford brothers, Robert (Nicholas Guest) and Charlie (Christopher Guest), who after being asked by Jesse to join his new gang strike up a deal with Rixley to kill his most wanted man for $15,000. While guests at Jesse's house, they finish dinner with the cowardly assassination of their host, with Robert Ford declaring, "I shot Jesse James."

Playing the man who pulled the trigger to create a legend is Nicholas Guest. Having grown up a child of New York City, Guest recalls devouring westerns and dreaming of the foreign vistas of the American West: "When I was a young kid growing up in the city I wanted to be Roy Rogers. I was fascinated with those superb early western films and TV shows; they had incredible characters. My dad worked at the U.N. so I grew up in New York and we went to London every other year; we spent a lot of time in England, and you always want the opposite of what you have. And as an actor, the western genre offers you a chance to be part of this grand mythical storytelling. It is simple writing, and I don't mean simple in a derogatory sense,

"I shot Jesse James!" Charlie Ford (Christopher Guest) and the coward Robert Ford (Nicholas Guest) make history in *The Long Riders* (1980).

but efficient and straight-to-the-point storytelling. You can feel what is being said in people's eyes and expressions. It lends itself to physical performance—it's the horse-riding, the accents, the costumes, everything. When we did our first scene in the film where we are walking through that hall with the music playing and dancing going on around us and we try to ingratiate ourselves with the rest of the gang, it really felt like we were stepping into that time. Having the people from the area and around that part of the country as extras helped immensely with that feeling. When it came to researching the man who was Bob Ford, I got everything that was available. I read books and looked at old photographs. I love to research. I read that after the Fords killed Jesse they went on tour and acted it out for people, so there was an element of them craving celebrity and of wanting to be known, which is a frightening concept. His catchphrase of 'I shot Jesse James' says it all really—if they were rejected by the gang, then not only are they going to get back at them by killing them but also by making money out of it."

In a casting move that lends immeasurable chemistry to the various relationships, and which could have encouraged accusations of gimmickry, Hill assembled a quartet of real-life siblings to fill the roles of the James, Younger, Miller, and Ford brothers. "I found nothing gimmicky about Walter casting real-life brothers to play the character brothers in the James-Younger Gang," says the film's property master, Craig Raiche. "If anything it was not too far from brilliant. Everyone knows that working with any movie or TV series crew does promote a fairly strong familial atmosphere. Working such long hours, and especially on lengthy location shoots, it's simply inevitable. Walter's screenplay repeatedly drove home the strong influence of family bonds in the lives of those outlaws, much more so than I could recall in any previous film version of the James gang exploits. That 'we take care of our own' attitude was a very nice touch in his retelling of the Jesse James story. *The Long Riders* principal cast members only contributed to that feeling and, to this day, that film tugs strongest on my heart."

"It was incredible that they decided to go with real brothers," Guest says. "There were other brothers who were considered to play the fourth set of siblings, the Fords, but they didn't want to do it and I don't know the full story behind that, but my brother and I were brought in just to have a chat with Walter. It was so unlike what happens now, to be able to simply go in and talk to the director. That is pretty rare these days, but we went in and were both put at such great ease with him, he just wanted to know where we grew up and what our background was. We did the audition and in the room was James and Stacy Keach, the producer Tim Zimmerman, and, of course, Walter. My brother and I had never actually done anything together. I was ridiculously nervous—he had done far more—and I think the nervousness was a great advantage because we became these bumbling brothers trying to join up with the James gang. And so they started laughing and said, 'Welcome aboard!' which also does not happen anymore. They started showing us pictures of the real people that we were portraying and there was great warmth and excitement about this notion of using real brothers; it really helped in terms of the chemistry because there is something unique to that sibling relationship. And all of the sets of siblings got along, which was remarkable; people who make movies often say 'we all got along' but it's not necessarily true, but in our case it really was true. There was an incredible support system."

The centerpiece bank heist had been depicted before in Philip Kaufman's *The Great Northfield Minnesota Raid*, a picture that suggests a more vicious Jesse James and a more benevolent brother Frank, though the film is primarily focused on Cole Younger (Cliff Robertson) as he and the James gang anticipate and fail to execute the robbery of the First National Bank in Northfield. Hill's telling of the James-Younger Gang's exploits demythologizes the more romantic tendencies of Hollywood to depict the characters as Robin Hood–style men of the people. There is little room for sentimentality in Hill's world and so he depicts the gang as being brutal when the situation calls for it. And while the director doesn't make any claim for the James-Younger men as heroes, by contrasting their morals with those of the Pinkerton detectives, our sympathies inevitably err on the side of the outlaws more than with the law. We are given a glimpse into the James-Younger milieu, which is that of family, friendships, and community, while the Pinkertons are devoid of any such humanizing aspects; they are mercenary and ruthless, government bureaucrats with a gun. The Pinkertons represent faceless antagonism; their targets are attacked from a distance, whether it's the James family home being set ablaze or the gang being ambushed in a barn on Mr. MacCorkindale's farm.

In the midst of all this macho business are several women who provide the comforting solace of home when these men are not out on the trail of loot, though perhaps the most noteworthy female character and performer in the film is the vivacious Pamela Reed as the feisty and wholly independent prostitute Belle Star. She, more than any other character, has the opportunity to elicit an emotional response in the usually stoic Cole Younger; he will even go toe-to-toe with her husband, the half-breed Sam Starr, in a knife duel. "Pamela brought an unusual presence to the film," Guest says. "She underplays it in the best sense and brings this understated sense of humor to the role. The manner with which she makes her comments throughout had people roaring with laughter in the first screenings of the film, and it is because of that unique way she has about her. It was kind of unexpected actually. I felt that was a really great casting choice. Her chemistry with David Carradine was superb. David was a true standout. He was effortless and absolutely brilliant. He was great to hang out with as well. He was a huge fan of Shakespeare and we would talk late into the night. I stayed in touch with David. He was one of the kindest people I've met."

"Walter was madly in love with David Carradine and you can see it," says *48 Hrs.* screenwriter Larry Gross. "Carradine is just fantastic in *The Long Riders*, it's one of the best things he ever did. In a way it is emblematic of the way Walter works in myth. You can see him just gravitate toward Carradine as the film goes on, and that's because he sees what a presence he is and that gives Walter various opportunities of textures and nuances. Walter is prepared to take the opportunity that an actor supplies and run with it. Under the right circumstance an actor is inspired by that. It's true of the work of a lot of directors and is very much true of Howard Hawks. A film is a record of the director's feelings of what the actors can do, and Walter's films are an exploration of that. It's a collaboration."

"Working with Walter is very liberating for an actor," Guest concurs. "He puts you at ease with his great sense of humor. There were times when he'd walk over to me and say, 'Hey, Nick, see that guy over there? Do you think you could beat him up?' It was just silliness but it is a great thing to have right before a take. When a director knows exactly what they want, as Walter does, it is incredibly freeing. It can be a horrible feeling when it becomes apparent that the director doesn't know what they are doing, but with Walter it was so easy because he was hands-off and trusting of his actors. The freedom that he affords actors allows you to do great work without any feeling of insecurity."

While the film is buoyed by the young and beautiful brethren, the presence of beloved Old Hollywood character actor Harry Carey, Jr., is a bonus for western fans. Hill was compelled to write a part for the inveterate supporting man of many a John Ford film upon the instigation of his close friend British filmmaker Lindsay Anderson. It was he, the director of *This Sporting Life*, *if...*, and *O Lucky Man!* who introduced Hill to Carey, Jr., one night over drinks in West Hollywood. "Lindsay Anderson was a great friend and a real character, one of the most wonderfully caustic people I've ever known," Hill says. "He made some really stunning movies and wrote that great book on John Ford, which I think is the best book anybody has written on a director. I cried when I heard he had died. And it was through him that I met Harry Carey, Jr. Lindsay rang me and invited me for a drink over at the Chateau Marmont. He said, 'Come on over, there's somebody I want you to meet.' That turned out to be Harry and his wife, Marilyn. She was the daughter of Paul Fix, who was in almost every John Wayne movie. He and Wayne were very close and, of course, they were all in the shadow of Harry Carey, Sr. But I was happy to meet Harry. He was a very friendly guy, good at telling stories. A little later Lindsay called and asked what movie I'm doing next, and I said, 'I think I'm doing this western with all these brothers,' and he said, 'Well, write a part for Dobe [Harry].'" He said, "'Don't let me down on this! Write a part for Dobe!' I didn't want to risk Lindsay's wrath, so I wrote a little part for Dobe to do the stagecoach thing. And then I did a couple of things with him later on."

One of the most notable things about *The Long Riders* is its adherence to authenticity in its sounds and visuals, both of which reiterate themes of the passage of time to both the audience and the characters of the piece. The Coles and Youngers are men out of time, outlaws of an Old West that will be replaced by a society that will have no place for them and their ways, a new world of impending technology; they are reminded of such when a steam tractor rolls mightily past them on the streets of Northfield just before their disastrous endeavor. Filming of *The Long Riders* took place in various areas throughout Georgia, including Parrott and Leary, and it was there where Nicholas Guest found legitimacy in his experience on location. "Being in that part of the country really gave a great sense of authenticity to the film," Guest says. "We were in a place called Clayton County and it definitely felt like we were in the 1800s; we used locals as extras, which added a great deal to it because they were to some degree still living that 1800s way of life. It was fascinating. So at that point I just wanted to blend in with that whole world. There was a great atmosphere, there was evenings of singing, it was like an ongoing festival. The locations had this kind of green that you certainly don't see in California, and it started raining when we were there and I think that added a further atmosphere to the film. The landscape is very much its own character and I felt that from the minute I arrived."

Another element of the film that draws us into the time and place of the narrative is the music of Ry Cooder, here providing his debut film score and one that marks the first in a prolific series of collaborations between the renowned guitarist and Hill. Unusually for a composer scoring a major Hollywood production, Cooder had no formal training in music, but is rather a gifted self-taught player proficient in myriad styles and sensibilities, though rooted in a very American idiom that translates to authentic blues, roots rock, and traditional sounds that would support and drive forward this tale of western myth. All the instrumental tools that reflect the period are present—acoustic guitar, fiddle, dulcimer—but Cooder manages to be both romantic and edgy, the former in salute to the Old West that is represented in the lifestyles of these anachronistic outlaws, but contemporary enough to acknowledge that these men are new antiheroes of contemporary cinema. "I love Ry," Hill states. "I got along very well with him. He is an amazing talent. I was a fan of his, that's how he got the job on *The Long Riders*. He did an album called *Jazz* and there were two cuts on it, old-time religious songs, which were done in the way things would have sounded in 1890, and I thought that was the kind of thing I was trying to do in this western. I didn't want the big *Magnificent Seven*–type score, although that was great in its moment. I was looking for something more atmospheric and of the time. With a score, I don't want to underline the drama, I want to surround it with atmosphere. One of my criticisms of most movies is that they have too much music and too in-your-face."

On hand to assist in re-creating authentic Missouri garb of the post–Civil War era was costumer Dan Moore, who would go on to work extensively with his director. Indeed, *The Long Riders* would prove an interesting test ground for Moore, who ditched a stable life in academia for the trenches of Hollywood. In 1979 Moore was writing his dissertation in the English department of Ohio State University when a movie came to town, and that movie was the Robert Redford vehicle *Brubaker*. Through a friend of a friend he got a job as a production assistant on that picture and was randomly assigned to the wardrobe department, working under costume designer Tom Bronson. "Because I did whatever I was asked to do, Tom thought, 'This guy is talented!'" Moore recalls. "He told me that if I was interested in taking this up he could get me into the union out in Los Angeles. I thought about it for about 30 seconds and I said, 'Sure, I'll come and do it!' I had already passed all of my exams for my PhD but I went out there and took a job on *The Long Riders*. We prepped the movie in LA and took off down to Georgia. We were going to use a lot of western string ties for when the boys got dressed up a little bit, so when Bronson and I were on the plane to Georgia, he had me tying these string ties on my leg for practice. I was the set guy, so I had to make sure all the brothers were dressed right and had their gloves on for riding, that kind of stuff. It was quite a challenge."

Hill recalls the sage advice of his Old Hollywood hero Raoul Walsh, who told his admirer of a costuming rule that would lend further authenticity to his characters:

"Raoul smoked like a chimney, and they were these unfiltered cigarettes that he would roll like a cowboy, with one hand; it was amazing. He was rolling a cigarette when I was saying goodbye to him out on the porch, and just as I was doing so, I told him that I would like to be a director and I asked him if there was anything I should bear in mind. He said, 'Always let the actors pick their own hat.' He grew up in an era when men wore hats and, of course, for westerns you always use hats, but his point was that actors are self-conscious, they need to feel confident to give you a good performance. He said that hats are very personal and if you give an actor a hat and they don't think they look right it's going to bother them, it will block their performance, that if you allow them to choose it themselves most actors will figure out the right hat for their character, which will make them feel good about themselves and the way they look. I thought that was very good advice and I put it into effect on *The Long Riders*. I had a couple of big barrels organized and sent them all in there at the same time to pick out their own hats and they inherently picked out good ones. I just told them not to look like a cowboy, it's not really a cowboy movie nor is it a traditional western. Allowing the actors to pick out their own hats was a direct aid to their ability to perform within the character they are trying to pull off."

The violent bank heist centerpiece of the film is one of the most impressively constructed and thrilling action scenes of any Hill film. The buildup to the scene is ingeniously taut with the image of a slow-rolling steam tractor, a symbol of imminent technology and a harbinger of the end of the era to which the James-Younger boys belong. Hill draws upon stylistic flourishes that he would use to more prominent effect in later films, such as the use of long-lens photography to derive a sense of intimacy with the characters as the anxiety of the scene reaches its crescendo and before all hell breaks loose. The ensuing bullet ballet of the Northfield raid unfolds in utter devastation, and Hill slows everything down so that we feel and hear every single shot coming and its subsequent impact. It is a stunning display of action cinema and a powerful depiction of violence with context. The scene is presented in a choreography of agony, with every movement and gesture an additional note of despair. Editor Freeman Davies introduces a form of montage to create a truly exciting action set piece, his formalist style heightening the impact of each gunshot. This notable aesthetic resulted in some comparisons being drawn to that of past masters of the genre, in particular to Hill's old friend Sam Peckinpah, whose unforgettable action sequences were edited with a striking mixture of slow motion and regular speed to create a montage of brutality unlike anything since the Odessa Steps massacre scene of Sergei Eisenstein's *The Battleship Potemkin* in 1925. Davies's editing style evokes a similar form and rhythm to that of Louis Lombardo's in *The Wild Bunch*, which is something Peckinpah himself questioned Hill on. Always anticipating the testing curiosity of his friend, Hill managed to explain the subtle differences in their use of similar technique:

"After *The Long Riders* came out Sam called me up," Hill recalls. "He had seen the movie and said some nice things. Sam was certainly friendly but in a reserved way; there was always a little edge to it all. It was like you were always being tested by him. So, we were talking about the film and he said, 'I hear a lot of people comparing the Northfield scene to my work, but that's not true, is it?' And I said, 'No, it really isn't, it's not true at all,' and he said, 'Well, why isn't it true?' And I thought, 'Oh, fuck! Here we go … the test!' I said, 'Look, when you are doing the slow motion you are extending the reality of the moment and the way I used the slow motion in the Northfield scene is actually the opposite, you are getting inside the characters' heads and turning it into a nightmare.' And Sam said, 'That's right, Doctor.' He used to call people 'Doctor' a lot. I never forgot that moment."

Joining the James-Younger Gang on the doomed raid are Chadwell and Pitts, a couple of lowlife robbers played by genuine hard men, Eddie Bunker and Tim Rossovich. Bunker was a convicted felon turned author and actor, acclaimed for novels such as *No Beast So Fierce* (1973) and *The Animal Factory* (1977); Rossovich was an NFL linebacker who also found a niche playing tough guys in Hollywood movies and TV shows. Another celebrated athlete bringing his commanding physical presence to the screen is Allan Graf, who would become one of Hill's most prolific collaborators, appearing in front of the camera as well as working behind the scenes as a stunt coordinator and second unit director. Graf appears in *The Long Riders* in two minor roles, playing a mouthy, hapless Northfield civilian and the train engineer who asks Bob Younger, "What the hell are you aiming to do?" to which the youngest Younger replies, "I ain't aiming to do nothing, I'm doing it!" Graf recalls the film's most famous sequence and its intricate stunt work: "It is incredible the way Walter put that Northfield action sequence together. How he works with slow-motion images and sound is incredible; the sound of the bullets, the way you hear them coming and then impacting was really good filmmaking. The scene has an incredible stunt in which the guys go through the window on horseback. Even though they prepped that for weeks, a guy almost got hurt coming out the back because he flipped over the horse, which just about managed to avoid trampling on him. To rehearse the shot they let the horses jump through the empty window frame with just Saran wrap in place where the glass would be. This got the horses used to making the jump through the window so that there would be no hesitation upon filming. And then when the time came to shooting the scene, they put the candy glass in the window frame and the horses jumped through and it was spectacular. Having that many horses doing that stunt at once was pretty big-time."

"Taking the horses through the windows, that was amazing stuff," prop master Craig Raiche says. "Back then we had the effects departments and the stunt departments working together to create these amazing sequences. Craig Baxley was the stunt coordinator on that and he came from a long line of stuntmen in his family; his father is Bob Baxley, and so he grew up in the business. They did things on that film which would be a little more vetted for safety today than it was then. It is the kind of stuff that would be all done using visual effects."

"I was nearly seriously hurt," Graf recalls. "I played the bank customer during the heist and when the woman screams I run out of the bank and start shouting, 'They're robbing the bank!' Then the gang shoot me in the back and I fall facedown in the street. There are seven or eight cameras going and people firing guns. We shot this in Georgia, in a little town called Albany, and they were using locals who had these teams of horses and wagons and when all this gunfire went off this one guy couldn't control his team of horses. So this one horse got loose and he was aiming

The daring horse stunt from the Northfield, Minnesota, Raid sequence in *The Long Riders* (1980).

right for me. I'm lying there on the ground and this wagon is coming right at me and they're yelling at me, 'Get out of there, Allan!' I didn't hear anything and I didn't want to raise my head and screw the scene up because they're shooting with long lenses on me. I didn't hear all the commotion but then I felt this wagon wheel roll right by my head and I felt the ground shook. I was thinking, 'Was that real?!' They yelled cut and everybody just freaked out, checking to see if I was okay. I asked what happened and they told me that I almost got ran over by a wagon. Then Walter says, 'Get that dummy out and put a real dummy in there!'"

Raiche continues: "Walter wanted the bullet hits on the James gang to be not just larger than life, but much, much larger. Our talented special effects coordinator, Larry Cavanaugh, did not disappoint. I recall one film critic proclaiming those bullet hits to be 'so over-the-top huge that everyone in the first four rows left the theater in blood-splattered clothing.'" Indeed, the film benefited from the sense of danger that came with Raiche, whose propensity for using live ammunition quite unnerved one certain cast member. "Quite unexpectedly, somewhere in the middle of filming, Walter greeted me one morning with, 'Hey, 'Live Rounds,' how's it going?' Of course, I asked what he was talking about and he said that he'd just read David Carradine's *Playboy* magazine interview in the next, upcoming edition. Apparently, David told the interviewer that the movie he was working on had a rather 'loose' prop master. Loose enough that I had used live ammunition in some of the scenes. Thankfully, David didn't identify me by name in the article, but Walter's nickname of 'Live Rounds' did stick with me for some time in the industry. The seventies really were a 'far out' time and being known—or, at least, suspected—as *a little bit crazy* was not altogether a bad thing. In truth, I had used live ammo to shoot an old barn door so that Walter could see the difference between that reality and the end result after being sprayed by 'bullet hits' from our special effects department. As anyone (except

Mr. Carradine) could imagine, I'd done this off set, out in a forest, and safely far enough away from all people."

Considering *The Long Riders* in the context of its place and time in western film history, it stands out as bold and as different as ever. It is unusual in many ways, particularly so for a mainstream studio release, as the picture does not function in the traditional manner of commercial filmmaking—it is a collection of scenes and moments that are character-driven rather than motivated as part of a direct narrative trajectory. The film is linear but the structure of the story is less concerned about taking audiences through the motions of beginning, middle, and end of an overarching story, preferring to take us directly to crucial moments in the lives of the outlaw ensemble. Many westerns of the 1970s were revisionist and Hill's vision feels reactionary to that, but unlike other films of the era, Hill has no intentions of turning the genre inside out or to mine for contemporary parallel socio-political themes; his vision is a restoration of a certain kind of elegiac picture that recalls Ford as much as it does Peckinpah. "We shot *The Long Riders* in '79 and it was released in '80," Raiche recalls. "There had been a number of classic westerns made in the seventies but well-made westerns were seriously on the wane. I don't think *The Long Riders* 'revived' western movies as much as it moved Hollywood studios to realize their folly in making so many cheap 'B picture' westerns that they had been doing. It doesn't matter how you slice any classic Western movie. It can be cavalry vs. Indians, land baron cattlemen vs. immigrant homesteaders, outlaw cowboys vs. lawmen or, well, just about anything really. It all boils down to good guys vs. bad guys and then it really depends on your own point of view as to what constitutes or separates the good guys from the bad guys. Surely, we all love a good antihero and *The Long Riders* was full of them. It was a great experience. A lot of fun."

"We made *The Long Riders* towards the end of the New Hollywood era," Guest recalls, "and United Artists were making *Heaven's Gate* at the same time. And in the end *Heaven's Gate* affected everything afterwards. I knew people who were working on that and it just went forever. It's a beautiful film in many ways but it was also a catastrophe in terms of production, and the ripples of which are still being felt today, so I'm not sure if they could make *The Long Riders* in the same way today or if it is something that a studio would ever consider doing now. The director had a lot more power back then than they do now. I worked on *Trading Places* around this time and even on that you could feel that the director was very much the person in power; he was able to reel in an amazing mixture of actors and could take more time making the film and not be dictated by the studio demands."

For Larry Gross, this film proved to be the one that instigated his interest in Hill, an admiration that would soon lead to several professional collaborations: "*The Long Riders* is one of those movies that made me want to meet Walter Hill. When I watched it I certainly saw the Peckinpah element, particularly in the action sequences, but it is also very John Ford. I've always thought the sequence where the younger James boy is buried is pure Ford." *The Long Riders* is also that rare western that is both incredibly violent and yet underscored with a subtle sense of humor, neither overshadowing the other as Hill strikes the balance exquisitely. Nicholas Guest concurs: "It is not an easy thing to balance humor and violence but Walter achieves it effortlessly. He brings some of his own sense of humor to the films as well. Even in the tougher scenes there is an element of humor which is very much Walter; it could be a gun not going off or something unimaginable going wrong. A fine example of Walter's sense of humor is on the train when Bobby Carradine says he wants a free copy of David Carradine's book and David says, 'No, you gotta pay!' There is also a certain toughness that he can describe and portray, and that comes with a certain vulnerability as well. He is a terrific writer. I mean he had written *The Getaway* for Sam Peckinpah! His incredible honesty and deep understanding of his subject matter allows him to bring great depth and truth through knowledge."

Gross agrees: "That is a terrific moment of humor where Cole Younger says, 'I'm going to write a book about my exploits which will make me even more famous than I already am,' and Frank James says, 'I hope I'm going to get a free copy,' and Cole says, 'No, you gotta pay, Frank!' The way Carradine delivers that line is unbelievable; Walter told me that Carradine improvised that line. The humor in Walter's movies has to do with the actors, what they can do and what they are able to do. Walter doesn't write very funny lines but he is extremely sensitive to and looking for what's in the actors."

"I can't say enough about how great it was to be part of *The Long Riders*," costumer Dan Moore says. "All of a sudden I'm in the union and I'm getting paid to do all of this fun stuff. It really was a fantastic time and it is a wonderful movie. Nobody sees it anymore but it is a great piece of work. Best of all was that I got to know Walter and I ended up doing a lot of movies with him."

"It all starts with Walter as a writer," Guest applauds. "He really is multifaceted, and he was so clear in his vision. That's what makes him a true auteur filmmaker. I feel so fortunate to have had the experience of making this movie; it was such a unique thing to have that amount of time making it and to become a family with Walter, who is a very kind person, and with all the brothers. I loved hanging out with Dan Moore talking about *Ulysses*. We all feel blessed to have done this movie. It was a gift to us, having that experience of making *The Long Riders*. It was a standout for sure. I'll always treasure it."

Following *The Long Riders*, Hill would venture deep into the Louisiana swamplands for one of his darkest, and greatest, films: *Southern Comfort*. The roots of the film go back to Hill's directorial debut, *Hard Times*, in which a sequence in Cajun country grabbed the attention of cowriter and coproducer David Giler, who suggested to Hill setting an entire film around this culture. The film would prove authentic in its milieu, with Hill and his crew going deep into the heart of some lesser-filmed land, shooting entirely on location in Caddo Lake, which borders Texas and Louisiana, across the fall and winter of 1980. Production would scout for suitable swamp settings in Florida, South Carolina, Mississippi, and Alabama, each too beautiful and thus unsuitable, before settling on the Louisiana location that would harbor all of the unsettling and unwelcoming character required. It would also prove to be one of the most physically grueling productions that Hill and his collaborators would ever partake in.

Trudging through the soggy bayou is a nine-member platoon of the Louisiana Army National Guard headed by Staff Sergeant Crawford Poole (Peter Coyote) and including Corporal Charles Hardin (Powers Boothe), Corporal Lonnie Reece (Fred Ward), Corporal Nolan Bowden (Alan Autry), and Private First Class Spencer (Keith Carradine). These and the rest of this disparate group end up at loggerheads as they go to war with a gang of Cajun trappers who are residents of the region. Corporal Reece immediately shows a lack of concern for his surroundings and its inhabitants when he casually cuts apart the trappers' net, which has been capturing fish for food. It is this indifference to the world they have entered that will lead to the disastrous events to follow. The terrain the men had mapped out to traverse is now under water due to heavy winter rains, leaving the men with two options: to return to base camp and start over, or take the chance of getting across the land using a trio of pirogues they come across without their owners' permission. The guardsmen's blatant commandeering of the boats shows little regard to those who own them, and the result is tragic. Bowden doesn't want to take them, but Reece immediately dismisses such a moral view and decides to "get in 'em and take off." Poole eventually agrees with Reece to appropriate the boats for the sake of making the shortcut across the water, telling Bowden to leave a note explaining their absence. Naturally, the trappers are not pleased when they arrive to discover their transport taken, and then things get serious after hotheaded Private First Class Stuckey (Lewis Smith) stupidly and carelessly fires blanks at the aggrieved indigenous folk in a display of gung-ho bravado. However, the locals duly return fire with real bullets, killing Poole. Reece blames the trappers for things turning fatal and uses their shooting of Poole as justification for going back to "get these Cajuns." This proves a tactical nightmare for the ill-equipped weekend warriors who are at the mercy of the merciless guerrilla methods used by the Cajuns to hunt and terrorize these inexperienced men whose limited

A Cajun trapper, played by Brion James (left), is interrogated by hotheaded Corporal Lonnie Reece (Fred Ward, center right), who is flanked by Private First Class Spencer (Keith Carradine, center background) and Corporal "Coach" Bowden (Alan Autry, right), in *Southern Comfort* (1981).

survival skills are severely tested. With booby-trapped trees, bear traps, and spear beds, the Cajuns have set the obstacle course of the damned.

As with many of Hill's films, *Southern Comfort* is intrigued with the idea of placing ordinary men in extraordinary situations and allowing the personal dynamics of those individuals to fuel the drama. While the central premise pits supposedly sophisticated contemporary men against those of a more primitive culture in a battle for survival within a treacherous environment, one of the key aspects of the film is the conflict of personalities played out in uncomfortably close quarters under intense circumstances. "We really covered all the bases with the characters in the film," Hill says. "Some of them are bright and some are more brute, and it is interesting to see them reacting in this situation which they are responsible for getting themselves into. I'm proud of the actors in it, they brought a lot of character to it, and we all had a tough time making it." Hill sets up the contrasting personas and their varying dispositions in the pre-credit sequence, clueing us in to the type of men they will be as the narrative progresses, clearly marking their respective moral perspective with great economy. Corporal Hardin is the new guy, having transferred his National Guard membership from his previous home base of El Paso, Texas, to Louisiana. His first exchange with Staff Sergeant Poole is fraught with barely contained hostility, and we quickly learn that Hardin is burnt out and cynical. Poole asks what he likes about being in the Louisiana National Guard, having come from El Paso.

> HARDIN: *"I don't. But then I didn't much like being in the Texas Guard either."*
> POOLE: *"Well, not liking the Texas Guard makes sense. Not liking the Louisiana Guard can get you into trouble with me. You got that?"*
> HARDIN: *"I got it."*

Elsewhere we get a quick insight into the personalities of the rest of the platoon, which also provides some foreshadowing of conflicts that will soon reemerge in the depths of the swampland, particularly between Bowden and Stucky. Bowden's volatility and no-nonsense demeanor is evident early on, and their feuding reaches a boiling point in a physical confrontation after Poole's death, which can be blamed squarely on Stucky's stupidity. In these early scenes we witness his brand of provocative juvenile behavior that will land the whole platoon in trouble—he indiscriminately fires his machine gun loaded with blanks at his peers, an act that prefigures his action later that will incur fatal consequences. "Stucky," considers Spencer, "well, he's not smart enough to read a dime novel." City boy Spencer is a macho archetype led by his libido and who clashes with the impatient and moralistic Bowden, who chides Spencer when he hears of him having six prostitutes waiting for them at the end of the weekend, a little something for morale, as Spencer puts it: "They'll fuck us in a more interesting way than the National Guard." "Women? What women? You mean prostitutes? This is a new low, Spencer, even for you," Bowden says. Spencer's jaded view of the Guard is tinged with sarcasm and cynicism. To him, the women at the far end of the swamp justify his presence in such a company. When Hardin tells him that they do things different in Texas, like watching the ball game, throwing dice, and sleeping, Spencer counters with, "The Louisiana Guard is a little different.

They have us out doing really important things like beating up on college kids and tear-gassing niggers ... we have a long, noble military tradition." When Spencer tries to make excuses for his fellow guardsmen's behavior and questionable morality, Hardin doesn't buy it, saying, "They're not okay, they're just Louisiana versions of the same dumb rednecks I've been around my whole life."

Underscoring such conflict is the class and cultural disparities among the group, such as that which exists between white-collar chemical engineer Hardin and some of his uncouth comrades. "A college boy!" Spencer says. "Not many of them in Texas." Spencer questions Hardin's domestic situation and assumes him to be living a comfortable life, though Hardin doesn't relate the sentiments of contentment that one would expect from the aspirational middle class. When bluntly asked if he loves his wife, he doesn't display much emotion, rather shrugging off the question by dispassionately saying "she makes me laugh." When Spencer assumes there to be a big house, Hardin tells him he doesn't even have a den of his own. Thus, we don't get the sense that Hardin is particularly content in life, despite the appearance of upward social mobility. Further strain emerges when the men's personal lives on the outside world reveal opposing morals, as when Pvt. Cribbs (T.K. Carter) pushes Cpl. Bowden's buttons by taunting the high school history teacher and football coach with the fact that he makes a living selling drugs. "I pick up a little cash pimpin' here and there, but mostly what I turn over comes from selling dope to high school kids." Despite the acrimony, it is Bowden who leads prayers over Cribbs's makeshift grave after he is killed by a spear bed trap.

Such discord and anxiety among the squad is heightened as the threat from the Cajuns increases, leading the guardsmen become dangerously unstable, turning on each other and forming alliances that sever any unity that might help them through the inhospitable environment. Even those of elevated social status due to profession are just as prone to violence and equally adept at the potential for barbarism as

The one-armed trapper (Brion James) gains the upper hand in *Southern Comfort* (1981).

those of more criminal tendencies. Tension mounts among the platoon after Spencer reveals that Reece has discreetly brought along live rounds "for his own use," meaning a limited supply of ammo is available that could save the men's lives. But Reece is not willing to divide and share his stock. Only when Hardin steps in and threatens Reece with a knife does he give up the bullets. And so, another feud is formed. Hardin proves he can be just as brutal when pushed and he succeeds against Reece in a bloody knife duel that is encouraged by the captive Cajun trapper, who sees an opportunity to escape with Reece out of the picture. Hardin's quick resolve to action proves vital when he saves Spencer by plunging a knife into the groin of a gun-toting hunter (Sonny Landham).

If there is any form of unity in the world of *Southern Comfort*, it is solely represented in the rowdy but close-knit Cajun community that we observe in the final act. Here we see a feast being prepared: hogs are hung, slaughtered, and roasted; crawfish are boiled; and music is performed as families gather and dance jubilantly. Their welcoming disposition is displayed in the potential for romance as a local beauty draws a dance out of Spencer; she is visibly disappointed when he is alerted by Hardin that trouble is brewing and must leave her alone on the dance floor. This climactic display of community presents a marked contrast to the disharmony that exists in the collective of so-called civilized urbanites and suburbanites who constitute the group of guardsmen. Here, Hill skillfully sets up a world that is both unfamiliar yet inviting, the first glimpse of warmth for the audience, seducing us into the spirit of celebration before we experience the paranoia of Hardin and Spencer as the trappers close in on them. Playing one of those pursuing trappers is Allan Graf, who recalls the less-than-salubrious location work. "*Southern Comfort* was one of the toughest shows I've ever worked on," Graf recalls, "and I have worked on a hell of a lot of shows! We shot it in Uncertain, Texas—they were uncertain if they were in Louisiana or Texas! We did it at a time of year when there wouldn't be as many mosquitoes and bugs, but we froze our buns off. We had to break ice to get into the swamps and underneath that water were tree stumps; you can't see them, they just rip you a new one. That setting was rough."

Prop master Craig Raiche was also knee-deep in the swamp waters of Caddo Lake, but working on a Walter Hill production meant a crew willing to persevere through the toughest of conditions to make the best possible film, as he recalls: "It was no secret that *Southern Comfort* was going to be a particularly difficult shoot, as the entire film took place in a swamp called Caddo Lake, in a city named Uncertain, Texas (population: 114, and that may have included their pigs and chickens), in the dead of winter, and some 80 miles from our hotel in Shreveport, Louisiana. Apparently, we actually *wanted* to test fate. Still, this was a Walter Hill film, so a good time was pretty much guaranteed for all … well, maybe. Morning after morning, our bleary-eyed crew boarded the bus that would take us to the location. Right next to our hotel there was a digital sign on the side of a bank that read '5:05 a.m./8 degrees' and then we'd hit the freeway on-ramp to Uncertain. Sometime around 6:30 my assistant, Bruce Kasson, and I would open the prop truck and remove two Zodiak inflatable boats. Bruce gathered up and organized all the working props for the day while I fired up a large propane heater, scraped off how many ever leeches were still hanging on to my wet suit from the prior day's work, and then hung it in front of the heater to thaw out. Eventually, I stripped down, climbed in, and we'd shoot until sundown. And so it went, more or less, for another 70 days or so. Nobody had it easy. Only a handful of crew were in the water as much as I, but 'solid ground' in that swamp was just as difficult to traverse. It's the kind of mucky mud that can suck your boots off at any time. Just getting to a director's chair could be something of a workout."

"It was a hard movie to make out there in winter," Hill concurs. "We had to shoot quickly when we were in the swamp, because once you set up and rolled the camera you had to get it within a few minutes, right before the bottom of the swamp would start giving way."

Costumer Dan Moore, who had given up the potential for a lofty life of academia for the heady lights of Hollywood on *The Long Riders*, was now plunged into the sludge with the rest of the crew. He recollects on the fraternal bonhomie that helped everyone move forward through the physically tasking production: "*Southern Comfort* was a physical ballbuster, but you just had to get out there and do it. The crews were all working together in those days, so we're out there in the swamps and slogging through it. We had a stunt coordinator called Bennie Dobbins and he would be out trudging through the swamps looking for a pathway for the actors to walk through; he would find a path and have the effects guys chop down these little cypress trees. But you can't always see them under the water and the actors would trip and fall; just doing all that stuff was really intensive. One thing about *Southern Comfort* is that because you can't see the breath coming out of the actors' mouths it looks like we were shooting on a pleasant afternoon in the fall, whereas it was actually freezing all the time and it was wet. The actors could barely keep their teeth from chattering while doing their lines. It was quite a challenge, but we were a band of brothers out there. There were great guys on that film, people like Powers Boothe and Keith Carradine, and there was a lot of admiration between the crew and the cast; we could see that Powers wasn't saving it for the prom, he was giving it everything he had. I miss those days a lot."

As fall turned to winter, the days were long and hard, but for Raiche, a bit of humor could be found in some of the more absurd tasks of his job, which included acquiring and overseeing the handing of all "properties" that were directly handled by the actors; in this case, the pigs that would be providing dinner for the Cajun ensemble in the climax of the film. The very pigs whose demise is captured on camera as the denizens of the village celebrate the culinary gathering.

"In *Southern Comfort* there was a scene where a local couple are driving their flatbed truck to an authentic Cajun boucherie. The couple comes across two of our lost National Guard soldiers and gives them a ride to the event. Also on that truck are two gigantic pigs (at their weight, hogs really), which were individually caged. A couple minutes before our crew broke for lunch, one of those hogs managed to escape and off to the swamp he went, never to be seen again. In order for us to continue shooting that sequence, I would have to forgo my lunch and get a driver to help me track down any local farmer who would sell me one of his hogs. Yes, all manner of animals are props too. That alone took about an hour and after a few more minutes haggling over the selling price, I was ready to head back to the set and have my lunch—or so I thought. I told the farmer, 'I'll take that huge one, right there.' The guy said, 'Okay, fine. You got any rope?' Shaking my head no, he said, 'I'll get you some.' When he returned with the rope I realized I hadn't made a deal that included the actual capture of said hog and/or getting it loaded onto our pickup truck—and he was not willing (or young or strong enough) to do either. Now, that was a comedy film that should have been shot: this city boy hopelessly trying to rope a hog into submission—no real help from the driver—in a nice big pen of hog slop. Eventually, I returned to the set prize in hand, so to speak, and I was absolutely covered, head to toes, in pig shit and mud. I needed a little medical attention for a bite to my hand and a kick to my face. Oh well, lesson(s) learned. Moments after their arrival at the boucherie, those two hogs were shot in their cages on the pickup truck, quickly strung up by their hind legs, bled out, and then disemboweled; we filmed all of it. Some could say we simply documented a very long-standing and time-honored Cajun tradition of a boucherie hog slaughter. Most filmgoers, however, were quite shocked to see such graphic footage. Still, in the end, that scene did have an upside in that I was able to arrange for a swift and proper delivery of that butchered meat to nearby charitable institutions."

Southern Comfort is a master class in narrative economy, hooking the audience from its opening frames and unrelenting until its final moments, a film that rarely allows the viewer a moment of respite from the onslaught of tension and obsessive pursuit. While the closest Walter Hill has ever come to directing a horror picture is *Supernova*, a film he ultimately took his name off, the other film that bears closest resemblance to the genre is most certainly *Southern Comfort*. Both this and his later film *Trespass* contain similar elements to his script for Ridley Scott's space horror *Alien* (1979) in that both films place a group of individuals of varying socio-economic status into a hostile environment of limited field and into contact with an enemy from an entirely different culture. Whereas *Trespass* assumes the generic form of a contemporary western, evoking elements of John Huston's *The Treasure of the Sierra Madre* (1948) and Howard Hawks's *Rio Bravo* (1959), *Southern Comfort* unfolds in the tone and tradition of the horror picture. It has been interpreted as an allegory for the Vietnam War, perhaps because it works in the vein of the combat picture. Of course, there is cause to compare it to such given the visual correlation of its landscapes, the military clothing, and artillery used by the characters to those that would be seen in a traditional war film set in South Vietnam. Indeed, at first glance *Southern Comfort* looks like it could unfold in combat movie fashion, but the deeper into the woods we go, the more akin to a folk horror picture it becomes. "*Southern Comfort* does feel like a horror film in places," Hill agrees. "I actually got in trouble once when I was talking about *Alien* and I noted the difference between horror movies and other genres. I said that action movies beat up men and horror movies beat up women, so I ended up getting a lot of letters. I wasn't recommending it, just pointing out the obvious." This chilling tale of men being stalked and terrorized by unfriendly backwoodsmen in the harsh Louisiana swamps is as terrifying as anything bearing more traditional bogeymen. And it was nothing new for Hollywood to present and reinforce cultural stereotypes of rural men as violent, almost animalistic, terrorizers of supposedly civilized visitors to their land. It is most famously presented in John Boorman's *Deliverance* (1971), Tobe Hooper's *The Texas Chainsaw Massacre* (1974), and Wes Craven's *The Hills Have Eyes* (1977). Like the Appalachians of Boorman's thriller, the Cajuns of Hill's film put to test the American ideals that the guardsmen represent: rugged individualism, pride, and fortitude. Even though the ethnic antagonists have been residents of the land on which the guardsmen tread since their ancestors settled in the 17th century, they are presented as an Other in the eyes of our heroes. As with the Hooper and Craven films, *Southern Comfort* also balances the generic registers of horror cinema with a great degree of verisimilitude and lack of supernatural elements, and just like those two films, it brings a sense of gritty realism to its nightmarish milieu, as the action and drama here are very much rooted in actuality. The Cajuns are presented as abnormal, savage, and deformed (Brion James's lead trapper is a wily and beastly one-armed man), deeply rural swamp rats who live an obsolete lifestyle that is perceived as uncivilized and uncouth. But as otherworldly as they may seem to us and to the guardsmen, they are as earthly as any of us. And therein lies the terror.

With a canvas of unfriendly fog-shrouded swampland, the stylish production design and cinematography brings us into the realm of the gothic and it offers up some truly disturbing images for the audience and its distraught characters to observe. Some of these are reminiscent of classic works of anti-war art, such as Francisco Goya's disturbing commentaries on the horrors of conflict, including *Grande hazana! Con muertos!* (*A heroic feat! With dead men!*), from his *Disasters of War* series of prints of 1810 to 1820. Hill serves us grisly shots of freshly exhumed bodies savagely mounted on poles and eviscerated animals put on display to taunt the remaining members of the squad. If the guardsmen held any romantic or idealistic notions about playing soldier, it all comes crashing down with these grim tableaus. In presenting these scenarios, Hill is going far beyond direct allusion to the war, for this is not the symbolism of the Hollywood combat film. He is bringing us into the realm of staged barbarism, of the horror film. The guardsmen are being toyed with by an elusive enemy that essentially disappears into the environment and is hell-bent on the most vicious vengeance, not merely protecting their plot of land from unfriendly fire but becoming the land itself. The nightmarish mise-en-scène of the maimed and slayed bodies of their comrades is shocking to the audience because Hill eases us out of the mundane maneuvers of the opening act and into the infernal landscape of the midsection of the film, before bringing us back to reality once again in the Cajun village where in the clear light of day slaughter still takes place, though it is normalized in the name of food and tradition. Indeed, the final act of the film provides a terrific contrast of diegetic realities, taking us out of the surrealist nightmare of the swamp and into the jolting reality of the village, which soon becomes just as treacherous. Much acclaim for this must go to the great cinematographer Andrew Laszlo. Having previously lensed New York City as a sprawling urban jungle in *The Warriors* and later converting the Universal backlot into a neon noir netherworld for *Streets of Fire*, here his photography skillfully creates a hazy, colorless world for the platoon to tread precariously. Only when we get to the Cajun townland is any life and light brought into the visual aesthetic, setting us up for a climactic showdown that takes place after Hill eases us into the warmth and seeming hospitality of the jubilant locals. Laszlo's photography iterates the harshness of the protagonists' struggle in this strange, hostile, and unwelcoming landscape. The deeper we delve into the swamp, the more Lazslo's monochromatic aesthetic mutes his palette of life and color, just as the characters become enveloped in the cloak of diffusion and fog. Craig Raiche recalls how Laszlo's approaches resulted in some premature R&R for some of the crew. However, they would soon be working their asses off in earnest.

"Andy's choice of film stock and other technical considerations allowed him to shoot with low levels of artificial light to achieve that look as desired by Walter, the unexpected result of which gifted two weeks of vacation time to the electricians—specifically, the first two weeks of shooting. And, had they not so openly flaunted their vacation in such a carefree manner, acting the maggot and all, they might have enjoyed that vacation all the way through the entire shoot. So there they were, the Little 'Lectric' Lads, floating around all hither and yon on the best houseboat available for rent in Uncertain, Texas, all comfortably stretched out on folding chairs and pool lounges with beverages in one hand and fishing poles in the other, smoking cigars, telling jokes and tall tales from past movie experiences, while the rest of the crew had as much fun as anyone else might have in a question & answer session with Tourquemada. And just as a topper, well, let me tell you, those boys made a right fetching sign for their floating man cave: *The Electric Lounge*. I never did hear the circumstances that caused their gift to just … float away, but something did happen and in right quick fashion. On the first day of week three, 'The Electric Lounge' had been shut down and confiscated. From that point on, there on the set, next to the cast and the crew and Tourquemada, there were also a couple of electricians and, sometimes, they brought a 9-light with them.

"There are two parts in the appropriated pirogues sequence. In the first half, our guardsmen gently paddle the canoes through the glassy-smooth waters of the swamp. Nothing is gentle or smooth in the second half as all hell breaks loose and its pure panic for the soldiers. We'd filmed all but one of the various scenes needed to complete that sequence—a tight shot of the bullet hit on Staff Sgt. Poole's forehead. Walter, along with Andy Laszlo, our director of photography, and Freeman Davies, our editor, decided to shoot that bullet hit scene at sunset/magic hour. It would help transition the light-toned sky seen in our canoe sequence to a darker-toned sky that is seen when they take cover on solid ground. Filming at 'magic hour' is often difficult because all ambient sunlight is quickly fading while the sky is continually darkening. Time, and light, will be working against you, and sometimes you'll lose that battle. As I recall, that bullet hit scene was not so much scheduled for any particular day as it was listed on every new day's call sheet as 'Possibly/Time Permitting.' To get that shot, all we needed to do was complete any one day's scheduled work and find enough sunlight remaining to shoot it. To no one's surprise, that day was not to be—unless we double-timed our pace after lunch to help ensure some remaining light. As the saying goes, 'Ya gotta do what ya gotta do,' and so we did. Our first assistant director, Pat Kehoe, in his normal disposition could bark out orders with the best of them. But in a 'crunch time' mode he could be a Captain Bligh. Yes, I've got whip marks.

"Working in water and thick, slippery, mud does not make for quick work, and if you're putting in 60-hour workweeks in that environment, then a double-time pace, even for a short while, can be exhausting … unless you happen to be sailing on The Electric Lounge. With 'the old college try' our crew was on the move, hustling from the previous shot in the swamp to the place where we would finally do the bullet hit scene. And with the approaching sunset, we are now 'losing the light.' By the time I got there, my assistant, Bruce Kasson, had already dragged the canoe along with a paddle and Coyote's personal props to the set. In doing that, Bruce had a fall resulting in minor injury, so I sent him back to the truck to get him off his feet. No biggie, everything I needed for the shot he'd already taken care of. Do keep in mind a few things here: this is a 'head shot' featuring a bullet hit on Sgt. Poole. We're filming this on a peninsula of land that's not wide enough to permit safe vehicular travel, so my prop truck—and a recuperating Bruce—are about 250 yards away. Andy Laszlo has two electricians and one 9-light on set. Did I say anything about the fading light and darkening sky? Andy had finished lighting the stand-in, and just as Kehoe was about to call Coyote to set, Andy said, 'Walter, I think this shot looks a little too bare. What if we put someone—we won't need the actor—but someone in uniform at the foreground. We could widen the shot, just a bit, to see an arm and shoulder in a paddling motion.' Before Walter said anything, I was trotting off to the prop truck for another M-16 and a paddle. To my left, I found a costumer, Dan Moore, trotting to his own truck for another uniform and a helmet. We were trotting a bit slower when we returned to set and did our business. The guy we dressed took a seat in the canoe and then Andy said, 'You know, Walter, it's still too bare. We really do need to put another soldier in…' but before Andy could say 'the back of the canoe,' Dan and I returned to the track meet for the next 200-meter event. With good-natured humor, some of the guys were calling out to us, 'Come on! Hurry it up! There's a barstool waitin' for me.' Again, we did our business but this time a little more out of breath than the time before. But now, again, Andy was about to say something else and I blurted out, 'Is this still a fucking head shot?' Walter said, 'Let's shoot this, as it is.' Andy wasn't really ticked off, but he did show me a look of mild disgust. Anyway, a couple days later, after wrap, I caught the last van going back to our hotel. I always used a side entrance that passed by our production offices, and then, a fresh, clean, and showered Walter Hill saw me and said 'Raiche, come here, I want you to see this.' I didn't know what he wanted me to see. But now I knew how much better I could look (by 8 p.m.) if I ever caught the first van back to the hotel.

"Leaving the bright hallway lights, my eyes slowly adjusted to almost no light in the small room that Walter brought me to. He'd been watching footage on a KEM editing machine and my first thought was, 'Oh, no. I screwed something up big-time and now he's going to show me the evidence.' Sure enough, he rolls film and … aha … it's the bullet hit shot on Poole. Well, overall, the actor is dark, the background is dark, the shot is dark, and, not even getting to the actual bullet hit, he stopped the film and asked, 'So, what do you think?' I said, 'Walter, there is nothing wrong with that shot … that another 9-light wouldn't have corrected.' Walter turned the lights on and, wow, I was very surprised at how crowded with equipment this room was and, oh, look … Andy Laszlo had been standing right behind me the whole time. It would be days later, but, eventually, and with a smile, Andy did tell me that he should have brought out another light. In the movie business, it's likely that some future day you'll find yourself working again with some of the same people you're working with right now. Andy and I would work again on *Innerspace* and *Streets of Fire*. Andy was a very good cinematographer and a really nice person as well. The same can be said for Pat 'Capt. Bligh' Kehoe. Walter kept a lot of good people close by."

A financial failure upon release, *Southern Comfort* has deservedly gained a status as one of Hill's best works, perhaps a definitive example of the director's position as an auteur of masculine action cinema. Though to cast Hill as a predominantly action-oriented filmmaker is to limit the scope of his storytelling talents, especially when one considers the diversity of character and milieu in the films that preceded it: *Hard Times*, *The Driver*, *The Warriors*, and *The Long Riders*. Hill's films may indeed be action-oriented and predominantly male, but he is wildly unpredictable when it comes to the generic contexts and narrative structures of his stories. However, it would be Hill's next film that would instigate and define the very male genre of the buddy-cop movie.

If *The Warriors* is Walter Hill's ultimate cult film, then *48 Hrs.* represents the director at his commercial zenith and most populist. A true "lightning in a bottle" picture, the mismatched duo of Nick Nolte and Eddie Murphy provided the template for a whole new genre in Hollywood in which the standard setup involved pairing two men of diverging cultural sensibilities, often of different race or ethnicity, always at each other's throats while harboring growing and begrudging respect for each other. Of course, the Hill-scripted *Hickey & Boggs* came before it and contained elements refined here, but what *48 Hrs.* does is to establish a tone of humor that plays on top of a serious thriller narrative that is executed with heightened production values, amplifying the more modest violence of the 1970s films and defining a formula that would be utilized relentlessly throughout the 1980s and 1990s. Therefore, without *48 Hrs.* there would be no *Beverly Hills Cop*, no *Lethal Weapon*, no *Running Scared*, no *Last Boy Scout*, and obviously no *Another 48 Hrs.*

Eddie Murphy plays streetwise criminal Reggie Hammond, who is temporarily released from prison for 48 hours in order to help renegade cop Inspector Jack Cates (Nick Nolte) capture Hammond's old partners in crime, jailbreaker Albert Ganz (James Remar) and his vicious associate Billy Bear (Sonny Landham). If Hammond successfully assists Cates in putting the pair away, he will benefit from not having to split the $500,000 that the gang previously stole from a drug dealer and which Hammond has kept hidden in a downtown parking lot. But Ganz and Bear are determined to get their cut, killing one former ally and blackmailing another in order to find out where Hammond hid the stash of cash. As the clock ticks, Hill raises the bar for creating slick, well-produced, and exciting action cinema.

The story of *48 Hrs.* originated in the mid–1970s with producer Larry Gordon, though it would take seven years and many drafts of the script before Paramount would put the film into production, reuniting Gordon and Hill several years on from the controversial release of *The Warriors*. "I told Walter about the idea for this film," Gordon recalls. "He was busy at the time and he suggested I go to a friend of ours,

Inspector Jack Cates (Nick Nolte) prepares for a showdown at the climax of an intense *48 Hrs.* (1982).

Escaped convict Albert Ganz (James Remar) holds former criminal associate Reggie Hammond (Eddie Murphy) hostage in *48 Hrs.* (1982).

Roger Spottiswoode, who was an editor but wanted to be a writer. Walter said if I let Roger write the first draft, then he would rewrite it and direct it. So I paid Roger to write the first draft and he did an okay job with it, then Walter came in and rewrote it and that's the movie we made." As well as Spottiswoode, future *Die Hard* scribe Steven E. de Souza would also come and go before Hill settled on working with a young writer by the name of Larry Gross, whose work in the industry at this point was mainly uncredited rewrites on films directed by Ted Kotcheff—one a picture about religious cults called *Split Image*, and the other being the original Rambo film, *First Blood*. It was on the former that Gross made an impression on *48 Hrs.* producer Joel Silver. "*Split Image* was made by a little production company called Polygram for whom a young producer named Joel Silver worked," Gross says. "Joel previously had a working relationship with his mentor Larry Gordon, but for a brief period he decided to go to work for Polygram Pictures around the time I was hired to rewrite *Split Image*. Although he was not directly involved in the film, he was very aware that I had been on set and done a lot of rewriting to make it into a film that could get finished and released on time."

Before being offered work on *48 Hrs.*, Gross previously met Hill in a social setting during the writers' strike in 1982, when the girlfriends of both men were pals. Gross's girlfriend asked him if he wanted to meet Hill, to which the writer replied in the affirmative. "I told her 'I do!'" Gross recalls. "I thought he was one of the best filmmakers in America, so I really wanted to meet Walter, which I did at a dinner. However, at that dinner we did not discuss working together, nor did we discuss much about his current prospects for making films in any practical way because the strike was on; it was kind of just blowing smoke, and blowing smoke is not something Walter was particularly interested in doing. We were becoming friends on a whole other series of topics unrelated to working together. I certainly made it clear in our first couple of meetings that I knew and respected his work. I said to him there are people who compare *The Driver* to the work of Robert Bresson and I asked, 'Does that seem ridiculous to you?' He said, 'You mean that guy who made the film about the donkey?' And in a very classic Walter moment, he said, 'I know that guy's work, he's a really good filmmaker, but you know at the end of the day he and I are in a different business and, quite frankly, I prefer our business.' Walter went on to discuss Bresson in such a detail which showed me he was completely versed in Bresson's work and understood that it represented a genuine aesthetic achievement. Walter's got such complicated and interesting taste and considerable knowledge. I'll never forget the day he came on the set and we got into this long rambling talk about Josef von Sternberg and *The Scarlet Empress*, which is exactly the opposite kind of movie that you would think Walter would have the slightest interest in or capacity to appreciate, but he totally got it and had a tremendous capacity to appreciate it. He has always exhibited that kind of complicated taste and an ability to take an interest in work which is very different from his own."

When the writers' strike ended, Paramount head Michael Eisner called Larry Gordon. He was in need of a property that was ready to go into production immediately. Eisner inquired about the producer's project that had been incubating for almost a decade. Pending a quick tune-up of the script, they would be ready to roll on *48 Hrs.* By this time Joel Silver had left Polygram Pictures and gone back to work for Gordon, and when it came time to bring in some new blood to update the script, Silver knew the right man for the job: Larry Gross. Silver was acutely aware of how Gross could save a film at the eleventh hour, and it didn't hurt that he was represented by the same agency as Hill. After almost 10 years, nine writers, and many drafts, Gross would be next to join the *48 Hrs.* rewriting party.

When it came to casting the film's lead costars, it could have ended up a very different film had the filmmakers' first choices accepted. "The people who played the lead roles were not our first choices," Gordon affirms. "We almost made it with Clint Eastwood, then we almost made it with Sylvester Stallone and Gene Hackman, for the role that Nick Nolte ended up playing." As with the script for *Hickey & Boggs*, Hill didn't envision the two protagonists with specific ethnicity in mind. In fact, Eastwood's interest was in playing Hammond, which would been a brave move for the star in the midst of his heroic *Dirty Harry* days. But Eastwood would satisfy his urge to play a convict elsewhere in Don Siegel's *Escape from Alcatraz* while the character of Reggie Hammond would become African American as the script went through further drafts. With only a few months before the film was due to go into production, Hill had the idea of making the convict character black, to which Michael Eisner gave him the greenlight to find a suitable actor for the role. But this was the early eighties, when there weren't many black movie stars bankable enough to play the lead in a major studio film. So the short list of potential stars was indeed short, with only Richard Pryor being considered as having the required commercial value, but he ultimately proved elusive, as did Bill Cosby. Next on their list was Gregory Hines, who was not a big star but was highly regarded. He passed on it. Then, a moment of inspiration struck one Saturday evening in the Hill house that encouraged the director to make the bold move of trying out a hot new talent who was tearing up the television comedy rulebook every weekend. Eddie Murphy was the rapidly rising star of NBC's *Saturday Night Live* but had no formal acting training nor experience behind him, but that didn't deter Hill from inquiring into the potential casting of the edgy and energetic comedian. Hill asked his girlfriend, Hildy Gottlieb, who also happened to be Murphy's talent agent, if she thought the actor could pull it off. The rest is film history. "I had rewritten *48 Hrs.* a couple of times," Hill says. "There were a lot of previous writers and it all came together pretty well. It's Eddie's first movie and that worked out. Nick was very good in it, held it together."

Casting such an untested performer as the lead of a major studio picture was not without some attendant issues, as Murphy's evident inexperience led to doubts over whether he could carry the film as equally as Nolte. There were periods of time at the beginning of production where it didn't seem like Murphy was truly getting the part and it became a question of whether he would work out or not. For two weeks the filmmakers were worried, but Paramount was more worried. The studio had such little faith in their leading man that it came close to letting him go, which would have proved a major detriment to the studio's finances throughout the rest of the 1980s, as Eddie Murphy became one of their most bankable stars of that decade. But Hill was determined to save his star's performance one way or the other, as Gross recalls:

"Paramount wanted us to stop the film and fire Eddie. There were periods at the beginning of shooting where we felt that we would have to cut around Eddie and rely on Nick, but Walter had several different things going on in his head about the situation and he had an absolute determination not to go along with this. Based on the pieces in the first two weeks that worked, I said to Walter that one thing is perfectly obvious and that is every time Eddie's character starts to talk about something that's happening, or has happened, off-screen there's a loss of energy in Eddie. He's not good

Walter Hill (center) directs Eddie Murphy (left) and Nick Nolte on the set of 1982's *48 Hrs*. (Photofest).

with backstory and exposition. What he is good at is what he's got from stand-up comedy, which is that a stand-up lives and dies in the moment of the delivery. At that particular point he was not experienced enough as an actor to be able to deal with off-screen material; that's a certain kind of developed skill. He became capable of it, yeah, but it was something he literally couldn't process at nineteen years of age, especially never having acted in a film before. So, I said we have to write every scene between them as something that's happening right in front of his eyes at that moment that he's reacting to. I think if we come into every scene in the movie like that then we will get the performance that we want. The joke that made us confident and made us put up with all the problems we were having happened on the second day of shooting and it was pure Eddie improvising. It was the scene where Nick is beating up David Kelly with the car door and Eddie goes, 'Man, you better tell him something. He's having a ball with that car door.' That's Eddie in the moment. We tried to figure out how to put him on track so that kind of reaction happened more and more."

Costumer Dan Moore recalls the precarious situation: "The one particular memory I have from my time of working on *48 Hrs.* is the fact that the geniuses at Paramount, who later became the geniuses at Disney—Michael Eisner and Jeffrey Katzenberg—didn't think Eddie Murphy was any good. The studio had such little faith in Eddie that they were surprised with how big a success that *48 Hrs.* became when it was released."

Gross continues, "Eddie's evolution as an actor happened during the course of the making of *48 Hrs.* because he'd never been in a film before. Sure, Walter was not satisfied with the performance Eddie was giving, but he believed, as I did, that there were glints of a good performance that we needed to work on. Walter said, 'I'm a director, I can work with my actors and get the performance I need them to give; the studio can't. This is too much the creative center of the movie for me to listen to what anybody else has to say, and if they want to fire me for not firing him, then so be it.' It was personal for Walter, it was about himself and his own authority, and he said, 'I'm not firing Eddie. I can see what he needs to do and what we need to do with him.' So Walter had a program, and one part of that program was for fixing his performance and the other part of the program was keeping the country and western bar sequence until the end of the shoot so that Eddie would be fully relaxed, confident, and a much more self-possessed Eddie in that scene." Also part of Hill's program was bringing in an acting coach to prep Murphy for his scenes, as Dan Moore recalls: "They actually hired someone to help Eddie along with his performance, and that was David Proval. David would go on to act in things like *The Sopranos* where he played a bad motherfucker, but back then he was working with Eddie in this little honey wagon, which was just like everybody else's because it was Eddie's first movie, he wasn't yet the huge star he would become."

The animosity between the two central characters is often infused with racial epithets, which added an additional layer of tension and no little humor to the script that would lead to further anxieties for those who had experienced the controversy and commercial ramifications that on-screen racial animosity could have off-screen. Gross recalls:

"Walter had done one pass through the script making the character black but most of that idea had not gone into the script when I first got my hands on it. I said that we have an opportunity here, we've got to make a little bit more of a big deal out of this than it is in the script right now. There were many things in the script that worked fine with the convict being white, it worked very much the same as they do in the current version, but there were other things we added such as the whole idea of the racial enmity between the two characters being intensive. There would always be enmity between the convict and the cop in any version of the story, there would be mistrust and suspicion, but obviously the racial component changed it. On the first week of the shoot Eddie showed incredible insight about one particular scene in the script when he walked up to me and said, 'Tell you one thing, man—that scene in the bar where I kick everybody's ass, I'm going to just kill in that scene, I'm gonna be great.' In that moment he understood that scene was his opportunity. When it came time to shoot the scene Eddie started playing around with the various things that we'd written. Certain important parts of it are exactly what I wrote and certain parts of it are totally improvised, but when Walter said 'Cut!' after the first take he turned to me and said, 'We're rich.' By that point Eddie had come completely around and was on, but the cutting of that sequence is another story…

"There was a lot of internal anxiety about the scene and the internal anxiety was prompted by the experience that Joel, Larry, and Walter had on *The Warriors* where people had gotten angry and ended up having gang fights in the movie theaters, which had cut into the box office of the film significantly. Larry was very paranoid about these things and concerned about it like any competent producer would be, so when the editors showed us the sequence, Larry said, 'We're in trouble here, guys, this is really going to provoke fistfights in the audience. This guy is wailing on the white people in such an aggressive way that we're going to get into trouble with this. You have to cut another version of this scene!' So we cut another version of the scene which was basically the same but everything was toned down, there was less cursing, less abuse, and on its own terms it was a perfectly adequate scene. But I had a very strong visceral reaction to what was wrong with it and I had a very special argument. I said, 'I know what you're worried about, Larry. I'm worried about it too, and we all respect your worry; I am not disregarding your concerns but what I'm telling you is this is not the solution to the problem, it is exactly the opposite of a solution. What we've done by cutting the scene back is made it more realistic and by making it more realistic we have actually increased the likelihood of the thing you're worried about.' Everything in the version we had before that was so over the top and so funny, and it is because it's funny that it has the hope. I'm not saying that there's no danger there, but that's our only choice, to give them a chance to get out of this alive. There's no version of this where we're not going to run the risk of offending people, but at least the funny excessive version has a chance of not offending them as much; by paring it down the scene moves in the wrong direction. When I saw it I just said, 'Whatever we do, we mustn't cut it like that because it is going to get us into worse trouble.' I was with Walter, Larry, Joel, and others at the first public screening of the film before it opened and I can honestly say that I won my arguments by about 3 percent, that is to say 53 percent of the audience was laughing and 47 percent was so shocked and quiet. We watched it like we just barely escaped with our lives; that was a recruited screening where nobody knew anything about the film and had nothing to expect. Two days after the film opened, I went into a theater and watched the film and people were laughing hysterically at the scene almost from the moment it started, and now 99 percent of the people in the theater thought it was funny, it had become the comic high point of the film and everyone knew it was coming because within two days it already had a reputation. I was right, but I was only barely right, and then the machinery of audience response took over."

Gross also drew Hill's attention to another element of the script that was trying to manifest more clearly, and that is the romantic and lascivious longings of the two men, particularly Reggie Hammond's mission to get laid after being banged up for several years. Hammond's negotiations with women usually result in comical failure. "There was sort of a bent romantic comedy trying to get out," the screenwriter recalls, "and Walter seized on this very early on as an approach to give Eddie stuff to do. We would have Eddie get distracted from any narrative event by whatever girl passed in front of him and whom he would end up pursuing." One of the funniest and most memorable moments in the film, and one that would be replicated in the sequel *Another 48 Hrs.*, is Reggie's enthusiastic high-pitched singalong with the Police hit "Roxanne." Murphy improvised the moment, but both band and song were unfamiliar to Hill, who was inclined to discard the take. This did not sit well with Gross, who saw the comedic value and pop-cultural crossover potential of the scene. "That is the only aspect of this process that I can take complete and total responsibility for," Gross says. "When Walter said, 'Don't print it,' I threw a fit. I said, 'You don't know this song and you don't know the Police! Joel, do you know the Police?' And he didn't. I said, 'You gotta trust me, this is huge, this moment and this song is huge, and if we can afford to use the song it will be very good for us and very big for us.' When the editor, Freeman Davies, saw dailies, he said, 'Guys, that scene with the Police song was so great. That was such a great idea, Walter!' From the moment people saw the footage of Eddie doing 'Roxanne' they had the impression that it was always an idea to do this. This one thing I was really 'responsible' for in this process of gleaning Eddie's improvisations and seeing something that the other two guys didn't. Ninety-nine percent of the time Walter could have made all the choices he ended up making without me; I only just ratified choices that he made. This has to do with the unique way in which Walter works with those people he wants to work with and people he gets along with and we were getting along well enough at this point that I was included and incorporated into the editing process and I got to be in the edit room all the way through production."

After all of the anxieties over Murphy's performance and with little support from the executive suites at Paramount, *48 Hrs.* would be released to wide acclaim and massive audience approval, resulting in a significant performance at the box office. "Before the film was released, Paramount had just shrugged their shoulders at us," Gross recalls. "We were a very small and inconsequential production compared to other things on their plate; we were not important enough for them. They were going through a crisis in management. Their previous head of production, Don Simpson, went on to an insanely successful but brief career as a producer, but he had just been fired and a new fledgling junior VP who was yet to make his bones and later become tremendously influential in the industry, Jeffrey Katzenberg, had taken over Simpson's position under Michael Eisner. Katzenberg was completely untried as a daily head of the studio and he was preoccupied. He came to our set exactly once and that was on the last day of shooting, at which point Paramount had officially ordained the film as 'great.' We had enough cut footage by that time for them to say, 'We were always really into this film,' but the truth of the matter was they were absent the entire time and I knew this was a lucky fluke. It could have gone wrong. If they didn't like the results they could have just buried the film and never looked at it. That's the way they usually treat the films they ignore. But by the end of the shoot they'd seen enough cut footage to know that the film stood a reasonable chance of being successful and they started taking credit for it. It's a widespread phenomenon in Hollywood, which is you don't know about something but then enough people tell you that something is great and then suddenly you know because you always knew."

"Eddie really enhanced the humor that was already there in the script," Gordon admits, "and being in the film really worked out great for his career because it became a big hit and a cult movie which started a whole new genre because it was the first real buddy movie."

"In my first couple of years in the business I had gone from working on *The Long*

Riders and *Southern Comfort* with Walter to then working on *E.T.* and *48 Hrs.* in the same year," Moore says, "and I remember one particular day on the set of *48 Hrs.* which made me think how lucky I was. We were filming the scene where we find the Chinese guy who has been shot right between the eyes and we were up on this hill in San Francisco with the wind blowing and the sun shining, there's this dead body slumped over on a bench, and I'm thinking, 'I can't believe they are paying me to be out here doing this! This is easy!' It was just such a thrill and I have experienced moments like that throughout all of Walter's movies. And then it came out and just exploded. It is probably the only film where Walter received the recognition that he deserved and that is because *48 Hrs.* was a totally new kind of movie. Nobody had seen that kind of action movie before."

Gross recalls the moment that someone took notice of a potential new genre that had been created with *48 Hrs.*: "A friend of Joel's named Sean Daniels, an executive who went on to be a successful producer, was at the premiere screening for the industry in Westwood and he walked up to Joel and said, 'You guys did something new here, this is an action comedy!' That's a fairly definitive statement. There hadn't been quite an action comedy before that. Walter and I could point you to movies like *Gunga Din* and to a lesser extent *Butch Cassidy and the Sundance Kid*, movies that have action in them and have funny things in them but they're not actually 'action comedies,' they are action films that have some funny stuff in them, and that's what we thought we were doing. I don't think we had any idea of how funny Eddie could be within the context of a conventional cop movie. We knew we were making an action film that had funny stuff in it, but we were utterly unprepared for just how funny the fun stuff could be and it was our obligation to follow where that led. The truth is that in our film the comedy and the action play with each other in a way that had not been done before and it became a very influential thing, not just with buddy-cop movies but also on the approach taken by the Marvel industry. How to make an action movie that's a comedy at the same time. *48 Hrs.* was one of those lucky coincidences that only happens once in your life."

"When you make a hit people think you've got a formula, but you didn't make the film any differently from how you made the other movies," Hill affirms, "you just shot what you thought was the proper way for the material at hand and with the actors that you had to work with. You can make movies for an audience, or you can make movies for yourself, or you can make movies for critics. Making movies for yourself always sounds noble but it can be awfully self-involved, and you are using other people's money. Still, that's what I do. But there are people that make movies with that audience in mind and that are very good at calculating what an audience will like. I have an instinct for it, but I've never been wildly sure. Most of the time I'm really drawn to hard genre stuff, and I like to see what I can do with it. If you are making a family entertainment you have a much better a chance at financial success, but I don't make family-oriented movies, I'm not interested in those kinds of stories. I've made a couple of movies for young people, including *Crossroads* and *Streets of Fire*, and in a sense *Brewster's Millions* too. Those are what I would call a kid movie, but most of the time I'm really drawn to the hard genre stuff like *48 Hrs.* I like to see what I can do with it."

Three

Tonight Is What It Means to Be Young

After a decade of directing some of the toughest films to come out of the Hollywood mainstream, Walter Hill felt the need for some respite, figuring it was time to branch out into new territory with films designed for the youth audience that was consuming contemporary pop culture at a considerable rate in the mid-eighties. And so Hill duly followed *48 Hrs.* with three films that cast a wider net for that potential audience: *Streets of Fire*, *Brewster's Millions*, and *Crossroads*. These three films would try to tap into the market that was enjoying MTV and *Saturday Night Live*. They were intrepid expeditions into the genres of comedy and the musical, of course, all achieved in Hill's inimitable manner.

The first, best, and most ambitious of these productions is *Streets of Fire*, released in 1984. The opening moments of the film are among the most exciting of Hill's career. It is, we're told, a "rock 'n' roll fable" and, sure enough, a rousing rock 'n' roll riff resounds to the rhythm of the rapid editing, an assembly of youth and energy in "another time, another place." That place: Richmond, a city in which the time is undefined, built on an aesthetic marriage of retro 1950s rockabilly rebellion and 1980s new wave quirkiness. The opening montage leads us into a heaving theater that is host to a hometown show by local hero Ellen Aim (Diane Lane). We are treated to the stimulating stomp of Aim's Wagnerian rock song *Nowhere Fast* before a gang of greased bikers called The Bombers, led by Raven Shaddock (Willem Dafoe), storm the concert to cause havoc and make off with the singer back to the dark side of town: the Battery. Thankfully for Aim, her mercenary old flame Tom Cody (Michael Paré) is back in Richmond and is reluctantly hired by Aim's manager and budding boyfriend, Billy Fish (Rick Moranis), to retrieve his star for $10,000. Cody is joined by tough tomboy McCoy (Amy Madigan) on a dangerous quest across town and in the process meets a variety of colorful characters, from Ellen Aim enthusiast Baby Doll (Elizabeth Daily) to a quartet of soul singers, The Sorels. Once Aim absconds from the Bombers' Battery biker bolthole, Shaddock demands an epic sledgehammer showdown with Cody.

After the massive success of *48 Hrs.*, Walter Hill was hot property, but typical for the maverick filmmaker, a repeat of the formula of his previous film was not a consideration. *Streets of Fire* was conceived in the euphoric closing days of shooting his mighty action comedy, with Hill and Gross thinking they could get a movie into

Going nowhere fast: Ellen Aim (Diane Lane) onstage in *Streets of Fire* (1984).

production quickly with Paramount, expecting the studio would want a first look at their new idea. In the end, the duo wound up making it at Universal. For anyone following Hill's career to date, *Streets of Fire* heralds an entirely new direction for the director. For a filmmaker whose work to this point had been somewhat anachronistic—timeless and yet steeped in cinema history—Hill revealed himself to be very much in tune with pop sensibilities of the day. "We were kind of in the jet wash of *48 Hrs.*," Hill remembers, "and suddenly we were great heroes to the industry, which doesn't happen very often. Larry Gross and I wrote the script rather quickly and we wanted a Homeric premise: a girl is captured, and you go to war for her. Before the change in administrations, Universal was looking to do something a little different and the old movie star kind of stuff didn't seem to be working at that moment."

"On the last week of production on *48 Hrs.*, Walter came to the set and said, 'This is what we're going to do next if you're interested,'" Gross recalls. "He told me about these three ideas that were in his head. When I heard them I said, 'Sure!' Walter's idea was essentially for a comic book film with the additional elements of rock 'n' roll and teenagers. He wanted to invent a comic book movie for which there would being no preceding comic book, and we did talk about designing a comic book to accompany the film. Walter had made a foray towards comics with *The Warriors*, and he was very proud of the comic book style as something that had not been seen before. When I say 'comic book,' what I mean is permission to depart from reality, permission to be abstract, permission to in a loose way sort of evoke and invoke myth. I trusted Walter's intuition about the comic book sensibility, but we kept revising our concept of it slightly as we were making it and we didn't know we were going to make it as stylized as we did. We jokingly told ourselves we could use the epigraph 'In a galaxy far, far away.' The subtitles for our two-word concepts were like, 'The other world this film takes place in,' it was all about 'the other world' and so we wrote it that way. The business of implementing it took certain surprising directions, but it was always part of Walter's thinking."

Prop master Craig Raiche realized how unorthodox a project he was about to embark upon from the get-go: "From the beginning, *Streets of Fire* had a distinctly different vibe about it," Raiche recalls. "It seemed a most ambitious project and we, Walter's group of regular players, went into it with a sense of renewed vigor and excitement. Its core story was still the same: strong antihero does the right things and wins in a bittersweet ending … but, really, 'a rock and roll fable.' Say what?"

"We had conceived of something weird," Gross confirms, "and then we discovered we didn't know how weird it was, where we didn't know how weird it needed to be, and we just kept on looking for more ways to make it weird. Two weeks into shooting Walter came onto the set one day and said nobody's going to get killed in this movie. I said, 'What?!' 'Cause, a lot of people were killed in earlier drafts of the script and Walter said that's not the reality of this movie, this is an abstract world and if people get killed it will be out of kilter with audiences. We're going to blow up motorcycles and not see what happens to the people that were riding them; we're not going to show any blood and we're not going to show any dead bodies."

There are certain shades of *The Warriors* in the film's depiction of youthful rivalries across demarcated patches of land claimed by local gangs, and while the comic book elements of that film were emphasized further in the 2005 rerelease in which Hill added comic book panels for transitional purposes between scenes, there is so much more to *Streets of Fire* in its construction and aesthetics, so much more that cost a whole lot more. The film proved to be Hill's most ambitious production to date, with a budget to match its elaborate aspirations. One of the more extravagant elements added to production was the tarping over of the Universal backlot, which would allow for daytime shooting of nighttime exteriors.

"That is a great example of how well Walter treats his crew," says actor and stuntman Allan Graf. "They were shooting on the backlot of Universal Studios and there was somewhere between 50 and 60 nights scheduled, and nobody likes nights, so what did he do? He had Universal tarp in the whole backlot, which cost around $2 million or something astronomical like that. He did this so he could shoot during the day. You arrived at the studio in daylight but you walk onto the set on the backlot and it was darkness. How classic is that? The crew loved it. But that's the kind of guy Walter is. And it meant he could control the light and the look of the film without having to shoot at night." Camera operator Lloyd Ahern concurs and recalls the massive scale of the production: "That was a huge set. It was the whole backlot of Universal, but by doing this it gave them complete control over everything, although building a massive city set and then putting a black tarp over the whole thing was a million-dollar commitment in itself. I don't think it has ever been done before or since. But that's Walter, he is practically a genius as far as knowing how to make a movie. He is the most unique director I've ever worked with, and I've worked with a lot of them. He could come up with an idea at the last second that is so much smarter than the idea that he had which was already really good just before then. He likes what he likes and he doesn't cater to the crowd and that takes big balls."

Along with exciting visuals and a thundering soundtrack, this most postmodern film benefits beautifully from vibrant and visually sumptuous production design and costuming, the aesthetics of which incorporates 1950s pop-culture symbols (cars, leather jackets, pompadours, etc.) to populate its distinctly 1980s neon-lit milieu. Costumer Dan Moore was on hand to assist costume designer Marilyn Vance to create the style of the street gangs and rock stars of the film. "Marilyn deserves all the credit for the style of *Streets of Fire*, that combination of eighties and fifties aesthetics. She went over to Italy to get prototypes for Ellen Aim and Tom Cody. I picked her up at the airport and looked at what she had and I thought, 'Oh my God, they're going to fire us tomorrow!' But Marilyn was very much part of the Joel Silver camp and Joel had his finger on the pulse of fashion and everything that was going on in culture. Walter was the visionary on that film but the end result was the product of everybody working on it: Walter, Larry Gordon, Joel Silver, and Larry Gross. Each of them contributed to making *Streets of Fire* what it is."

"Walter chose a stylized mix of different looks by combining iconic 'bullet-nosed' Studebaker cars of the fifties with Madonna's 'material girl' fashions of the eighties," Raiche affirms. "The cars and the buildings were conspicuously 1950s in appearance. They were drab and dirty—not quite postapocalyptic but very far from crisp, clean, and modern. Storefronts and businesses featured brightly colored neon signage that perfectly tied in with our female costuming. Elevated train tracks heavily hinted at Chicago, but the look of our downtown city achieved Walter's desired effect of being kind of everywhere but nowhere. We were shooting crowd scenes that take place prior to the rock concert with Ellen Aim & The Attackers. We shot it on the city streets of Universal Studios backlot. For a couple of legitimate reasons (to stay hidden from prying eyes of tourists on the Universal Trams and intentionally scripting those scenes as 'Exterior Night'), we had fabricated and installed a famous million-dollar tarp that literally tented us inside."

The film's electric musical energy is matched by the stunning work of three credited editors: Hill regular Freeman Davies, James Coblentz, and Michael Ripps. As if anticipating the aesthetics that would become known as "the MTV style," the film's musical segments are filmed and cut as if they were a montage destined to accompany pop singles. Closing the film is a duo of numbers, one from Ellen Aim (the epic "Tonight Is What It Means to Be Young") and one by the film's soul quartet, The Sorels ("I Can Dream About You"), which provide the perfect high notes to bring the curtain down on a most exhilarating film. "Someone wrote something in the *New York Times* recently and while they were saying nice things about the movie overall, I thought they misunderstood it," Hill says. "They were seeing it as an action piece whereas I've always thought of it as a musical. Universal wanted to sell it as an action movie. And it is certainly an odd mixture of an action film and a musical. It is as close as I could ever get to making a straight-ahead musical. *Streets of Fire* was supposed to be a film for a young audience. By the time the movie came out, MTV was with us and there was comment that we were inspired by MTV, which was ludicrous. I don't think I had ever seen a music video before making *Streets of Fire*. It was well after the movie came out before I saw one. But yes, oddly enough the film did prefigure the style that became associated with MTV."

When it came to casting the film's youthful ensemble, Hill would be impressed with a number of young actors who came with limited screen experience but who brought their own set of unique skills. Assuming the lead role of Tom Cody would be Michael Paré. The handsome actor had few credits to his name when he was brought on board to headline this major studio production, the magnitude of which wasn't lost on him. Though as he would find out, being thrust into the spotlight to headline an expensive mainstream picture brought its own kind of particular pressures. "At the time we made *Streets of Fire* I was really new," Paré says. "Here's the story: I went to the Culinary Institute and I'm living on 101st Street on the Upper West Side of New York while working at Tavern on the Green. One day there's all this commotion in the neighborhood, people are like, 'Hey, they're shooting a movie!' and it was down the street on Riverside Drive. They're saying, 'Hey, if you go down there and heckle them they'll give you 20 bucks to shut up so they can roll!' So of course I do that and then four years later I'm on the set of *Streets of Fire* and there's David Sosna, the first A.D., and he was the guy who paid me 20 bucks to shut the fuck up on Riverside Drive a few years earlier. So in those few years I went from being a cook with no aspirations of acting to being the star of a Walter Hill movie. That's how new I was! I had done *Eddie and the Cruisers* and then I went off and did this weird period thing in Australia called *Undercover* and then I came back and did *Streets of Fire*."

"Michael Paré was not our first choice," producer Larry Gordon says. "We initially went for some bigger stars before casting Michael. He was really a beginner, but Michael did as good a job as he could do." Meanwhile, Larry Gross contends that the actor "did some good things. He certainly worked hard, he was a good guy, and we tried to make it work with him and we came pretty close, but he had limitations that we never entirely overcame. We initially brought in Willem Dafoe for Tom Cody but for various reasons we moved him over to the other character, Raven Shaddock. Kathryn Bigelow was dating David Giler—Walter's partner at the time—and she knew about the project so she told us about this guy Willem Dafoe and showed

Michael Paré stars in the lead role of Tom Cody in *Streets of Fire* (1984).

us her short film that he was in. I wish his part was bigger—he's only in the film for 12 minutes or something like that—but that moment of him coming out of the flames is one of the best things in the movie."

"Michael was the kind of actor who would show up and say, 'What do you want me to do?' And that is the director's dream, of course," Hill says. "There is something that I say to actors these days that I didn't earlier in my career. I say: 'I'm a movie director; I am not an acting coach. If you want to talk about the script ahead of time, fine, but when we're out there shooting we're not going to reinvent. Just get out there and perform it.'"

"After *Streets of Fire*, I realized that directors are not acting coaches," Paré says, "they expect you to do your job, but I was still learning my job. When I would turn to Walter for direction, he would say, 'Michael, just say the line. Don't try to act.' That's about as in-depth as it got between us as director and actor. As a director, Walter doesn't like to talk too much; he and I didn't have a lot of polite conversations. In retrospect, Walter's direction of 'don't try to act' is something you hear over and over again and it means that as soon as you start acting people know you're acting. But soon after I began working on the film I discovered that Walter wasn't used to working with kids and I don't think there was anybody over 30 there, except maybe Rick Moranis. I don't know where Walter is from, but I was just like this wild guy from New York who just dropped out of the sky and he was probably thinking, 'I don't know how to handle this animal!' or he didn't feel that he had to … perhaps it was more my responsibility to figure out how to handle him. I was young, I didn't have anybody around to say, 'Michael, don't expect Walter to be your friend, and you have to be careful about trying to be his friend.' Put it this way: there were only two chairs on the set: one for Walter and one for Andy Laszlo. On the back of Walter's chair it said, 'Lone Wolf,' and that tells you a lot about him."

If Hill seemed impassive to some, to others his demeanor suggests something more in line with the way he considers his privileged and powerful position as a film's director as one that sets a standard of responsibility and accountability for the overall experience on-set. "Walter has utter contempt for two schools of thought," Gross affirms. "He is totally contemptuous of the idea that you have to suffer in order for the movie to be good. He thinks that is utterly ridiculous. And he is totally contemptuous of the director who thinks he has to impose himself on a recalcitrant crew and beat them in order to get a good result. He said countless times that it's hard enough to make the films well, so you don't have to make it harder by being an asshole. He knows that just doing your job is hard enough and elicits enough attention, energy, and discipline, and so he abhors the idea that you've got to beat on people to get their best out of them."

As with Paré, the supporting cast were relatively new to acting for the big screen, though they brought considerable chops from the live-performance worlds of theater and comedy—Diane Lane and Willem Dafoe came with much stage experience while Rick Moranis had emerged from the Canadian comedy scene, known for his popular inclusion on *Second City Television* and its spin-off feature film, *Strange Brew* (1983). "We cast *Streets of Fire* with some wonderful people," Gordon says, "Diane Lane was spectacular, as was Rick Moranis, but as with other movies we had other people in mind that we wanted to cast. Had we gotten any of our first choices it would have been a totally different movie."

"I think the pleasant surprise was Amy Madigan," Gross says. "I think she really was brilliant. Rick Moranis was great, he was Joel's idea as they were friends, and Walter had a great time with him. Diane Lane is great, particularly in the beginning and end of the film. She is very Ava Gardner-ish, I mean she's just beautiful and romantic and I love her performance. Let me put it this way: If everybody in the cast were at Diane Lane's level, the movie would have had a chance to be a hit."

"There was a lot of wining and dining and cultivating Diane," Paré recalls. "It was always 'Diane, Diane, Diane.' She had been on Broadway for two years and worked with Laurence Olivier, she was already a seasoned actress. Working with her felt a lot like Tom Cody and Ellen Aim—she was incredibly talented, beautiful, and soft, all those things you want in a woman. But they didn't encourage anything between us at all. Believe me! They would be very nervous if they ever saw me and Diane talking, Joel would be helicoptering us. It was very easy to look into Diane's eyes and fall in love, but I knew it wouldn't work for us, it would have been a great sin to pursue a romantic relationship with her. As with Tom and Ellen, it's like 'you're going places that I ain't gonna go. But if you ever need me, let me know.' Kissing Diane was the most fun I had on that movie, and that scene in the rain where I throw the money at Rick Moranis and I run down the stairs and Diane follows me ... man, I could have run away with her. But it's a good thing I didn't."

The actor continues, "Amy [Madigan] and I were friends, we had done a movie of the week together for ABC called *Crazy Nights*, in which she played my girlfriend. Willem came out of this Soho-based experimental theater group called the Wooster Group. He was one of those guys coming out of that New York scene but he was just this cool guy from Washington State. Then there was Rick Moranis. Comedians are—and I don't want to generalize here—but they are protected. A comedian can gibe at you all they want, but when you're on a movie set and someone pisses you off, you can't hit them. You just can't. It's like when people get a little too comfortable on social media when they say things and they know you can't punch them in the face, it's the same with comedians. They get away with saying what they want but you can't react the way that you want. So that makes for a complex situation."

Having come from the modest origins of smaller, quieter fare, Paré was now thrust into an elaborately produced action picture and tasked with all the complicated stunt work required of a leading action hero. Luckily for him, skilled stunt coordinator Bennie Dobbins was on hand both for physical and moral support.

"Bennie was the most help to me on the set, he was like a mentor to me on that movie. At the time there weren't a lot of things to give me confidence; the director wouldn't talk to me, my costar had been on Broadway, and I had no allies. But Bennie was really there for me throughout. There was one time when we were shooting in Long Beach at some oil processing plant, which was the location for the Bombers' headquarters, and they told me that my stunt double, Jerry, was going to walk across this pipe bridge that was four stories up, and I said, 'Let me do that!' And Bennie said, 'You want to go up there?' 'Yeah, I can do that!' So he takes me up there on this ladder and then he sees me standing at the edge and I said, 'You know, this would be better with sneakers,' and Bennie replied, 'No, you gotta wear the boots!' And then I'm like, 'Ah, I don't know about doing this,' and he said, 'Good, because I wasn't going to let you do it anyway!' They had real Hell's Angels there and they gave them a clubhouse and a keg of beer on the set, they were there smoking marijuana and hanging out. Meanwhile I'm thinking, 'I'm the lead in the movie, I'll go over there and pal around with them,' but when Bennie sees me wandering over there, he grabs me and says, 'You stay the fuck away from them!' The big fight scene in the diner with Deborah Van Valkenburgh where I beat up those guys, that was the first fight sequence that I had done and Bennie just said, 'Don't worry about it, everything's a weapon. You can pick up the coat rack and whack 'em in the face,' and I said, 'Really?' and he said, 'Yeah, he's a stuntman, you can't hurt him! This is a movie, kid!' Okay, 'Bam!' Bennie was like that character Mickey in *Rocky*—'You're indestructible, kid!'—he would talk like that. When Bennie was on the set I knew it was going to be okay; when he wasn't there I didn't know who to turn to. When I'd say that to Bennie, he would say, 'What the fuck are you talking about? You're Tom Cody! Nothing can hurt you!' and I would feel like, okay, that's it.

"I asked Walter if I should take some boxing or martial arts lessons and move around like Bruce Lee. Well, this is a piece of direction he gave me: he said, 'Michael, there were these two actors, one was named Tom Scott and one was named John Wayne...' And I said, 'Who is Tom Scott?' and Walter said, 'That's the point! John Wayne wasn't a boxer but he knew how to fight on film, but Tom Scott was a boxer and he thought he should fight like a real boxer on film, and nobody has heard of him.' So it was like, 'Aha!' He said, 'No, don't practice any real martial arts, just do what Bennie says,' and it ended up working out very well. Those words really helped, 'Just listen to Bennie and make sure your punches are the way he shows you,' and I did. Bennie choreographed the fight and I did what he said; that little bit of direction helped me tremendously. I'm told that fight scene between me and Willem is one of the classic Walter Hill scenes. We shot that scene for two weeks and for me that was the most fun. I would be there early, I wouldn't want to leave the set to go eat; it was like, 'Yeah, I can do this, I'm doing a good job here taking the punches, doing the falls!' The hammers we used could have been an issue because they were aluminium, so if you got hit with one it would really hurt, and they wanted to do this shot where I almost hit Willem and they put this little capsule on the end so that when I hit the cement piling it would be like, 'Pow!' They were only two and a half pounds but if you get hit with a pipe hammer it will knock you out, but there was not a single mistake made. There were a lot of things that I did for the first time on that movie: my first love scene, my first fight scene, a lot of physical stuff. I had to do the motorcycle ride in Chicago but I had never been on a motorcycle before and nobody asked if I had or not. When I told our prop master, Craig Raiche, about this, he said, 'Hold on a minute' and he hooked me up with one of the local drivers and he put me on a motorcycle, so I rode up and down the alley and then the next day we shot it. I had never shot a gun before but I have this big .44-caliber handgun that probably weighed six pounds, so Craig took me to a shooting range, although they would only let me use blanks because of insurance. So I had never driven a motorcycle, didn't know how to shift gears, had never driven a standard transmission, I had never shot a gun, but Craig taught me about all of those things; I learned all of that on *Streets of Fire*."

Raiche recalled his first meeting with Paré:

"Our first day of shooting on *Streets of Fire* was in Chicago. I had about a week of prep time there and I'd just begun to get geographically familiar with that city. Our hotel, big and grand as it was, had only limited parking space so our many production vehicles and picture cars were being stored in a nearby warehouse. On the day before our first day of shooting, I went there and gave my prop truck a last going-over. Satisfied that all was well, I locked the side door and the liftgate and walked over to the transportation cubicle to arrange my ride back to the hotel. It was early/midafternoon and only a handful of crew people were in the warehouse at that time. I noticed an unfamiliar person getting up close and personal with the customized lead sled that Michael Paré would be driving in our very first scene … the next morning. I went to see who it was and lo and behold it was Paré himself. During prep we talked by phone a couple times but for the most part this was really our first in-person meeting. Being a car guy, I said something like, 'Hey, she's a real beauty, what do you think?' I thought his look of incredulity meant that he, too, was just another fellow car guy that was drooling with admiration over such a beautiful car. He was slow to respond but, finally, he said, 'This is a stick shift … on the steering column!?!' That's when I realized that his facial expression wasn't saying, 'Hey, this is a really cool ride!' It was really saying, 'Holy shit. I've never driven a stick!' To offer encouragement and alleviate his anxiety, I said, 'Don't worry, it's easy-peasy.' Before doing a thing, I let him know that a gear shift on the steering column was known as a 'three-on-the-tree' and I twice demonstrated the action for each gear and reverse. 'Here, try it,' I said. 'Just get in the driver's seat and I'll watch to see how you work the clutch and go through the gears.' At that point, Michael turned to me and said, 'Actually, I don't have much driving experience at all.' Now, it was my facial expression saying, 'Holy shit. He's a typical New Yorker who doesn't drive!'

"Hey, sometimes information 'falls through the cracks' but, somehow, this little tidbit of info had fallen into the Grand fucking Canyon. With a quick and purposeful step, I zipped over to the warehouse cubicle and had the local driver call Ronnie Baker, our transportation coordinator. Ronnie couldn't be found in our production office at the hotel and this was decades before the time of cell phones so we 'beeped' him. About 10 minutes passed without his response. I looked back at Michael and he was still in the driver's seat dutifully practicing his shifts. That's when it hit me. Through the very large and open doors of the warehouse, it was disturbingly apparent that shadows had grown long and nightfall would soon be upon us. With that, I made a rather hasty, but necessary, executive decision. I told the driver I wanted to show Michael something about the car, but I would need the keys. Of course, he obliged. I got back to the car and asked Michael to slide over into the passenger's seat. I sat down behind the wheel, turned on the ignition, and drove away onto the busy downtown streets of Chicago even as that driver was yelling very nasty things at me.

"After a brief five minutes of demonstrating, in moving traffic, the action needed to shift gears and how to smoothly engage and release the clutch, I pulled to the curb and told him it was his turn. Michael was not joking when he had told me that his driving experience to that point was almost nil, but he was a very quick learner. Not even a half hour had passed before Michael, with no more trepidation, confidently pulled back into the warehouse and parked the car. I can still feel the 20 lashes I received for what Ronnie and UPM Gene Levy called an irresponsibly reckless and illegal action. Many times since, I've delighted in wondering how comically bad it might have gone so early the next morning when everyone first discovered that missing tidbit of info floating downstream in the Chicago River. Oh, well … that's just so much water under the canyon."

Streets of Fire looks and feels like a definitive movie of its moment. MTV had just emerged and the film zips along on the same manic energy as the music videos being broadcast on the new channel. It is populated with beautiful actors poised to become stars, boasting a powerhouse producing duo and a director who had just reached the commercial peak of his career. And yet the film floundered upon release. It went out against other high-profile summer blockbusters and suffered in doing so, making back merely more than half of its production budget. Larry Gross realized that *Streets of Fire* was becoming an increasingly uncommercial project as production progressed, as he recalls that "it just became a more resolutely abstract film as we went along, and that has to do with why it is not a commercial success. There's ways in which the average mainstream tent pole comic book movie humanizes and sentimentalizes things to be more commercial because it helps those films reassure everyone that they're watching something that isn't too different from what they're used to. But we really tried to have the courage of our aesthetic convictions in a way that a lot of people working in this genre don't always do. The failure of this film is one part of the story of how I didn't become a director. It makes all the difference in the world between having one hit and having two hits. It's a huge difference, and I'm not saying I would have become a great director, but my chances would have increased. So I was devastated when *Streets of Fire* wasn't a hit. Walter and I didn't work together again until *Another 48 Hrs.*, and I'm sorry that it was *Another 48 Hrs.*"

Dan Moore recalls an acerbic quip from producer Joel Silver just days after the film opened to muted response. "*Streets of Fire* came out one weekend while we were working on *Brewster's Millions* and I remember something Joel Silver said on the Monday morning after it was released. One of the big songs in the film is called *Tonight Is What It Means to Be Young*. Well, that morning on the set of *Brewster's Millions*, we asked him: 'Well, what about the opening weekend, Joel?' and he replied, 'Tonight is what it means to be dead!' There was a lot of expectation on that film. When we were making it we were the biggest, hottest film in town, but by the time we got it ready to deliver, people had begun to get tired of the hype, so there was a backlash against it. I was just a humble crew member at the time but I remember thinking it just seemed really unfair that people instantly didn't like it when it came out. They didn't see it for what it was and how great it was in its own way."

As the face of the film, and one who was new to the spotlight of Hollywood stardom, Paré pondered upon the film's failure and agonized over whether the responsibility rested on his shoulders; but considering the commercial competition at cinemas that summer, it is more likely that audiences were just seeking out the safer haven of decidedly more old-fashioned material for their taste of escapism. Sometimes a work of art is too ahead of the curve to be appreciated in its own time, as *Streets of Fire* most definitely discovered.

"Joel Silver was really excited because of what he was seeing in the dailies. He thought he had a big fucking hit on his hands. But he didn't. We opened against *Indiana Jones* and the film failed. It was an expensive movie. They put a tarp over the set so we could shoot day for night, which made it easier for all of us and they probably thought it was more economical because they didn't have to pay night rates or whatever, but that tarp alone cost $2 million! Everyone at Universal was running over to 20th Century–Fox, so the studio didn't really care if the film worked or not. I wondered what I could have done better, because, of course, I felt responsible—I was carrying this big, expensive studio film, and it was terrifying! But who fucking knows? The idea of being on what was an enormous-budget Hollywood movie at that time was shocking to me. It was a hit everywhere but the United States; the Japanese brought me over there because it was in their top 10 movies ever made. I mean they brought me over to meet the fucking prince of Japan! That's a big deal when you're 24 years old. Three years before that I was working in a kitchen! So when I look back at that movie, I remember every fucking day and every scene; I know exactly what was going on in my head just before we shot and just before we moved on to the next scene. If only I knew then what I know now, how important that film was going to be. You gotta be cool, you can't let them see that you are scared or that you are nervous, but I needed to be told to calm down and do my fucking job and make it look easy. I was just fucking amazed that they gave me the role."

Almost 40 years after *Streets of Fire* seemed destined for obscurity, Larry Gordon celebrates the fact that his production is being rediscovered in the age of streaming and nostalgia for all things eighties, with the film receiving critical reappraisal and cultural reevaluation amid lavish home video editions being released by boutique labels such as Shout Factory and Second Sight after years of neglect by Universal. "*Streets of Fire* was an original script that Walter wrote which was very different," Gordon says. "The movie looks very good; it has great production design and has that film noir thing with the darkness and the wet streets, which gives you that great lighting. It is a very unique movie but it was not a success at the box office. But even though it didn't do well at the time it has become a big cult movie which has really found an audience that loves it. Part of that could be to do with the soundtrack, which everybody seems to enjoy these days. The film has been rediscovered and is very popular right now. You never know which movies will last. Some of those which fail upon release find themselves having a second life."

Without doubt, one of the most surprising and unlikeliest projects in the Walter Hill canon is *Brewster's Millions*, a broad comedy based on the 1902 novel of the same name written by George Barr McCutcheon. The book centers on the efforts of a young man named Montgomery Brewster, whose fortunes change after being tasked with spending $1 million of his deceased grandfather's inheritance within a year in order to earn a $7 million inheritance from another recently deceased relative, a wealthy uncle who had been feuding with the elder Brewster. The terms of the cash prize dictate that every penny must be spent, though not on any assets or property that could yield further income. This source story would be adapted into a stage play and six film productions before Hill would take on the material, beginning with Cecil B. DeMille's 1914 version and including Allan Dwan's notable 1945 release as well as a 1961 British adaptation, *Three on a Spree*, directed by Sidney J. Furie.

By the mid–1980s it seemed as though the time was right for a contemporary version of the classic social satire, and so screenwriting duo Herschel Weingrod and Timothy Harris were tasked with bringing a story that originated at the turn of the century into the booming 1980s. In this updated adaptation, Montgomery Brewster (Richard Pryor) is a middle-aged semipro baseball player for the minor league Hackensack Bulls, a team so impoverished they have to stop midplay to allow for a functioning railway line to operate through its outfield. After a successful game, the relief pitcher and his best friend/catcher Spike Nolan (John Candy) hit a bar and flirt with a couple of ladies who happen to be the girlfriends of some opposing teammates, which results in a bar brawl that ends in Brewster and Nolan arrested. The pair are subsequently bailed by a man working for Manhattan law firm Granville & Baxter, who invite Brewster to New York to discuss a matter of great importance and greater fortune. Just when life seems to be throwing him one unfortunate curveball after another, Brewster learns that he is the potential heir to his great-uncle Rupert Horn's vast fortune of $300 million. But there's a catch: to qualify for receiving the money, he is tasked with squandering $30 million in 30 days in order to inherit the full amount. His other option: to invoke the "wimp clause" and take $1 million up front with no obligations. Spending $30 million sounds easy, but there are malicious forces plotting against him, notably Granville & Baxter, who as executor of Horn's estate conspire to have Brewster fall short of his spending spree, which would leave them to misappropriate the bulk of the inheritance.

Brewster's Millions takes a satirical and socially conscious look at what happens when one man is handed a skewed and corrupted version of the American Dream. Weingrod and Harris had previously scripted the similarly themed *Trading Places* for Paramount, in which a wealthy commodities broker (Dan Aykroyd) literally trades places with a destitute hustler (Eddie Murphy) after a mischievous bet is placed by a pair of miserly millionaire brothers in the form of a twisted social experiment. The screenwriting duo met while holidaying in Crete in 1970, a time when both were emigres in London, where Harris had attended the London Film School and Weingrod was a Cambridge student. The pair were there enjoying a break in the sun with their respective English girlfriends when the two long-haired Americans struck up a friendship and ended up staying in touch. Harris was a published novelist and accomplished prose writer, while Weingrod knew how to write screenplays, and so when they wound up back in Los Angeles, the pair pooled their talents and began writing scripts together, finding early success with John Landis's aforementioned 1983 Christmas comedy before they were approached by producers Larry Gordon and Joel Silver for a project that would be right in their wheelhouse.

"Larry and Joel had acquired the remake rights to the 1945 version of *Brewster's Millions*, which was directed by Allan Dwan," Weingrod recalls, "and prior to that it was a novel and a play; one of the early versions starred 'Fatty' Arbuckle and there's even a British version called *Miss Brewster's Millions*. It's a classic premise, a comedy of frustration which has been remade over and over again: the hero has a secret that he shares with the audience and he can't tell anyone else what the secret is, which is that in order to inherit a fortune he has to spend a certain amount of it in a certain number of days and have nothing to show for it. The 1945 version was about an American soldier, Montgomery Brewster, who comes home from World War II and is broke but then is approached by these lawyers who tell him he is due to receive a massive inheritance, although there's a catch. Of course, there's a romance with a girlfriend whom he can't tell and it is very frustrating and he has to figure out a way to work around that. So Larry and Joel had Timothy and I look at all of this previous material and asked us if we would have our own take on it. We said: 'How about Bill Murray as an out-of-work astronaut so broke that he is relegated to selling knock-off jeans on the streets of New York?' That was actually very common at the time, there were all these knock-off jeans, jewelry, and bags being sold on the streets, so the idea was to have Bill Murray playing one of these guys and he is approached by some lawyers who tell him he will inherit all of this money if he does this and that. So that's the way we wrote the script."

As amusing as that premise is, it didn't remain for long. With Silver and Gordon spearheading the project, it was only natural that they would approach their old friend and collaborator Walter Hill to direct the film. Following the commercial disappointment of *Streets of Fire*, *Brewster's Millions* was an opportunity to potentially reclaim some industry clout with a populist hit comedy. The first thing Hill suggested upon receiving the script was to change the central character from a former astronaut slumming it as a street vendor to being a washed-up baseball player for an ill-funded minor league team. Weingrod was thrilled to hear that Hill would be the man to bring his script to the screen, having admired the director's accomplished screenwriting work from his experience as a story analyst and reader for English company British Lion (which became EMI Films in 1976). While Weingrod was employed by British Lion, they were making Michael Cimino's *The Deer Hunter*, Sam Peckinpah's *Convoy*, and Hill's *The Driver*, and he was particularly impressed with Hill's script for his sophomore crime thriller, noting it as a brilliant piece of taut, lean screenwriting.

"I saved that script for *The Driver* because it is a perfect example of how to write a screenplay," Weingrod applauds. "It was really a definitive script for illustrating how to keep a reader's attention and wanting to turn the page. And then I had a chance to see Walter work when I was on the set of *48 Hrs.* I watched him shoot the scene in Torchy's Bar with Eddie Murphy because we were there to talk to Eddie about the script for *Trading Places*. I saw that Walter is the ultimate professional and a really good artist, he is not just a craftsman. In my brief time on that set, I could see that Walter is a very economical filmmaker, he is not flashy, he knows where to put the camera and he's got a really good eye. One of Walter's greatest strengths is his preparation—he knows exactly what he wants before he is on the set, and that kind of confidence and certitude gives an immediate sense of relief to cast and crew, knowing that they're in capable hands and can freely go about their jobs. Therefore I knew we couldn't have a better director for *Brewster's Millions*."

While the straight comedy context of the picture may initially appear to be out of Hill's comfort zone as a filmmaker, it doesn't take long for him to introduce his distinctive filmmaking style. Hill punctuates the film with moments of great visual flair and deftly handled aesthetic flourishes that suggest this is more than a mere journeyman work. He utilizes montage sequences that feature spinning newspapers, editorial wipes, and some decidedly old-fashioned comedic tricks when the film's more farcical elements call for some audio and visual accentuation. This kind of visual comedy is deployed in moments such as when Brewster is buying an expensive rare stamp; the character's eye is comically enlarged when framed through a magnifying glass to emphasize his wonder, giving the shot a cartoonish edge. Hill also is not above using an old-fashioned sliding kazoo sound when called for. "It was unusual for Walter to make a comedy at this point in his career," producer Larry Gordon says, "but he showed that he had a flair for comedy and did a great job with the material. And we had two brilliant lead actors in Richard Pryor and John Candy."

Brewster's Millions neatly fits into the 1980s milieu of yuppie satires and cautionary tales of money-motivated moral corruption with its fantasy of wholly endorsed consumerism. The film skewers the yuppie ideal of flagrant spending and accumulation of material goods as our hero Brewster digs himself deeper into misery the more excessively he spends. As with Murphy's character of Billy Ray Valentine in Weingrod and Harris's *Trading Places*, the opportunity afforded Brewster to ascend the social ladder offers him a glimpse into an exclusive lifestyle, but in both cases the men are privy to the emptier side of the bourgeois world that was once a fantasy beyond their reach. "The 1980s was the 'Greed Is Good' generation and that was always ripe for satire," Weingrod states, "so we wrote these scenes where we have these so-called entrepreneurs come in to see Brewster with these harebrained ideas, which he loves because he knows they are going to flop and he will have no assets once he invests in them, such as putting an outboard motor on an iceberg and having it float from the North Pole to New York. He sinks all this money into an election campaign that is obviously not going to make money unless he wins and gets the job, in which case he will have to find a way to somehow dispose of his income. Another device that we brought into it was the rare stamp. We were doing research on rare stamps for another picture and we decided we could introduce an element of that into this script; we thought it would be great if he actually bought *The Inverted Jenny*, which, even today, is probably the most valuable stamp there is. But then he licks it and it is stamped over by the post office and sent in the mail, so it becomes worthless. This means he can't be accused of purchasing it as an asset. Another thing I read about was a minor league team in Mexico who were so poor that they played in this field which had a railroad track running right through the grounds; they would often have to stop the games because these freight trains would come rumbling through the outfield. That's all true. We kept looking for ways to keep it more and more frustrating for Brewster. John Candy's character thinks he is helping them make money but Brewster just keeps getting more pissed off with all of his friends trying to help him."

Brewster's Millions costume supervisor Dan Moore recalls that this story of American excess was reflected in the off-screen expenditure as well. "One of the interesting things about *Brewster's Millions* is that it is a film about spending money and yet both Joel Silver and Marilyn Vance had pretty good reputations as being money spenders. This was my first job as the costume supervisor and it meant that I was watching how the money was being spent as well as being out there making sure everything looked right. So I was having a nervous breakdown over how much money was being spent, especially when Marilyn would come in and say, 'Oh, here's these receipts I forgot to give you.'"

One of the more ingenious implementations of various film versions of *Brewster's Millions* was to make the titular character of blue-collar origin, thus making his transition into the world of wealth an aspirational though ultimately cautionary tale. In George Barr McCutcheon's original novel, Brewster already comes from money and is part of high society, becoming a pawn in the wicked game being posthumously played by two deceased rival relatives: his grandfather and his uncle. Subsequent screen versions brought Brewster down to earth by alternately making him a soldier returning from World War II, a pauper, or just another working stiff clocking in and out of an office. But as these characters accept their new social mobility, they do so as their soul erodes. As a story about the pitfalls of capitalism, it must show the character going through with the stunt for him to become part of the system that working- and middle-class people can only dream about. And Brewster duly feels out of place among this high society that rarely associates with people of his economic milieu—"Guys, do you think I'm a lowlife?" Brewster asks the tailors of his expensive suits. "Oh no, not with these clothes," they reply. By rendering Brewster a struggling baseball player in the minors, it gives him the dual stature of sports hero and inspirational everyman; he is that rare cinematic entity: a working-class athlete. The sport itself is presented not just as a profession but a way of life—it alludes to a bigger idea of the sport as America's favorite pastime. When Brewster can afford to, he even finances an exhibition game for the Hackensack Bears to play the Yankees; this act of buying dreams for other people suggests that Brewster would make for a conscientious and altruistic millionaire.

If Pryor and Candy are the blue-collar hearts of the film, then bringing the bourgeois pomposity to be skewered mercilessly is effeminate junior lawyer Warren Cox (Stephen Collins). Cox is the kind of man who says he doesn't drink alcohol, that is until he is handed a $100,000 donation from Brewster and wishes to further ingratiate himself with his newly moneyed and seemingly generous acquaintance. Cox's allegiance is sold to the highest bidder. Cox's fiancée, Angela Drake (Lonette McKee), is the Granville & Baxter paralegal assigned to track Brewster's spending; she also becomes the object of Brewster's affections. She claims to be dedicated to Cox, declaring him to be a true humanitarian and careerist—and "a sincere feminist"—which leaves little time for their romance, but his sacrifice is supposedly noble and absolute. Cox is immediately set up as a complete contrast to Brewster. He proudly proclaims to be part of a committee to ban contact sports—"You guys ain't messing around with baseball, are you?" asks a wary Brewster, to which Cox replies, "No, no, no; boxing, football, ice hockey … you know, the truly barbaric sports." Cox's masculinity is lampooned often, as when Brewster taps into the yuppie's secret passion for interior decorating, hiring Cox at a premium rate to expensively design his apartment.

The film's depiction of an underdog unwittingly thrown into an extraordinary

Brewster (Richard Pryor) on the mound in *Brewster's Millions* (1985).

situation of wealth and power instills the film with its Capra-esque fable quality. On the surface its scenario recalls that director's 1941 dramatic comedy *Meet John Doe*, in which Gary Cooper plays a down-on-his-luck baseball star who is manipulated into becoming a political pawn by unscrupulous newspaper tycoons, but inadvertently becomes a popular man of the people. Hill affirms, "I was reaching for a social comedy with a heart which goes back to Frank Capra and Preston Sturges. I've always said all good drama ends with a tear, even a comedy. There's a slightly melancholy ending to *Brewster's Millions*, it's not just joy, joy, joy. There is something about having taken the journey that has made them all something else in a more positive way and in a way that makes them reflect."

"It goes back to the films of the thirties and forties, like *Meet John Doe*, *Mr. Deeds Goes to Town*, and *The Great McGinty*," producer Larry Gordon says. "These are all favorites of Walter's. In fact, for years Walter and I have talked about remaking *The Great McGinty*. Walter wanted to do that for a long time. But *Brewster's Millions* is as close as Walter has come to making something like a Frank Capra movie."

As with Capra's scathing satires, Hill and his writers bring a similar cynicism of the American political system when they have Brewster embark on an expensive mayoral election campaign for which his subversive slogan urges the electorate to vote "None of the Above." But in running for office to spend money quickly, he accidentally becomes a man of the people with his iconoclastic approach to the political and voting system—"Who's buying the booze? Who's buying the food? Who's trying to buy your vote?" Having a civilian successfully disrupt the political establishment in such a manner and with status-quo-upsetting rhetoric offers a hint of commentary that Capra would have exploited further, but *Brewster's Millions* is so busy with its narrative trajectory of having Brewster meet his deadline that little time is given to this interesting diversion of the story, although some fine montage sequences suffice. "Billy Wilder, Frank Capra, and Preston Sturges were very much our inspiration for this kind of social comedy," Weingrod recalls, "a story where the underdog comes up against great power and big money. We had done that before with *Trading Places* and we approached that the same way with those same influences informing it. The themes of that film are much the same as *Brewster's Millions*, it's all about the working-class guy coming up against moneyed elitism. There were some little things that we pulled out of the news and one of those was a story about a local election in San Francisco where a group of nuns were voting against the incumbent and their platform was 'Vote: None of the Above,' and so we had Brewster running for mayor of New York and saying, 'Don't vote for me, vote for None of the Above!'"

The character of Brewster was previously played by prominent male Caucasian actors of their respective periods, including Edward Abeles (1914), Fatty Arbuckle (1921), Jack Buchanan (1935), and Dennis O'Keefe (1945), with only Bebe Daniels breaking the format as the sole female version, Polly Brewster, in *Miss Brewster's Millions* in 1926. Richard Pryor broke the mold in 1985 by being the first African American actor to assume the role. "To his credit, Richard said, 'I don't want this to be about race at all,'" Weingrod recalls. "He told us, 'I don't want this to be anything like my other films, I don't want it to be like my stand-up, and I don't want it to be ghetto. In fact, I don't want race to be an issue in the film at all. I don't want race even mentioned in it, and by the way, when you write my dialogue, I don't want you to feel like you have to make me sound like I'm black; I'm just a guy who has this dream to pitch a game against the Yankees!' So that is how we approached it." Pryor was one of the stars of the American comedy club boom of the 1970s and 1980s who embraced the medium of cinema to further their profile on the national stage. Hill had previously brought Eddie Murphy to screen prominence in *48 Hrs.* and in

Vote None of the Above. Brewster (Richard Pryor, center) attempts to lose millions of dollars but wins millions of hearts in his campaign that ends up appealing to the common man in *Brewster's Millions* (1985).

doing so discovered a massive talent and screen presence. By 1985, Pryor was already a seasoned screen veteran and had amassed fame and acclaim as one of the edgiest comedians of the previous decade, but he was able to parlay affability and sweetness to his performance of Montgomery Brewster and indulge in a romantic role once again with erstwhile screen lover Lonette McKee; the pair previously starred alongside each other in the 1977 labor relations comedy *Which Way Is Up?* As he did in Alan Metter's socially-conscious 1988 suburban satire *Moving*, Pryor brings genuine pathos to balance the laughs with some drama.

"There was kind of an ugly phrase in those days that people used when referring to a certain kind of film," Hill says. "They called them 'slob comedies' and I didn't want to do that kind of film. I wanted it to be about the acting and I wanted it to be more dramatic. I wanted it to be comedic but not about jokes and gags, a good story with comedic performances, and that is why Richard did the movie. He got a chance to act in a part in a more formal style and not just do the 'Richard stuff,' and he really appreciated that, he very much liked the movie. He was not a guy who held back his opinions, but he was fond of the movie, though he liked it a lot more in retrospect. I got along with him fine, but he'd had a big fight with one of the producers—not Larry—and I was never really sure what it was all about. He had a rough journey. He had recently been diagnosed with the illness that took him in the end and it took years of living with it. Being diagnosed with an incurable disease doesn't do a lot for your spirits. It was not a happy time in his life." Larry Gordon similarly recalls Pryor's health at the time of production: "Richard was very weak from his accident, he was recovering from his terrible near-death experience, so he didn't have all of his strength at that time, and it influenced his performance."

Indeed, it is bittersweet to consider the tragedy of the joint talents sharing the screen in *Brewster's Millions*, as we are witness to the meteoric rise of costar John Candy, who would succumb to his own tragic circumstances a decade prior to Pryor. *Brewster's Millions* was one of four films released in 1985 to costar Candy, along with *Summer Rental*, *Volunteers*, and *Sesame Street Presents: Follow That Bird*, marking a prolific year for a talent poised for leading-man stature, a title that would be afforded him by eighties titan John Hughes with classics like *Planes, Trains and Automobiles* and *Uncle Buck*. "I worked with John on a project just before he died," Weingrod recalls. "John actually put himself in a diet facility so he could exercise and lose weight for the role. He really wanted to get in shape as a baseball player. He was a really lovely guy and was so committed to *Brewster's Millions*." Larry Gordon concurs: "John Candy was spectacular, a great fun guy. His dying so young was a terrible tragedy."

Brewster's Millions brought in a relative fortune of its own for Universal, being one of the top 20 highest-grossing films of 1985. "The movie did well but it wasn't a massive success," Gordon says. "I didn't like the way it was marketed. But we had a wonderful experience making it."

"The whole experience of *Brewster's Millions* was a pleasure," Weingrod says. "I was there on the location in New York for maybe two weeks and when we shot the baseball scenes in Long Beach; the studio flew us out to New York because things happen during production where the writers have to come in to fix something—the weather might change or production is behind schedule and so you have to compress things and make things better. I have nothing but really fond memories of making that film and it is really about the relationships and the people, not just with Walter but with John Candy, Richard Pryor, and Joe Grifasi. Yakov Smirnoff, who played the cab driver, was very funny. He was actually a fairly successful stand-up comedian here doing that whole shtick of a Russian guy who comes to America and makes fun of the fact you can buy 30 different brands of toilet paper—'America, what a country!' Hume Cronyn was there too, an Old Hollywood guy, and he was great. They were wonderful actors and wonderful people. I just have a really warm feeling towards that movie. It holds up pretty well."

With the box office success of *Brewster's Millions* proving Hill could work in populist genres as well as he could with more hard-edged material, he would become involved in several projects within the next couple of years that were of a decidedly more commercial nature, though audiences would prove elusive. Coproduced by Hill and David Giler, Hugh Wilson's *Rustler's Rhapsody* is a featherweight comedy that some may look upon as a timely parody of the western genre, which had been enjoying a brief resurgence of popularity in the mid–'80s. However satirical it may be, one would argue it is much more a sincere love letter to the early B-movie subgenre of the singing cowboy that was once the domain of Gene Autry and Roy Rogers. It works for the most part, due in no small part to the presence of Patrick Wayne (son of John) along with Andy Griffith and Fernando Rey lending some credibility amid the absurdity. Another film that Hill was involved with, one that is perhaps less popular than any film that bears his credit, is *Blue City*. A tale of civic corruption in small-town Florida based on Ross McDonald's 1947 novel of the same name, Hill adapted the book into a screenplay with Robert Aldrich's regular writer, Lukas Heller (*Whatever Happened to Baby Jane?*, *The Dirty Dozen*, *The Killing of Sister George*, and more). In transposing the story from the forties to the eighties, the film wrongly set its targets on the youth audience, most obviously so with the curious casting of Brat Packers Ally Sheedy and Judd Nelson. Both actors were fresh off successful roles in John Hughes's *The Breakfast Club*, a film that had been produced by Ned Tanen's Channel Productions and coproduced by Michelle Manning, who would make her directorial debut with *Blue City*. After helping to bring the Brat Pack to cultural ubiquity, Manning brought in Sheedy and Nelson perhaps thinking they could parlay some of that box office stardust to *Blue City*. However, the casting is entirely wrong for the hardboiled plot. "*Blue City* as Lukas and I had written it was supposed to have a more mature cast," Hill says, "but they turned it into a Brat Pack kind of thing. The script was not designed for a Brat Pack sensibility. I had been talking about doing it a few years before it got made but ultimately Michelle Manning directed it. Michelle had previously been Ned Tanen's assistant at Universal and then she landed a deal at Paramount when Tanen took over. While he was there he decided he was going to give her a shot as a director and so she reviewed some things and decided upon the *Blue City* script I had written with Lukas. Michelle asked me if she could do it and I said sure. It wasn't something that was on my plate because I was getting ready to go do *Crossroads*. In fact, when they were making *Blue City*, I was mostly down in Mississippi shooting *Crossroads*. So, I didn't see anything until they were well into postproduction, and it was then I realized they changed it a lot. And they didn't give Michelle enough money to make it properly."

While Hill is characteristically modest about his involvement in Manning's step up to the camera, others have noted the importance of the opportunity he afforded the young USC graduate, while also recalling the support he offered them. Maggie Greenwald is one such, having cut her teeth on several Hill films, first as assistant ADR editor on *Streets of Fire* and then as assistant sound editor on *Crossroads* before becoming a noted filmmaker in her own right with the likes of *The Kill-Off* (1990), *The Ballad of Little Jo* (1993), and *Songcatcher* (2000). "Walter was friends with Michelle Manning and he was instrumental in her getting that first directing opportunity on *Blue City*, and that is because he was quietly proactive in supporting women moving into directing. At that time, it was a big deal for a woman wanting to direct. I got to meet Walter when I was spending time around the editing room with Freeman and Carmel Davies; Freeman told him that I was an aspiring director and that meant Walter took notice and was really supportive of me without ever saying, 'Oh, can I see your work?' To have a big director like him to acknowledge me and to offer support by just being respectful and interested really meant a great deal to me as a young woman and aspiring filmmaker."

"Michelle was a girl coming up out of USC with ambitions to be a director," Allan Graf recalls, "so Walter, along with Paramount, gave her an opportunity with *Blue City* and that became her directorial debut. That's the kind of guy Walter is—a very supportive person who has given great opportunities to people. I even got a nice part in *Blue City*, playing a thuggish bodyguard."

Hill returned to the director's chair with *Crossroads*, a mystical musical road movie that pairs an eager young guitarist with a cynical old blues man as they hit the road to the Mississippi Delta in search of a mythical lost song that was cut by the legendary guitarist Robert Johnson. Eugene Martone (Ralph Macchio) is a prodigious music student at New York's prestigious Julliard School, but he is far from devoted to the staid bourgeois milieu of his classical studies. Rather, his passion is for the elemental power of the blues. He is obsessed with the legendary recordings of Robert Johnson and when he learns that Johnson's old bandmate Willie Brown (Joe Seneca) is languishing in a downtown minimum-security hospital, the avid fan gets a job at the facility as a cleaner to make contact with Brown and encourage him to help find the elusive track. But Willie is wary and agrees to share what he knows of the song only if Eugene will break him out of the institution. With Eugene's help, Brown absconds, and the pair set out on an eventful journey down to Eugene's spiritual home: the crossroads where Robert Johnson is said to have sold his soul to the devil and where it is revealed that Willie Brown did the same in exchange for his skills as a bluesman. When Old Scratch appears once again, Willie states that he wants to end the contract, but as this is the devil's business, he proposes a challenge: Eugene will play a concert battling hell's own guitarist, Jack Butler (Steve Vai), and if Eugene loses, then his soul is destined to languish in purgatory. If the young guitarist wins, then Willie reclaims his soul, the contract with the Devil null and void.

Like the hero of *Crossroads*, screenwriter John Fusco was a young New Yorker with a great fascination with the blues and who felt the pull of the Mississippi Delta.

Eugene Martone (Ralph Macchio): blues man in *Crossroads* (1986).

His love of southern rock music engendered a curiosity into the roots of that sound, which led him to the legend of Robert Johnson and the myth of the crossroads. Fusco left school early and headed south to seek out the sound behind this music that he loved. "It wasn't enough to say I was going to play covers of the Allman Brothers Band or Elmore James," Fusco says. "I wanted to know who influenced Elmore James and where that sound came from. Part of my motivation in heading down south was the ethnomusicologist Alan Lomax and the mystery and magic of the old field recordings, the idea of going into these remote places and finding living connections to Robert Johnson. I recognized that Robert Johnson was the Holy Grail behind all this music and wanted to find living connections and links to that, so I left home and went on the road to the Mississippi Delta. I worked in sawmills, and I got involved in the last vestiges of the hobo culture, traveling by rail with migrant workers who would go from town to town working car wash to car wash. That experience exposed me to authentic Delta blues. I did that for several years and then I wound up in New Orleans and wound up in north Florida, before heading back up north to write and perform music. Then at a certain point I burned out on the music scene, and I realized I had abandoned my first love, because everyone was trying to beat it out of me, which was filmmaking."

During Fusco's five-year odyssey he was writing all the time, eventually deciding to follow his literary ambitions by studying film in order to pursue his passion. However, Fusco had no high school diploma to even be considered for college, so he enrolled in night school to further his education. After building a portfolio of writing samples drawing upon the unique experiences of his alternative lifestyle on the road, Fusco got accepted into NYU, the Tisch School of the Arts. "I was an anomaly," Fusco says, "because a lot of the students were coming directly from high school or were working on their master's degrees and were very articulate in the world of film, whereas I was this traveling blues hobo. But the thing was I had material, I had stories to tell which were very different to what the instructors had been seeing. At that point everyone was trying to write the next *Star Wars* or very erudite playwright kind of things, but I had this story of a young white guy who was obsessed with the blues, a semiautobiographical screenplay that I wrote called *Crossroads*. I wanted to tell my story but take it to a creative place. My wife and I were working day jobs in New York City, trying to save up some money to get an apartment; she was working at an assisted living home, a rest home, and she called me one day and said, 'Hey, you might want to come down here after work. There is an old black guy from the South who has been admitted here; he has all these harmonicas in his top drawer, he sits and draws pictures of the South, and he is really cool.' On the 20-minute drive over I came up with this whole scenario, like what if he turns out to be that guy I always wanted to find who was so deeply connected to the mystery and the secret of the blues and we end up going on a road trip and he takes me back to where it all began, to the deepest regions of the crossroads. So, when I got to NYU I had my guns loaded, I knew that was the story I would write."

It was at NYU that the budding screenwriter had the immense good fortune to attend a masterclass taught by not one but three of the legendary blacklisted screenwriters: Waldo Salt (Oscar-winning writer of *Midnight Cowboy*, *Serpico*, *Coming Home*), Ring Lardner, Jr., (controversial member of the Hollywood Ten and writer of the Tracy-Hepburn romance *Woman of the Year*, among other pseudonymous work), and Ian McLellan Hunter (*Footlight Fever*, *Captain Sindbad*, *The Amazing Mr. X*). Places in the classes were limited, with only a select few students making the cut based on material submitted for perusal by the powerhouse three. Fusco was accepted and it was Salt who took a particular interest in the talented student; it was in this class that Fusco developed *Crossroads*, with Salt guiding the student to write what he had in his heart. Fusco recalls his conversations with the veteran writer:

"Waldo kept me after class one day and said, 'What's your deal?' I told him my story and he said, 'Do you know that I hoboed with Woody Guthrie?' And then Waldo became like a mentor and encouraged me in writing this road movie. So I had good guidance in that class, but I had the thing already written. Those instructors were the type of writers who believed in the purity of the vision, and I asked Waldo if it was alright to write this song into the script and if a director would feel like I'm stepping on his toes by doing that. Waldo said, 'Fuck the director! The writer is king. This is your story, you control this thing, and you put in any song you want. This is yours.' So, I completed the screenplay in that class, and it was actually my second script; my first was called 'Blues Water,' and it was another blues-based movie set in Florida but it didn't have enough of a commercial angle; it did, however, win first place in a national award which was sponsored by Nissan. The first prize was a brand-new automobile, and they flew you out to LA. That was literally my first class assignment, and I won the Nissan, which I was able to sell in order to continue going to school; then I got into that masterclass with Waldo, finished *Crossroads*, submitted it to the same national awards, and I won first prize again. So, I received a second Nissan and signed with the William Morris Agency. They ended up putting a clause into the rules of the competition called the Fusco Clause, which said you couldn't win two years in a row anymore."

The win and the attendant attention led to Columbia Pictures buying the script, meaning Fusco didn't have to tend bar anymore. Suddenly, agents were telling him it is the hottest script in town, every director wants to make it, and Tom Cruise wants to be in it. The script was optioned by producer Mark Carliner, who encouraged Fusco's input on choosing directors for the project. For the writer, there were two names expressing interest that stood out: one was Swedish filmmaker Lasse Hallström, whose *My Life as a Dog* left an impression on him; the other was Walter Hill, from whom Fusco received a call hailing the script. Fusco was a fan of Hill's work and felt that the director was a man after his own heart: a rugged individualist and the last of a rare breed.

"I was like, 'Oh, man, this guy came up under Sam Peckinpah!' and is the closest thing we have to a new Peckinpah. The name 'Walter Hill' is a brand, it's an icon. A movie is a Walter Hill movie in the same way it's a Peckinpah movie or a Leone movie or a Ford movie; he is the last of the real-deal rugged Americana directors, and I could relate to that. So, when it came down to those two directors, I told Carliner that I would go with Walter. The next thing I know is that Walter is directing it and they flew me out to LA to meet him. I remember walking into his office, and he is sitting behind his desk wearing sunglasses and the first thing he said to me was, 'Hey listen, kid, I don't want you to think I'm some Hollywood asshole sitting here with sunglasses on, I've got an eye issue.' I'm like, 'It's cool! It's cool!' And then we got talking about the script and he says, 'Where did you come up with this shit?' and I told him my story and about the jobs I worked; I described myself as a late bloomer and he goes, 'Ah!' and he starts laughing and says, 'A late bloomer? You're 24 years old! I was driving trucks at 24! It took me longer than that.' It began as a real good initial writer-director relationship and then we went down the road of casting."

Among those considered for casting were Tom Cruise and Sean Penn, but both were beat by Ralph Macchio, who was then what Fusco calls "America's sweetheart," a popular heartthrob coming hot off the success of *The Karate Kid*. As such, Columbia was keen on capitalizing on Macchio's burgeoning stardom, even if his casting meant that some would use the surface similarities in the plots of *Crossroads* and *The Karate Kid* to influence their unfavorable judgment of the film. Casting Macchio at the height of his success may have seemed like the right choice at the right time considering his popularity, but this connection may be something that ultimately tainted the film in the eyes of critics. The film was released between the first and second installments of the *Karate Kid* franchise and the surface similarities between the two—young apprentice and old master overcome personal obstacles and battle malevolent forces—was a little too close for comfort.

"Ralph was selling Coca-Cola for Columbia at that point," Fusco says. "He was their poster boy. So, we were getting a lot of support from the studio in casting Ralph but at the end of the day it was Walter's choice to go with him. One of the things Walter has said is that we weren't aware that critics wouldn't allow us a separation from *The Karate Kid*, and that was because there were some similarities between our film and that film. Critics will always look for the dirty laundry and they perceived our story as some premeditated contrivance; they thought, 'Well, *The Karate Kid* was a hit so they're doing it again here.' They never looked deep enough to find out that I was living in a doorway and living this life just a couple of years prior, and so it got an undeserved knee-jerk reaction upon its release."

"I had a fight with the studio in the beginning," Hill affirms, "because I said it wouldn't make sense unless we did it with the kid as black, but they said they wouldn't make the movie because it wouldn't be commercial. So, as usual, I lost that fight. However, I now believe that they were correct. I think it makes the movie more universal, but I think you can argue for it either way. I think it's meant to be a story about the power of music."

With camera rolling on his script, Fusco set out to join Hill and company on location, even if it meant toiling in the production trenches with the crew to be there and observe his creation coming to life. Not that he would have to, but if that was what it would take, then the screenwriter was more than willing.

"I went to the Delta for the shoot after I called Walter and asked if I could be on set. Initially he said no, but in the nicest way that he could say it. He said there is not much for screenwriters to do on the set, and I said, 'Well, how about I haul cables and carry shit?' which made him laugh. But, I said, 'Walter, I'm serious!' and he said, 'You don't have to do that, but okay you can drop in.' I had this great feeling and idealistic hope that Walter would become my Peckinpah in the way Peckinpah was with him when he wrote *The Getaway*, that he would bring me up under his wing. I thought, 'I'm going to be the new western guy' and I did end up the new western guy with *Young Guns*; with that film I brought back a genre which had been dead for two decades, it was the first hit western in years! But that relationship did not come to fruition. There were times that I have been resentful about getting cut out of the process and of the film going in a different direction, but in hindsight I don't feel that anymore, now I realize what happened. Walter described it as a great strain—and I remember that word 'strain' specifically, and it was a strain between him and the producer, Mark Carliner. I'm not sure what that was about exactly but I think the whole thing was complicated by the fact that I was so tied in with Carliner. When I showed up to the set I found there was this posse, it was Walter's posse, and in that you had Ry Cooder, Tim Zinnemann, and some other guys, and I wanted to be part of that but it was very much a closed circle; I wasn't allowed in because I was seen to be Carliner's boy. It was Carliner who got me interviewed by the *New York Times*, he was signing me to his next projects; he felt that I was his discovery, and I was his goose that was going to lay the golden egg. Carliner essentially said, 'John's my guy!' and Walter reacted with, 'Okay, he's yours then!' That's where I think I suffered from that 'strain,' and I never got to become part of the posse. I tried to bring my lunch tray to their end of the table, and I was just closed off. My feeling was, 'Hey, man, see where we're sitting? I was stretching out on trains in the Clarksdale railyard like three years ago. Lightning Boy is me! This is my story!' But I realized it was going to be Walter's story and I didn't get to have that writer-director mentor relationship with Walter that I had hoped for."

The blues is the force that brings Eugene and Willie together, but while that music is intrinsically tied to Willie's culture, Eugene's experiences of the blues have been largely academic. But as a duo in search of elusive meaning in life via music, they eventually find common ground and experience to develop their previously tentative relationship into one with a solid foundation of trust and mutual respect. There is toughness at the heart of Eugene and Willie's relationship, a friendship fraught with Willie's old-world masculinity and tough love that the coddled college boy must come to understand as part of his training as a bluesman. These kinds of male relationships are something that Hill has been specializing in and ruminating on since the beginning of his career.

"I was initially thrown by the fact that Walter gravitated to this story," Fusco says, "because the script I wrote was a relationship story, but it had its rugged beats because I based it on real stuff, such as the scenes in the motel room with the girl. One of the things Walter and I talked about was bluesmen being more like wandering gunfighters or wandering swordsmen; they even packed guns. So there was a toughness that spoke to Walter that he was able to lean into; he brought an American western vibe to the Mississippi Delta. Some of my favorite moments in the film are those traveling shots that capture the shotgun shacks with Ry Cooder's slide guitar playing on the soundtrack. Ry brought in a guy named Jim Dickinson on the film and Walter loved Jim, he was the real deal, and they introduced me to him during the rewrites so that I had another resource to go to for cross-referencing. The story had an inherently authentic Americana aspect that Walter responded to. He brought muscularity and deep understanding of male relationships, making it a little bit more hard-boiled. Walter would go through the dialogue and if there was anything he felt was too nice, he would say, 'We need to toughen this up.' But before all that, many people were saying this film would be an interesting choice for Walter Hill."

"If I may take a personal moment…" Hill pauses. "I had the luckiest thing that you could have in life, which is I had two really good parents. It makes the biggest impression upon how we all go down the line. My father, who had been a very healthy man, had suddenly gotten catastrophically ill and he was clearly in final decline. My appreciation of music, such as it is, comes from my father being quite musical. I was simply an appreciator, but he was a percussionist playing with bands in bars at night; he was a factory worker, that's how he supported our family. But he loved jazz and he particularly loved blues and Dixieland. When this script showed up, I thought that it all connected for me. *Crossroads* was an opportunity to go out into America, go down south and to explore the myths and legends of the land and the music that came from there. I immersed myself in the delta blues and the myth and legend of Robert Johnson."

"It was a tough time for Walter," Fusco confirms. "His father died during the production of *Crossroads* and his relationship with his dad was a big influence on him while making this film. The original ending in my initial script has Willie Brown dying on the side of the road. It's the morning after and they are camped out but Willie is gone and they hold a burial for him behind a church, but there was something about that which Walter didn't like and he wanted to tweak it, so he got me to work on it further and had me rewrite it so that Willie dies on a Greyhound bus with the kid sitting beside him; the kid tells him it's time to wake up and he realizes Willie is dead. It's Ratso Rizzo in *Midnight Cowboy*, so it goes back full circle to Waldo! So, we wrote that and filmed it two weeks after Walter's father died and I remember it was hard for Walter to shoot that scene. And then we went back and did reshoots and one of the scenes we reshot was the ending, so now in the final cut it ends with Willie being alive and saying, 'I'm ready for something new, how about Chicago?' And maybe that's one of the reasons why the film didn't land."

Hill has been successful in finding the intimacy in tough male relationships, but for some people the resolution of these two men's affection for each other doesn't feel authentic; it feels like a contrivance too far for Hill's erstwhile screenwriting collaborator Larry Gross, who considers the film to be a rare experiment in sentiment within the director's oeuvre. "There is a ton of interesting stuff in *Crossroads*," Gross says, "and there's a lot of things which are characteristic of Walter; however, there is something about it, and I don't know how to put my finger exactly on it, but there's something missing from the story, or something he just didn't connect to. It is the one film that Walter made where I think he miscalculated the material and his own understanding of how to do it. It was maybe an experiment, or he was just setting aside his normal operations. I think he connected personally and subjectively to everything in the movie, and I do know he cared about it deeply and was fascinated by the whole legend of Robert Johnson, stuff he knew backward and forward anyway, but it's the only film of his that I feel is in any way less than all of his other films. *Crossroads* is a movie for which you had to really be sentimental to make it totally work, and I don't know whether Walter could do that at the end of the day. That's what it boils down to. You had to be invested in the softness of it and the sweetness of it and I don't know if that was something Walter could access."

"The biggest difference between the two scripts," Fusco says, "is that in my original first draft the third act was never designed for the sky to open up for a

Willie (Joe Seneca, left) and Eugene (Ralph Macchio) make it through the crossroads on their way to Chicago in *Crossroads* (1986).

metaphysical crossing of spiritual planes and genre bending. Walter described it in an interview recently as 'metaphysical postmodern poetry' or something like that, and there are people today who love it, particularly musicians. In my original version of the script, the old man brought the kid to Clarksdale, just off the crossroads to an old railyard with fires burning in trash cans and flatbed boxcars; it was a combination of *Fight Club* and a modern-day rap-off with blues men from down there cutting heads, and from the old man's perspective this was the duel with the devil, and maybe Walter was right to change it to what he did, but my version was grounded in reality. You would think it would be something that Walter would really lean into, and there's no doubt about it, I wrote that guitar duel like a gunfight. To this day, if people ask me about my favorite gunfight that I have written I always say *Crossroads*, and Walter brought so much to that scene. It's iconic, it's classic. He wanted to create what he called 'The Devil's Church,' but it was literal to the point of them tearing a contract and that was not my vision, but that's where Walter wanted to take it. Rex Reed said in his review that he sat through the movie bewildered that Walter was going down such a refreshing road by getting into character relationships with this deep friendship between a young white kid and an old black man but then it collapsed into metaphysical silliness. That was the big difference in how I imagined the story and how Walter executed it."

After bouncing back from the financial failure of *Streets of Fire* with the roaring success of *Brewster's Millions*, Hill would once again experience having a film released by a studio unable to sell it to an indifferent audience. "The movie did not do well," Hill admits. "We did it very cheaply, but the studio didn't know how to sell it. The marketing was nonexistent. This was when Columbia had just gone through a big changeover when they were bought by Coca-Cola. I was surprised the movie didn't find more of a path of acceptance with the music critics; some did like it, but it was the white-black thing that especially made many of the music critics uncomfortable. If somebody else had made it and allowed the relationship to be more sentimental it might have been more commercial, but I make things to my own taste. You make them as best you can, and you send them out and sometimes you catch the wave but sometimes you don't."

Fusco recalled, "Before they flew me out to meet Walter, I talked to him on the phone and the first thing he said to me was, 'Do you have a fireplace mantel?' and I said no. Then he says, 'Well, can you get one? Because you are going to need it for your Academy Award for Best Original Screenplay.' That was the very first thing he said to me and I remember thinking, 'Wow! Holy shit!' and then he said, 'If you don't win it, it's because I fucked it up. The only way you won't win that Oscar is if I fuck it up somehow.' When I heard that I just felt like he was an even bigger hero to me than he already was. But then the movie came out and in the firestorm of attacks on the movie Walter was interviewed by *American Film* magazine and I remember my heartbreak when I read Walter's answer to a question about why it failed. He said, 'Let's face it, the script wasn't exactly *King Lear*.' To go from telling me to clear off my mantel for the Academy Award to saying that, I remember thinking, 'Damn, that's a shame.' But I want to be clear about this: I understand what Walter was dealing with and I think that I had to pay the price for it. For many years I was resentful only because Walter was a hero of mine like he is a hero of yours, Wayne, and I felt like, 'Why didn't he take me under his wing? Why wasn't he helping me with *Young Guns* and pushing me and making the handoff?' That just didn't come together, but you get older and, as they say, 'sadder but wiser,' and you understand more about how people were feeling when they say certain things. Walter took a real risk with this material and over time I have come to realize that what he was saying wasn't really about me."

Despite the initial lukewarm reception to the film, the influence of *Crossroads* is still being felt today, though perhaps more prominently in the music scene than in cinema culture. The film introduced people to the blues and to the music of Robert Johnson who may otherwise have never been exposed to such; Hill's mythological journey into the history of the blues is an enrapturing experience to viewers with an interest in the power of music. Such is the strength of the film's exploration of the blues and the authenticity of Ry Cooder's sterling soundtrack that the ultimate impact and legacy of *Crossroads* may be found in the grooves of many a musical recording. "After this film, so many men and women went down south," Fusco says. "There are people in Clarksdale right now running blues businesses, young white guys who saw the film and went down to find the crossroads and never left. It is enormously rewarding to see so many people influenced by this film, hearing that it introduced them to the blues, or Robert Johnson, or that it inspired them to pick up the guitar. But it did take me many years to be able to stand back from it and appreciate that. For years and years, it was hard for me to look at it, but over time so many people ranging from Eric Krasno to Devon Allman, Duane Betts and Tom Morello, Jonny Lang, all these guys have been in contact with me and telling me that *Crossroads* influenced them to pick up the guitar. The movie shaped my future, and it shaped the future of music, because a lot of people who are dominating on guitar right now got into music because of this film and because Walter created an unforgettable cutting heads tournament scene which has been so influential to young people."

Fusco continues, "I think the film missed some opportunities from the original script, but it also created some really good stuff by way of Walter. But the movie opened with $4 million and was absolutely hammered by the critics. I know it was hard for Walter to have a movie opening to $4 million at the box office, it had to be tough. But Ralph himself recently quoted [Francis Ford] Coppola when he said, 'Movies are defined by time,' and over time Ralph has inspired a generation of musicians, as the movie has; it has become a cult classic, and nobody holds that against us anymore. *Crossroads* has become defined by time. Walter and I are proud of where it sits, and I'm proud that I got to work with him. What Walter created has stood the test of time and become its own thing. There's a lot to be said for Walter's vision."

Four

"Blow something up!"

With his detour into more youth-oriented fare on his last three films, Hill proved himself to be a studio filmmaker of auteur sensibilities and chameleonic ability in the mold of his Old Hollywood heroes. But the commercial mainstream milieu of the film industry in the 1980s was unpredictable and its audience fickle; this was the era in which the franchise sequel to high-concept, low-risk fare was becoming the studio system's stock-in-trade. *Crossroads* may have starred Ralph Macchio as he was becoming a teen idol, but it was the brand familiarity of *The Karate Kid* that viewers really sought, just as they did the sequels to *Friday the 13th*, *Lethal Weapon*, *Back to the Future*, *Beverly Hills Cop*, and so on. Even Hill became involved in franchise fare by cowriting *Aliens*, James Cameron's bombastic follow-up to the 1979 Ridley Scott–directed and Hill-scripted horror picture *Alien*. Further on, Hill reluctantly but successfully gave Paramount a hit sequel with *Another 48 Hrs*. But following the tepid response to *Crossroads*, the director's next move would be a return to the mature hard-edged action cinema that he had become celebrated for in the first decade of his career. John Fusco recalls a time when, deep into the process of making *Crossroads*, he often overheard Hill saying, "Don't worry, the guns will be back in the next one! The guns will definitely be coming out on the next movie." And the director stuck to his guns indeed, as *Extreme Prejudice* contains more firearm fireworks than any other film in the Hill canon.

In this wildly entertaining alternative western, Michael Ironside plays Major Paul Hackett, the commander of the covert Zombie Unit, a team of soldiers presumably so called because each man, including Hackett, is officially listed on military records as having been killed in action, making the shadowy group untraceable in the event of being caught in their conspiratorial activities. The team includes Master Sergeant Larry McRose (Clancy Brown), Sergeant Buckman Atwater (William Forsythe), Sergeant Declan Patrick Coker (Matt Mulhern), Sergeant Charles Biddle (Larry B. Scott), and Sergeant Luther Fry (Dan Tullis, Jr.). The men descend upon an acrid border town in El Paso, Texas, to execute an assignment on behalf of the DEA, which is to rob a local bank that contains the ill-gotten profits and financial accounts of a former informer turned drug lord, Cash Bailey (Powers Boothe). Bailey is also the target of Texas Ranger Jack Benteen (Nick Nolte), who has been busy waging war on local dealers in these rural badlands. Benteen blames the lawlessness that rips through his town on Bailey, but things are complicated by the fact that the two are former friends, having grown up together in the same small town that is now being plagued by Bailey's product. Locals who have fallen on hard times are now taking payment from Bailey to transport his drugs across the border. Further complicating matters is the woman who has captured the hearts of both men, barroom songstress Sarita Cisneros (Maria Conchita Alonso). Sarita is Bailey's former lover but is now with Benteen, and she is torn between the lifestyles that the men offer her. After Hackett's bank robbery goes awry, Benteen arrests several Zombie Unit soldiers, while others become casualties to the dangerous mission, including Sergeant Fry; the futility of their deaths leads to tensions rising among the unit. "My buddy's in a body bag," screams an exasperated Sergeant Biddle, "and he ain't in Lebanon or Honduras ... fuckin' Texas!" Benteen is drawn into their mission when Hackett informs him of their plan to bring Bailey to justice, leading to the irate ranger joining them on their mission, which will pit the Zombie Unit against Bailey's private army and the friends-turned-foes going face-to-face in an ultimate showdown. But further espionage is revealed when Hackett suspiciously orders his men to kill Benteen in the ensuing battle, reasoning collateral damage in the pursuit of achieving their target of capturing Bailey. But the Zombies admire Benteen and find it odd and unreasonable that they would be ordered to terminate a civilian peace officer loyal to their country. When Buckman discreetly alerts Benteen to his imminent danger, the ranger now has both Bailey and the corrupt Hackett to deal with.

Extreme Prejudice contains one of Hill's most well-cast ensembles, led by the taciturn Nick Nolte, never as lean and chiseled as here, stiffly encased into his pressed uniform of the anachronistic lawman who seems more suited to the ways of the old west rather than the contemporary milieu. He is joined by two genuine Texans in the form of a memorable Rip Torn as the gruff rural sheriff Hank Pearson, who chomps cigars and chews scenery, emphasizing every gesture and drawl to the point of parody; then there's the formidable Powers Boothe, handsome and swaggering as Cash Bailey. The film is the finest example of when Hill says he always makes westerns even when they're not westerns. Given the southern setting and all the iconography of such (landscape, wardrobe, weaponry, etc.), the film feels as much a western as any legitimate genre entry of the era. Under all the political themes and extravagant violence is a tale of two men who wrestle over the love of a woman and over the moral conflict that has divided their friendship. It has been the trope of many a western to put two old allies against each other, from the Monogram B pictures like *Across the Plains* (Spencer Gordon Bennet, 1939) and *Across the Sierras* (D. Ross Lederman, 1941) to major studio oaters such as *Last Train from Gun Hill* (John Sturges, 1959); it is also a theme most excellently explored by Sam Peckinpah on multiple occasions with *Ride the High Country* (1962), *The Wild Bunch* (1969), and *Pat Garrett and Billy the Kid* (1973). However, Hill inverts the traditional western notions of good and evil, allowing for what is the traditional hero of the piece, Benteen, to be informed with a more ambiguous set of morals. He dutifully complies with the role of the western lawman in looking out for his community and protecting it from the scourge of nefarious outside sources, though he essentially admits that were it not for his badge he would not be infallible to being bought; that shield, a symbol that cannot be sold, is the only thing that can keep him from following his old friend to the other side. "The only thing that ever scared the hell out of me, Cash, was myself," Benteen says, "so I come home and I put the badge on and things are right."

Benteen's moral ambiguity complicates the binary forces that are often so clearly marked in black and white, and the film duly subverts the visual references that we associate with those markings: Benteen is decked out in the dark clothing of his ranger's uniform while Bailey shimmers in pristine white; the visual codes of the western hero and villain are reversed. Bailey is no black-hatted bad guy. His clothing represents a new class of 1980s antagonist: the yuppie criminal who is financially competent and dresses impeccably well—sleek, slick, and well-manicured. In a way, Bailey represents an ideological opposition, a modernization, and even corporatization of the old western values. Spending his time flying around in his expensive, high-powered helicopter and living the kind of exclusive lifestyle that is the reserve of the few, he is far removed from the humble farming community from which he and his old friend originated. His rough edges have been superficially smoothed out with a bourgeois veneer.

When Bailey and Benteen meet after an explosive device is detonated in town on behalf of the former, they converge on their old stomping ground where they once hunted deer together. But before they begin to trade threats to eliminate each other, they immediately jump back to their old bonhomie, as Bailey recalls them having "rode the river together" and played on the same football team, dated the same girls, and even shared some of the local weed. However, this rekindling of old times still ends in Bailey placing greed over friendship, noting menacingly that "I've got a feeling the next time we run into each other we gonna have a killin' … just a feelin'." Bailey covets the one thing Benteen cares about, and which is the other source of conflict between the two men: Sarita, whose loyalty is torn between the

Old friends Bailey (Powers Boothe, left) and Benteen (Nick Nolte) share a moment of reminiscing before parting as enemies in *Extreme Prejudice* (1987).

opulent rogue who could provide unending riches, albeit illicitly, and the moodier man who could provide a modest but honest life.

Aside from a similar display of balletic bloodshed, there are multiple thematic elements shared with Peckinpah's 1969 masterpiece *The Wild Bunch*, notably the central relationship being the hero and villain who are former friends now operating on opposite sides of the law, just as William Holden's Pike Bishop and Robert Ryan's Deke Thornton are old pals turned foes. Then there are the more subtle references, such as the scorpion imagery, which is something that figures in the opening moments of Peckinpah's film, when a scorpion is toyed with by a gang of children before they gleefully burn it; when we first meet Bailey he plays with a scorpion before crushing it. What may feel most familiar though is the thrilling montage of action in the ultimate showdown that takes place in the Mexican plaza as revelers celebrate Independence Day. This is perhaps the scene that invites most comparisons, due to several factors, though Hill is quick to distance himself from such conspicuous resemblances, noting that the imagery of the western is so evocative and definitive that it makes it very easy for such likenesses to be drawn.

"You call it an 'alternative western' and I would go along with that," Hill says. "It has been said that the film is kind of an ode to Peckinpah and *The Wild Bunch*, but I think people get confused. If you shoot a gunfight in a Mexican town plaza, in a place that looks western, you inevitably get drawn into those comparisons. But Peckinpah did it best. If you go back to *Vera Cruz* or *The Magnificent Seven*, any one of *The Magnificent Seven* films, they have the same tropes of the Mexicans fighting Anglos who have come down to Mexico, but I think Sam did it better than anybody and it hangs in everybody's memory."

"Walter looked up to Sam Peckinpah big-time, he always admired him," actor/stuntman Allan Graf says. "You can see that influence in the action sequences of *Extreme Prejudice* in particular. But Walter just loves westerns. If he had his way, every film would be a western. I mean what stops *Extreme Prejudice* from being a western? Very little. It looks and feels like a western, so it might as well be."

The ensuing carnage of the climactic showdown is excessive to the point of Peckinpah parody if not pastiche, but it is not merely the violent glory of the scene that would have viewers reaching for comparisons with the 1969 film, as the stylish montage editing recalls an aesthetic that people may associate with Peckinpah's own due to his prolific use of such. But this style was nothing exclusive to Peckinpah, and though it seemed like a relatively new tradition in popular cinema of the 1960s, the style goes much further back than that. It was Hill's own knowledge of this that saved his hide after catching the wrong side of Peckinpah when word began to spread that his kinetic style was lifted from Arthur Penn's *Bonnie and Clyde*, a film that uses a similar rhythm and juxtaposition of slow-motion and regular speed with rapid editing in its climactic montage of the film's antiheroes being gunned down. "I got in trouble with Sam one day when we were working on *The Getaway*," Hill recalls. "The script was pretty much done but he was still prepping, and my office was down the corridor but I came into his office just to say hello. His inner door was shut and I said to his assistant that I was going to say hello to Sam and she said, 'Oh god, don't! He is in a terrible mood.' So I ask what set him off and she

Ranger Jack Benteen (Nick Nolte) draws while Sarita (Maria Concita Alonso) fears for her man during the final shootout of *Extreme Prejudice* (1987).

said that there was some article in *Newsweek* that said he was an imitator of Arthur Penn because of all the slow motion that they used. Well, Sam was not an admirer of Arthur Penn's for starters, and then for it to be said that he ripped off Arthur Penn was too much for him. But I saw him that afternoon and I said, in my jocular way, 'Don't worry about that article, nobody that knows anything thinks you took it from Arthur Penn. Everybody knows you stole it from Kurosawa!' and he didn't think this was so fucking funny! I misread the mood and he didn't speak to me for about three days. But in the joke is a truth. What Sam did is he took matters of technique from Kurosawa and extended them way beyond what Kurosawa had done with the material, with the action. So, it made it uniquely situational and his own."

The kinetic camerawork of *Extreme Prejudice* was orchestrated by acclaimed cinematographer Matthew Leonetti (*Breaking Away*, *Poltergeist*, *Weird Science*, *Jagged Edge*), who made the crucial connection to Hill through his work with producer Joel Silver, with whom he collaborated on the 1985 Arnold Schwarzenegger spectacle *Commando*.

"Joel and Walter knew each other at that time and a lot of the people who worked for Joel also worked with Walter. One guy said to me, 'We're trying to pimp you to Walter!' So, they kept pushing me towards Walter and then we met and got along well. He took the recommendations of those people we had been working with and that's how we got acquainted and how I got the job to do *Extreme Prejudice*. Walter would give you a lot of freedom on how you approached it, although he was very specific about how he wanted the close-up shots and certain other shots like that. He didn't do a lot of wide masters, he would shoot medium shots, tight shots, and tighter shots. All the coverage was three sizes: one about the belly, one about the chest, one about neck high. He was very specific about that; it gave him some choices in the editing room, and he would always print two takes of each size. One of the things Walter likes to do on his movies is to use long lenses, and especially on *Extreme Prejudice* because when we were outside we could use 600mm or 400mm lenses, and he just likes the look of long lenses so that was one of his prerequisites. One time he asked me what lenses I use, and I said I like to put a zoom lens on because that way you can vary the size of the shot in an instant. If you have a 50mm on the camera and you want it tighter and want to move in by 5mm, well, then you've got to tear dollies apart and all that, but with the zoom all you have to do is crank it a little bit; it wasn't used as a 'zoom lens,' it was used as a fixed lens. Back then, as they are today, they are so good you couldn't tell the difference. I used to own a company that manufactured a 35mm sound camera, the Ultracam, and we used that on the shows, and they worked well with the Cooke zooms, so Walter was happy with that. It made life easier, it simplified it. When I do a movie, I try to keep it simple and try not to make it too complicated; it makes production go smoother and increases the speed by which you work and gives the director more time with the actors."

Leonetti had some of the best cameramen around to help capture the action, including Michael D. O'Shea and Bobby LaBonge. Prior to becoming a cinematographer, O'Shea had come off a series of films as the camera operator for noted cinematographer Nick McLean—the man behind the framing of such hits as *City Heat* (1984), *The Goonies* (1985), and *Short Circuit* (1986)—and excitedly embraced this opportunity to work with Hill after a tantalizingly brief experience on *Streets of Fire* and a missed opportunity on *The Long Riders*.

"Not doing *The Long Riders* is my one regret," O'Shea admits. "The director of photography, Ric Waite, was courting me to be the A-camera operator on that film but I ended up not doing it because I had a problem with the production manager when I was trying to make a deal for myself. I didn't know much about Walter Hill at the time, but I knew it was a great script and I knew we were going to Georgia for three months. However, it was a money thing and I got stubborn about it, and I really regret it because I missed an opportunity to work with Walter even earlier than I did. The next experience I had was when they were making *Streets of Fire* and the A-cameraman called me up to come on to work the C camera and that was the first time I met Walter. I remember being struck by how quiet he was, but that is because he knew exactly what he was doing; he was so well-prepared, every camera had a direction. I was really impressed with him. The next time I worked with him was on *Extreme Prejudice*, when I was the camera operator for Matt Leonetti, and I really got to know Walter on that one. We were down in Texas for the first six weeks, and he was just one of the guys, he creates such a good environment for his crew to work in. Sometimes when you go to work and it's for a big director that you haven't met before, you kind of get a little fear, but I never felt that with Walter. He is a very humble guy. Sometimes you wouldn't even know that he was the director on-set. In fact, he's the kind of guy who if I saw on the street, I'd put my arms around him."

Like O'Shea, Bobby LaBonge had worked on some major titles early on in his career, including *Star Wars: Return of the Jedi* (1983), *Weird Science* (1985), and *Three Amigos!* (1986), before joining the crew on *Extreme Prejudice*, the first of his many collaborations with Hill. "I had known Walter's name for a long time," LaBonge says, "but *Extreme Prejudice* was the first movie I did with him. Our director of photography on the film, Matthew Leonetti, is a good, solid cinematographer. I came in as the first assistant cameraman on a B or C camera, I was not the main A cameraman. Walter always respected the craft of whatever your job was; if you were the first assistant cameraman and you needed to get some focus marks, he would say, 'Okay, Bobby gets his focus marks and then we roll!' He doesn't discount or minimize your job. He would say, 'If that's what you need, let's do it and then we will roll.'"

O'Shea recalls one memorable moment of filming that speaks to his director's assuredness and trust of his collaborators: "We had three cameras on *Extreme Prejudice*. Michael St. Hilaire was on the A camera, I was on the B camera, and Ed Morey was on the C camera. One day we were filming the big shootout where Rip Torn gets killed and it was a tough shot, we had a wide shot, a medium shot, and a tight shot. Well, Rip is rigged up to all these squibs, he's jumping and moving around, and then he drops to the ground, and he goes out of my frame; but I caught up with him. I say to myself, 'It's okay, Michael or Ed will have gotten it,' but it turned out none of us got it! We all missed it when Rip dropped to the ground. So now we had to go tell Matt Leonetti when he yells 'Cut!' and asks how the shots went. Michael said, 'Well, Matt, I missed it.' And Matt says, 'How about you, Mike?' and I told him I missed it, and he goes, 'Really?' Then he turned to Ed, expecting him to say he got it, but Ed said he missed it too. Matt looks at us and says, 'I've got 60 years of operator experience here and none of you got that shot?!' He was cool about it, but then he says, 'Now I gotta tell Walter.' So, now we're all shitting our pants. He calls Walter over and says, 'Walter, I gotta tell you, the operators missed Rip hitting the ground, they caught up to him later.' Walter then looks at all three of us and goes, 'Well, Matt, I can't ask Rip to do this again, it will take two hours to squib him.' And in such a calming way he says, 'Freeman will figure out how to cut around it, boys. Don't worry about it.' Freeman Davies was Walter's editor, and he had enough confidence in Freeman that they would be able to work it out. When we watched the final cut of the movie you would never have known that we missed this shot. But that's Walter Hill right there. Missing that shot was a big deal, especially because of what Rip had to go through to get the shot. And we had a lot of years behind us as operators, so we were expected to get the shot; but for Walter to say, 'Don't worry about it, Freeman will fix it,' that's a mind-blowing experience."

"I was pretty careful about hiring people to make this movie," Leonetti admits, "and both Bobby and Mike were very good. They contributed. When they had an idea, I would listen, and they had great suggestions about camera placement and things like that. Contributions such as those are able to happen because of Walter. He would give the crew that kind of freedom while he was watching what was going on."

"When you are on a set with Walter, you know who is in charge," LaBonge says, "and he knows what everyone's job is and he respects that job; he gave you the time to get what you needed. You always had to be on your A game. You came to work knowing you are working with a really special filmmaker, so you were going to be super-focused. That is always prevalent with Walter."

O'Shea continues, "I never saw Walter dictate to actors what he wanted, and that applies to the crew as well. He hires you for what you can do, and he takes everybody in to feel part of it all and to feel like you are really contributing. He is open to things, but he knows exactly what he wants. If you can make a shot better, that's not a problem, he accepts all that kind of input. I used to listen to Walter and Nick Nolte going back and forth on ideas and I always like to listen to directors giving direction, so I was in awe of how Walter worked things out with his actors. Nick would have a point of view on a scene and Walter would listen to him and maybe come back and suggest something else. It was never a case of 'I am the director, and this is what I want you to do!' Whether it was Nick Nolte or Rip Torn or Powers Boothe, or even if it was Lloyd or Matt or myself, Walter would listen to every word, and I could feel that he was interested in what you had to say. If you had an idea that could make something better, he was always open to considering it."

Behind the elaborately staged action, multilayered plot, and intricate issues of military espionage and policing of the drug war, Hill distills the film down to a David and Goliath tale that pits a man who represents the noble ideals of Small Town USA against formidable adversaries that would seek to corrupt the values of such. In this case, a local lawman of limited means goes up against two far more powerful and well-resourced forces: a dissident paramilitary commander and a drug lord. Ranger Benteen is the sole, individualistic hero in these nihilistic badlands where conflicts are heightened by the fact that in this small town both the law and the outlaw rub shoulders, and in some cases they are family, friends, and neighbors. Sheriff Pearson talks of seeing these criminals growing up as children before they went down the wrong path; he reminisces about knowing their parents, fishing with their fathers, and how they were sweet boys before turning out to be mad dogs. Benteen reveals to Sheriff Pearson that he and Bailey were among the youth who used to evade his capture, much to the sheriff's bemusement. While these emotional insights into the town's culture and social fabric give some added depth to the film's milieu, many of those ne'er-do-wells are dispatched with extreme prejudice in the fierce shootouts, regardless of family history. "Now look it here, I'm just a poor old dirt farmer," says cornered drug mule TC. "It ain't right, Jack, you trying to take me in. I'm just trying to make some money at something besides chopping cotton." However, there is no time to consider the unfortunate circumstances these young men find themselves in, those who could have been decent citizens but who chose the wrong life out of desperation. Once the gun is in their hand and they aim it at Sheriff Pearson or Ranger Benteen, they might as well be paper targets at the shooting range. "Just another raggedy-ass dirt farmer gone broke trying to hold on to his piece of the world by running dope across the border … for Cash Bailey." Jack sounds almost sympathetic until his elliptical pause and proclamation of who is pulling the strings. Not lingering on the moment for pathos or sociological discourse, Hill reveals just enough information to inform us of the level of conflict that has been bubbling under the surface of this town, and which has now divided the community into opposite sides of the law.

This fabulous entertainment was produced by Carolco men Mario Kassar and Buzz Feitshans, themselves no strangers to extravagant action cinema, having worked together on the increasingly hyperbolic *Rambo* films and who knew how to make terrifically cinematic spectacles. The film opens on a hyperbolic note with a truly invigorating score by James Horner, and the film sustains this tone all the way through to its climactic crescendo of choreographed carnage in its beautiful ballet of bullets. "Now you get to wear the white suit," Benteen says as he hands power over to Bailey's lieutenant, Lupo, as the bloodied body of Bailey lays on display, the formerly gleaming white suit now crimson, soaked and asunder, with his hat the only thing remaining intact. *Extreme Prejudice* remains one of Walter Hill's most overlooked and underrated works; the film oozes style and operates on a knowing sense of itself. In what feels like a self-referential nod to the fact that the film is an absurdist over-the-top piece, Sergeant Larry McRose says to Major Hackett that they'll need a diversion to pull off their ambitious bank heist in daylight, to which Hackett replies, "Blow something up! A building, barn, school, church … something!" And blow something up they surely do, as actor/stuntman Allan Graf recalls: "We blew up a lot of things on *Extreme Prejudice*. I didn't coordinate that film, but I died in it about seventeen times. I played different guys all over the place getting killed in different shots. That scene we did where they are at the dinner table and they all get shot up was incredible. What we would do is tear up pieces of paper so that when we blasted stuff it's as if it's coming from the guns; all this paper would fall and you don't know where it's coming from, but it adds such a richness to the look of the shots. It is the kind of thing that if it weren't there you wouldn't miss it, but once it is there it makes the shot that bit more visually interesting. Little tricks like that are the kind of things that make a difference. *Extreme Prejudice* is a tough, kick-ass movie and such an underrated one at that, but then again so many of Walter's movies are."

If there was a dream ticket for fans of action cinema of the 1980s, it was the pairing of the preeminent action auteur Walter Hill and the foremost towering star of the genre, Arnold Schwarzenegger. That ideal partnership would come to pass when the two teamed up for the excellent buddy-cop movie *Red Heat*. The picture pairs Schwarzenegger with James Belushi as cultural contrasts Captain Ivan Danko and Detective Sergeant Art Ridzik, the former a no-nonsense Russian bureaucratic officer following a gang of Georgian drug dealers headed by the vicious Viktor Rostavili (Ed O'Ross) to the United States. When the clean-cut Danko encounters the slovenly Chicago cop Ridzik, their different methods of law enforcement clash, as do their political and social ideologies, to successful comic effect.

Red Heat was cowritten by Hill along with Harry Kleiner and Troy Martin Kennedy. Russian-born Kleiner had previously worked on the script for *Extreme Prejudice* and his previous work includes a collaboration with Sam Fuller on *House of Bamboo* (1955) as well as providing the screenplays for Rudolph Mate's western *The Violent Men* (1955) and Peter Yates's *Bullitt* (1968). It was on the latter film that Kleiner would meet Hill, who was working on the film as second assistant director. Also contributing to the script was Scottish screenwriter Troy Martin Kennedy, whose considerable credits include *The Italian Job* (Peter Collinson, 1969), *Kelly's Heroes* (Brian G. Hutton, 1970), and the 1970s British TV success *The Sweeney*. The film is one in a long line of eighties action thrillers that deals with Cold War tensions and uses a subtext of political contrast to underscore what is essentially a simple generic premise. Cinema of the Reagan era saw pop-culture heroes like Rocky

Balboa (in *Rocky IV*) and James Bond (in *The Living Daylights*) go behind the iron curtain and toe-to-toe with communist adversaries; the political standoff between East and West was also the foundation for dramatic films such as *Red Dawn*, *Firefox*, *No Way Out*, *White Nights*, and even comedies such as John Landis's *Spies Like Us*. Hill keeps his film politically neutral and has a lot of fun using the respective cultural identities of the two central characters to contrast the men's ideological and personal differences before allowing those dissimilarities to fall by the end of the picture. Indeed, *Red Heat* plays to the simple but effective formula of the buddy-cop movie that Hill clearly defined with *48 Hrs.*: bringing together two disparate men who bond in the face of adversity. Belushi walks a tonal tightrope; on one hand his jocular humor could end up seeming to be farcical in front of the stoic reserve of the Russian. Danko may be nicknamed "Iron Jaw" for his serious disposition, but Schwarzenegger allows Danko his own subtle sense of humor to balance out Belushi's boorish behavior. As a result, the film is no solo stand-up show for Belushi. Rather it gives both men space to bring their contrasting comic sensibilities to play. In doing so, Hill provides a fine canvas for Schwarzenegger to showcase his understated comic abilities, which he would soon successfully parlay into outright comedy with films such as *Twins* (1988) and *Kindergarten Cop* (1990).

By the time Hill cast Schwarzenegger in *Red Heat* he was well and truly one of the biggest and most recognizable film stars in the world, having crafted a well-defined screen image that began inauspiciously with the 1970 independent film *Hercules in New York*. The actor garnered greater attention with his supporting role in Bob Rafelson's *Stay Hungry* (1976), though it was the 1977 docudrama *Pumping Iron* that displayed the Austrian athlete's considerable physical prowess and screen presence, that which led to his first significant leading role in John Milius's *Conan the Barbarian* (1982). This would be followed in swift succession with

East meets West when Ivan Danko (Arnold Schwarzenegger, left) and Art Ridzik (James Belushi) collide in *Red Heat* (1988).

several star-crafting roles, including that of the titular android of James Cameron's seminal sci-fi actioner *The Terminator* (1984).

"Arnold is very good in *Red Heat*," Hill enthuses, "and I've always said that I think it's his finest performance unless he is playing an android, then he is excellent, but as a human being I don't think he has ever done a better performance. Arnold is so many different things, a man of many different modes, but he is also a cheerful, positive guy about his own success and his appreciation for the country and his coming here and doing well. I liked him very much, he was fun to be around and to work with. I had no idea he was going to become a governor. Arnold is a phenomenon; it goes way beyond acting. He would be the first to tell you that he is not an actor in the normal sense, he is a world figure, and he became a governor. He is a Theseus to his audience. He's a businessman, he's a star, and he is a good guy. He is like Stallone in that he brings that star quality and everything that comes with it to the screen; able to reach audiences across different cultures and languages. They have come under criticism on a talent level, which is ridiculous. When they are on-screen you don't watch anybody else, they command your attention."

"Arnold is a nice guy with an easygoing demeanor, he really worked hard on *Red Heat*," says cinematographer Matthew Leonetti. "They had a gym set up for him anywhere we went so he could work out during the day. Shooting Arnold is easy, he is a good-looking guy. It's not like shooting a woman in her 50s and trying to make her look 30, you could put a light anywhere on Arnold and he would look good. He said to me once, 'You should really use top light,' because it would show his muscles. That's the way they would photograph bodybuilders, you create a shadow. I said to him that when you use top light your eye sockets go dark, so I chose to use three-quarter fronts and half lights, which did the same thing in showing the shape of the body and I thought his face looked better than using top light. I did propose that we use smoke, so there's a bit of that in the film, but it was getting a bit annoying and about three-quarters of the way through filming Walter said, 'You know what? Maybe we shouldn't have done this the whole time.' When you use smoke you have got to be careful to keep it consistent; you don't want it to look like smoke, you just want it to give a little flavor to the film. I thought it would look pretty good and Walter went along with it and ended up liking it."

Red Heat was the first Hollywood picture allowed to shoot in Red Square, and while a minimal crew was there for only three days, the production didn't go unnoticed, nor did the larger-than-life presence of its star. "We largely worked in Budapest, Hungary, for four or five weeks to simulate Russia," Leonetti recalls, "and the crews in Budapest were good. They were to work 10 hours a day and on the very first day of shooting I turned around to tell the dolly man to move the dolly back for something and I realized he was gone, they all left. The next day the production manager came in a with a sack literally full of cash and after 10 hours he started distributing cash and they stayed on for 12 hours. We were only actually in Russia for a few days because we couldn't easily get into the country and film. It was just me, Walter, an assistant director, an assistant cameraman, and Arnold. We went and shot the title sequence where Arnold is standing in front of the Kremlin and some other pieces of footage around Moscow. A funny story: we were getting ready to get on the plane back home and some Russian soldiers stopped Arnold and were looking him up and down, asking him for his ID, and just harassing him for about three or four minutes before they finally let him on. They knew exactly who he was. When we were in Russia people would recognize him and you realized that he was very popular there, even though it was a socialistic place."

"When we were getting started on *Red Heat*, Jim Belushi was acting a little bit like a movie star," costumer Dan Moore recalls, "that is until Arnold got on the movie. After that there was no more Jim Belushi being the movie star. And that wasn't Arnold being a dick or anything, it was just Arnold being a good example. When it came to getting in there and making the movie and being out there in cold, wet weather and all-night shoots, Arnold was really a champ. There's a lot of leading by example when you are making movies, you've got to have the Big Fella and on a Walter Hill film, Walter is always the Biggest Fella. It also helps to have Arnold be the Big Fella as well. That is how movies get made."

"*Red Heat* can be quite a tough movie, especially when you have Arnold Schwarzenegger in it, then it becomes a larger-than-life action film," says actress Gina Gershon. "Although Arnold is very funny in it too, he brings some humor through his toughness. We became pals. I ended up going out with his brother-in-law Bobby, and I had met Maria, so Arnold and I already had a little bit of a connection." Indeed, bringing some female vitality to the largely macho proceedings is Gina Gershon as Viktor's wife, Catherine "Cat" Manzetti. Cat is a former prostitute now working as a dance instructor since taking payment from the criminal so that he could marry her for a green card, but now she is in danger as a potential witness to his misdeeds. Gershon made fleeting appearances in several films, including *Pretty in Pink*, and was featured in an episode of the eighties iteration of *The Twilight Zone*, but *Red Heat* would prove to be her first major film role, although it wasn't originally written as substantial as it became in the final version. When Gershon was initially cast, the part of Cat Manzetti was but a minor role; however, she and Hill got along so well that he suggested she be the female lead.

"I think it's fair to say my character was the heart of the film," Gershon says. "Walter kept making my part bigger. He would tell me he was going to add another scene with my character here or there, and I said, 'You can do that?' and he would say, 'This is my magic pencil, I can do whatever I want! Remember in *The Warriors* where the guy gets hits by a train? He wasn't supposed to get hit by a train, but I brought out my magic pencil and he got hit by a train.' My character's original name was Latisha, and Walter said, 'You don't really seem like a Latisha, why don't you figure out a name and let me know what you should be called.' I was just like, 'Really?' I mean he wrote the script, and nobody ever said anything like that to me before. I was really excited thinking about a name, and I called Walter up and said, 'I've thought of a name! I think the first time we see her they should call her Cat and she turns to them and says, 'It's Catherine!'" Right there it would set up the idea that she doesn't consider herself what she used to be, it set up the idea that she is someone who is trying to run away from her past, and Walter said, 'Yeah, I like that! That's good!' That really set the tone. I knew then I could bring more to it than what's on the page, and the part just kept getting bigger and bigger. I got really into the dancing thing, and

Gina Gershon plays villain Viktor's tragic wife, Cat Manzetti, in *Red Heat* (1988).

I was dancing so hard because I wanted that part to be really good and because of that I started losing weight without realizing it. So, Walter said to me one day, 'Gina, I think you are losing weight. I'm sending you home for the weekend, you've got to gain five pounds and come back,' and I've never heard of a director saying that to anyone."

"Gina is a livewire," Hill says. "She has got a great sense of humor. *Red Heat* was one of her first movies and since that she has gone on and done terrifically well in so many things."

Gershon continues, "*Red Heat* was a big learning experience for me. Walter was such a teacher, it was like Film Acting 101. He rarely did master shots. The way he would direct is he would put his hand to his waist or to his chest to let you know what kind of shot it was going to be, he would let me know that I didn't have to move around much because it is a close-up. It was very helpful because it was my first real part. I did another film where we did like 30 master shots and Walter said, 'Well, that director doesn't know what he is doing, then. He doesn't know what he really wants and is wasting time. I edit the film in my head.' Walter already knows what he wants to do."

Like *Extreme Prejudice*, *Red Heat* benefits from a late-eighties industrial milieu where cartoonish, exaggerated violence was acceptable and wholly embraced by cinema audiences and pop culture at large. With Schwarzenegger on board, the film had license to inflate the mayhem to comic book extremes, with the action star having delivered successful over-the-top pictures such as *Commando* and *Predator* to the box office in recent years. The terrific action set pieces of *Red Heat* are the work of two of Hollywood's finest action experts: stunt coordinator Bennie Dobbins and stuntman Allan Graf. "I had already worked with Walter on many movies, including *The Driver*, *The Long Riders*, *Southern Comfort*, and *Streets of Fire*," Graf says. "We were together for years but I really showed Walter what I could do on *Red Heat*. I drove the buses smashing through downtown Chicago, did all the major stunts, and I acted in the film as well. I was in the prison scene with Belushi and Schwarzenegger. I did stunts on that film that hadn't been done before, long before CGI, so it was all real and in-camera. I think Walter appreciated that; it showed him how much I would do for him. After that I started as Walter's stunt coordinator on *Johnny Handsome*. That was 1989 and I've been with him ever since."

"I have always liked the movie but there are a couple of things about it where I made an error," Hill admits. "I did the movie backwards; I should have had the American cop go to the Soviet Union. The best parts of the movie are in the first 15 minutes, that was really good stuff, especially the scene where Arnold breaks off a criminal's wooden leg and finds cocaine stuffed inside of it; that's the best scene in the movie. The rest of the movie is fine, but I just didn't think it had as much energy."

"Working on *Red Heat* really set me up for the rest of my career," Gershon says. "I was just so happy to be in it; it was such a really wonderful experience, it was my first big role as the lead actress, and it gave me confidence moving forward in my career. By Walter trusting me as he did, it allowed me to trust myself. I was lucky that he was my first real director. If anyone says they don't like working with Walter, then they have their own problems, because he is just so straight up, he doesn't play games. There are some directors who are very good, but they are very difficult to work with and you have to go through all of this craziness to protect your character and protect your performance, and they like that chaos; but Walter doesn't like chaos, he just says, 'Let's do this and make it as pleasant as possible.' So it's all about the work with Walter. It sounds crazy, but that's not a given. I came to this movie with a small part and Walter ended up making me the female lead, and in doing so he gave me my first real part in a film, my big break in Hollywood. I adore him forever; I will be forever grateful to Walter."

After the hyperbolically violent action duo of *Extreme Prejudice* and *Red Heat*, Hill would move toward darker territory with the modest and moody film noir drama of *Johnny Handsome*. A brilliant adaptation of John Godey's 1972 crime novel, *The Three Worlds of Johnny Handsome*, this is the story of a man who has no place in society due to his unfortunate physical appearance, and after he is humiliated one too many times he decides to take revenge on those who would double-cross him. John Sedley (Mickey Rourke) is a disfigured man who leads a lonesome life in the criminal underworld of New Orleans, that which is the only pocket of society that accepts him. And just barely at that. His frightful appearance has earned him the ironic nickname of "Johnny Handsome," and as the movie opens we learn that he has only one friend in this world, Mikey (Scott Wilson), who is in desperate need of funding to buy out his scheming partner in a sleazy downtown booze joint. However, the only collateral this "poor boy from Shreveport" ever had was his Smith and Wesson, so going to the local bank for a loan isn't going to be an option. Thus, Mikey enlists Johnny for a jewelry store heist, for both his planning skills and "for old time's sake." Unfortunately, to pull the job off they get involved with a gang of cutthroat thieves that includes the devious Rafe Garrett (Lance Henriksen), the despicable Sunny Boyd (Ellen Barkin), and Bob LeMoyne (Allan Graf).

We are quickly privy to the kind of scum that Garrett and Boyd are as they ridicule their supposed accomplice-in-crime—"Why don't you give us all a break and put a bag on his head," Boyd oozes. Her comments don't stop there, soon attacking his muffled speech: "Sounds like he's already got a bag on his head … a scumbag." We see Mikey comfort his friend as he receives the vile insults, then scolding the wicked woman as he reminds her that it is only with Johnny's logistical skills that the heist will be successful. Good help is hard to find and so the heist goes ahead, but not according to plan. Once they've got the loot in their hands, Garrett and Boyd kill Mikey and Bob and then open fire at Johnny, fleeing the scene of the crime believing they have left him for dead. But Johnny evaded their bullets and lives, only to be picked up by the police.

The ominous Lt. Drones (Morgan Freeman) tries to glean information from Johnny, but he won't talk because the criminal code is the only code he knows and which he lives by. And if that isn't enough, he takes the rap, gets sentenced, and ends up in a Louisiana prison for a 20-year stretch. Even that's not good enough for Garrett and Boyd, so they hire somebody to knife him to death in prison so that they will finally be rid of him, should he ever talk. Miraculously, doctors manage to save Johnny. A well-meaning surgeon, Dr. Steven Fisher (Forest Whitaker), proposes that he undergoes years of reconstructive cosmetic surgery procedures and reeducation to deal with his demons; they will give him a new identity and let him out. And so, with Johnny now looking like Mickey Rourke, he will have a better chance of happiness and living a normal life. Right? Wrong. Johnny sets out on a quest for vengeance that will take him back to the darkest corners of New Orleans to wreak havoc on those who betrayed him and took away from him the only love he knew: his friend Mikey.

Johnny Handsome began life when screenwriter Ken Friedman was commissioned by his friend, producer Charles Roven, to adapt Godey's book, for which he had acquired the film rights. Friedman met Roven socially in the early eighties

Postsurgery Johnny displays the handsome features of Mickey Rourke in *Johnny Handsome* (1989) as he looks at love interest Donna McCarty, played by Elizabeth McGovern.

and the pair became fast friends and collaborators. The first production they made together was *Heart Like a Wheel*, the biographical film based on the real-life drag racer Shirley Muldowney, which Friedman wrote, Roven produced, and Jonathan Kaplan directed. It was an inauspicious debut for the man who would go on to produce major studio successes such as *The Dark Knight, Man of Steel, Suicide Squad*, and many other box office hits. Friedman supplied up to seven drafts of *Johnny Handsome* over seven years for various directors who became involved at different times. One of the high-profile directors attached was Harold Becker, whose notable credits included *The Onion Field* (1979), *Taps* (1981), and *Vision Quest* (1985). Becker's attachment attracted stars to the project, including Richard Gere, who was lined up to the play the titular character. Friedman recalls the development of the film that could have been but, thankfully, never came to be. "I worked with Harold on his version of *Johnny Handsome* and received all of his notes," Friedman says, "and at this stage in my life I can tell you I am no friend of Harold's. He is a nice man and an intelligent man, but I didn't really see eye-to-eye with him. We had a meeting at the Imperial Gardens in Los Angeles with Harold, Chuck, and Richard Gere. Harold took my script that I had worked on with him for three weeks, slid it across the table at Gere, and said, 'Don't worry, we can fix this script.' At that point Gere dropped out, but I think that was always the plan because Harold really wanted Pacino to play Johnny. Then Pacino came on board and I left. Three or four well-known writers were hired to rewrite the script for the Becker-Pacino package, and it went through three different studios."

However, the film would never be made in this form. Pacino dropped out of the picture, and he was soon followed by Becker, meaning *Johnny Handsome* went back to square one. However, the script would find a home at Mario Kassar and Andrew G. Vajna's Carolco Pictures, the successful independent production company that had just worked with Walter Hill on *Extreme Prejudice* and *Red Heat*. The property found its way to Hill, who perused the many early versions of the script and ultimately chose "Ken Friedman treatment number three" as his preferred draft, which meant Friedman was firmly back on the project. From there the writer would work with Hill on what would become the shooting script. "Kenny Friedman's script for *Johnny Handsome* was excellent," Hill applauds. "Of all the movies I have ever done, I had less input on that script than any other one."

"I felt reenergized when Walter came on," Friedman says. "I was compensated well throughout all of the stages of this movie's development and I wanted to give them the movie they wanted, but when Walter came on board to direct the film I was incredibly energized because the movie he wanted to make was the movie I wanted to really write all along. I was aware of what a great writer and what a great film historian he is, so I knew it was going to be a very pleasant collaboration."

This was not Friedman's first encounter with Hill, the pair having met in the early seventies when the writer found himself out in LA after he won an award at the 1970 National Student Film Festival as an NYU attendee. The accolade led to Friedman receiving a telephone call from Roger Corman on the recommendation of Martin Scorsese, after which he traveled west to LA. Once there he met with Roger's brother Gene Corman, for whom he began developing ideas before going on to work with director Jonathan Kaplan on the 1975 Columbia Pictures film *White Line Fever*. Also working on the Columbia studio lot was Walter Hill, there making his directorial debut, *Hard Times*. Friedman recalls, "We had an office on the Columbia lot which was in a row of semipermanent offices that they built on the parking lots of the studio that we called 'The Motels' and Walter was there as well working with the producer Larry Gordon on *Hard Times*, so we got to know each other. Walter made an enormous impression on me, as he and several notable writers, including William Goldman, Eric Red, and some others of that era, redefined what a screenplay is in terms of the job of the writer; before these guys came along, the studios liked a lot of wordy scripts, they really wanted to know what they were getting. They were paying high-price writers like William Faulkner to come in and do rewrites, but when the studio system broke down and screenwriters weren't on staff anymore we were out there trying to sell ourselves as writers or we were writing spec scripts and trying to sell them. I had read the script to *Hard Times* and when I went to see the movie I realized how close it was to the script, and it is like the best first movie ever made. Walter has that great capacity as a writer to put you in the film and he was really my introduction to a new style of entertaining, aggressive 'this-is-the-movie' screenwriting, he was at the forefront of that. A lot of the lessons I learned from Walter's writing are still relevant today, which is to create the most images with the fewest words."

For Friedman, it was Hill's interest in the moral crux at the heart of the story that meant that the film had found its ideal pairing of scribes. "The book had some interesting 1940s gangster dialogue," Friedman says, "but it was the concept that was most intriguing: a lifelong criminal gets his face changed. Will he seek a better life for himself now that he looks like Mickey Rourke instead of looking like the Elephant Man? Will he prioritize putting the life of crime behind him or will he get revenge on the people who screwed him over? Walter was keen on exploring that."

Indeed, *Johnny Handsome* functions in the mode of the classic film noir whereby the protagonist sets out on a fatalist course with destiny. No matter how well-executed his revenge plays out in the proceedings, he will never feel a sense of satisfaction. No matter how handsome or verbose he becomes, after years of disfigurement and inability to articulate, he will never achieve the sense of value that he craves and that had been given to him by his only friend, Mikey, now deceased. Johnny's doomed path is atypical of the road taken by the cynical antiheroes of Old Hollywood. Also hearkening back to the visual aesthetics of noir films out of the past is the muted color palette, almost but not quite black and white, the frame drained of life just enough to suggest the genre conventions that lay ahead for the audience. Composer Ry Cooder's moody blues exquisitely set the apposite tone as Johnny wanders the streets of New Orleans like a man who has no place in the society around him.

"Walter really saw the picture the way I saw the picture: as a film noir," Friedman says. "Walter wanted it to be about the character of Johnny and his destiny, and that is what film noir is about. Like many of the movies in that canon, our character is doomed from the start but will kick and scream and fight and claw for success as he defines it, for meaning in his life, only to be cut down at the end. That is the way I saw Johnny Handsome: you can fix his face, you can fix the way he talks, and you can try to fix his heart, but in the end he is just like James Cagney on top of the oil tanks in *White Heat*—'Top of the world, Ma!' The shipyard robbery was inspired by the meat packing robbery in *Gun Crazy*, and another film that Walter and I talked about was Fritz Lang's *The Big Heat*. In that film you have a character who was destined to end up sitting behind that little desk; he goes through his wife being killed and seeing several other women die, everybody he knows goes through hell, but it does not change who he is or his destiny in life. And that is a very dark Fritz Lang thing. These are the kinds of conversations that I would have with Walter and which Chuck would be involved in."

As a contemporary film noir, *Johnny Handsome* benefited from being able to go further in depicting the amoral lives of its underworld characters than the classics of the Golden Age ever could. One of the nastiest villains to grace a Hill picture is present in the form of Ellen Barkin's femme fatale, Sunny Boyd, a former prostitute plucked from a Texas trucker bar by Garrett and where he threatens to return her to when she displeases him.

"Ellen Barkin's character is definitely the meanest character I've ever written," Friedman admits. "There is a certain amount of sympathy for Ellen because she carries so much fury, she is just like Johnny Handsome. You know the kind of background she had; she was treated as a whore, she was beaten, God knows what kind of life she lived, and that is something you don't have to spell out, you know it the second you look at her. The fury at the hand that she was dealt makes her and Johnny Handsome bedfellows in a way, and that adds another level to the movie. He goes to bed with her, but it is all part of his revenge, he doesn't get any satisfaction from it. That's another part of the film noir element: nobody in film noir gets any satisfaction. Johnny Handsome can't live in this world, he's too damaged."

Sleazy underworld criminals Rafe Garrett (Lance Henriksen) and Sunny Boyd (Ellen Barkin) wonder whether they should trust the handsome stranger who knows them too well in *Johnny Handsome* **(1989).**

Friedman continues, "When you're working in genre, in this case film noir, you already understand the basic motivations of the characters, so I don't have to restate anything unnecessarily; the action of the story, which is the sense of betrayal and revenge, is right there in the first scene. Johnny's motivation never changes, his goal is to get out of jail and kill these people; it wavers, but it never changes, and Walter understands that Johnny doesn't waver. So, if casting means there needs to be some minor changes to the script, then we did that. I was very gratified by the way Ellen's character turned out from the script to the screen. There were nice touches such as once Ellen's character is established and she takes a job at the shipyard and shoots her supervisor who had been giving her shit, I thought that was great."

With the inconvenience of heavy makeup application, Rourke preferred to keep dialogue to a minimum, meaning Friedman moved some dialogue initially written for Rourke to various costars, resulting in a more verbose Morgan and Barkin than what was initially envisioned for their characters. These adjustments were ultimately made for the benefit of the picture, and Friedman details such an example:

"We shifted a lot of the dialogue from Mickey to Ellen and she was happy with that because she wanted to say more. Mickey preferred to be sort of a listener and Ellen preferred to be the screamer, which makes sense to the story because at one point Ellen says to Mickey, 'Don't talk, you're not a talker.' Of course, he's not much of a talker, he just learned how to talk a year ago, so he wouldn't be a verbal guy anyway; it makes sense to viewers of the movie that Mickey wouldn't be saying much, and she wanted to embrace that. The scene where Lt. Drones visits Johnny in the jail cell was written as having Johnny say to him, 'You got me wrong. I'm ready to start a new life. I've been given a second chance and I appreciate the opportunity, so I'm not going to screw it up.' That's the subtext of what the character was saying but Mickey didn't want to say all that, so when we shifted the dialogue, Morgan would come in and say, 'I know what you're thinking, you think you can pull one over on this cop. But it ain't going to happen, I know who you are.' It shifted from Johnny carrying the scene to Lt. Drones carrying the scene and it is much better for it. Neither Lt. Drones nor Dr. Fisher were originally written as being black. So, you have this poor trailer trash white criminal on one hand, and you have these two black authority figures on the other hand; one representing hope and possibility, while the other is cynical and jaded. Drones respects Johnny because he understands him and he understands the life he lived, the hell that he lived, and because of that he knows where he is going. The heroes and antiheroes in film noir don't go quietly while kicking and screaming and Lt. Drones knows that, while Dr. Fisher is a scientist, a psychologist, and he tends to look at things the way they should be rather than the way they are. I thought it was interesting to have these two terrific actors playing those roles of the angel and the devil in Johnny's ears. You can't write a Morgan Freeman part; he just brings those qualities himself. Casting a role in a certain way sometimes means some rewrites. It becomes a different movie with Mickey Rourke than it would have been with Al Pacino. Not that Pacino wouldn't have done a great job, but it would have been a much more theatrical performance. Scripts are always in development until the movie is finished. Sometimes it is studio interference, sometimes it's misconceived voiceovers, or bad camerawork; things can happen during the making of a film, so I always like to remain involved, though not on the set, but involved in the development of the script because things change.

"Walter is not only a great writer, and a transcendent screenwriter, he also has tremendous respect for other writers and we have tremendous respect for Walter. Ninety-five percent of the time, his instincts about what will work in a script are right. In the original script we had made the character of the nun who helps Johnny Handsome learn to speak again a Vietnamese immigrant, an escapee from the Vietnam War who had to learn a new language all over again. So there would be some nods and echoes to the Vietnam War, although this was about five years past, and Walter said, 'Why don't we make her a nun?' Making her a nun asked other questions about redemption, about faith, about whether you can be saved. So either way she was not going to be an important character that had an arc, she is just somebody who was going to be in a couple of scenes. I thought about it quite a bit for a while and as a writer I just generally never say no. I'll state my opinion to my producer or to my director and say, 'This is why we made her a Vietnamese woman, but let me try writing it the way you suggest.' Instead of having theoretical arguments about story elements, instead of being defensive or being egocentric, it is often a lot quicker to write the scene the way they want to see if it works. And maybe I'll end up saying, 'Hey, maybe I missed something, maybe this is better!' I owe that to the director and I owe that to the producer, I owe it to whoever is paying me. My philosophy as a writer is 'I think I have good answers, but I may not have the best answers.'"

Not all potential script changes were welcome though. With a popular Hollywood leading man headlining the picture, pressure was on to have his audience leaving the theaters knowing their hero will live on with his new love, and the premise of Friedman's draft cowritten with Roven reflected the producer's desire for such a happy ending. This would have meant maintaining a measure of redemption in the character that played in the tradition of the more positive films noir, an idea that love could conquer all and that Johnny Handsome could start a new life. But, thankfully, that was never going to happen on Hill's watch. "There were pressures to have an ending that was more hopeful than the true destinies of the character. I was never comfortable with that," Friedman affirms. "There was a positive message in it for sure, and I knew going in that it was my job as a contracted writer to deliver the story that they wanted, but that message didn't sit right with me. I thought that it was trying to be commercial and anticipate an emotional response from the audience. And Walter was never going to make a movie with an ending that he felt was inauthentic."

"I liked making *Johnny Handsome*," Hill admits. "Mickey was Mickey and he is fine in it, but we made the movie just as his popularity was going into a real nosedive, which had to do with a lot of different things. He has become an even more exaggerated figure now than he was then. I loved Lance and Ellen in it, they did a good job. The only issue that arose was there was the usual studio horseshit. They wanted a happy ending. Both Kenny and I told them the story would never work that way. We shot two endings. They accused me of throwing the fight because the happy ending clearly didn't work. I think the ending in the movie is one of the best things in it."

"My pitch for the story before Walter was ever attached went as such: Johnny

Handsome is born with all sorts of physical defects, kind of like the Elephant Man, and because of that he feels rejected by society and was always treated like a freak." Indeed, Johnny is reminded throughout the film that behind his newly chiseled features is the soul of a social outcast, criminal or otherwise; it is this perception of him as an unlovable outsider that has haunted him all his life and which will remain regardless of cosmetic rearranging of his features. "You've probably got a lot of people feeling sorry for you, because you're such an ugly son of a bitch," says Lt. Drones, "but not me, because I know what you are on the inside ... nothing but a cheap crook."

"The story is all about identity, loyalty, and the criminal code, so you can't change the character's destiny just by giving him a new face and social skills," Friedman says. "There was only one element of society that would deal with him, and that was the criminal element because he happened to be really smart and was very good when it came to planning robberies and heists. But even those people had little tolerance for him. He had no chance of ever falling in love, no chance of getting a job, no chance of ever having a meaningful life. The film goes to great lengths to make the operation plausible, and in the end he is disfigured again when he gets his face cut up, so before his death he gets restored to who he was. I thought the ending was incredibly fitting, it was very satisfying. It's more exciting for him to go and get revenge, even if that means he dies at the end, than it would for him to say 'live and let live' while staying with Elizabeth McGovern to raise some kids while working at the steelyard and riding his dirt bike at the weekends. I don't think that would have been a very exciting film. If they had made the film around the time the book was published it would have been like the Bogart film *Dark Passage* where they put the bandage around his face and then he's a new character, but by the time the film was produced in the late eighties plastic surgery had come a long way from the time the book was written."

For *Johnny Handsome*, Hill once again returned to the Louisiana city of New Orleans, the distinctive architecture of which provided a rich backdrop to craft this tale of moral decay. "For us, it was always New Orleans, it is such an evocative city," Friedman says. "I always tell my students to never write their script to be based in a nondescript place, always set it in a major eastern city or southern city. Always be specific because further ideas will be drawn from that specificity and authenticity will spring from the reality of such a setting. I had been to New Orleans a few times and we went there when we were scouting locations. You write specific to a location but you're not married to it, you might have to change it according to how the movie is financed, but I was always pleased that we went with New Orleans. I was down there most of preproduction and a couple of weeks into shooting."

"The French Quarter in New Orleans, it is so unique," cinematographer Matthew Leonetti says. "There is no other place in the United States like it. Anywhere you point the camera you are going to be in good shape. Walter was very careful about picking locations but New Orleans is always great as far as the look of the film goes, and using the long lenses means it brings the background closer to the actors. We shot it mostly handheld and we didn't shoot anamorphic, we shot 1.85, and I remember shooting the jewelry store robbery scene where I suggested shooting the whole thing using a 50mm lens. I believe we ended up doing that, so we backed off a little bit with the master because we could get wider shots with the 50mm and maybe we'd go to a 40mm; doing that seemed to give it some sort of a look, for a lack of a better word. It was intimate enough yet also wide enough to see the set. We were always going to use the long lens because that's what Walter likes."

After working as an actor and stuntman on many of Hill's films beginning with *The Driver*, Allan Graf had proved himself to be a no-nonsense man of action who could get things done economically and as Hill wanted them done. Graf got his opportunity to become the director's go-to stunt coordinator following the tragic death of Bennie Dobbins, who suffered a fatal heart attack on location in Russia while making *Red Heat*. Graf recalls receiving the awful news: "I was working on the TV show *MacGyver* up in British Columbia when I got a phone call and it was Walter. He said, 'I hate to tell you but Bennie Dobbins has died and I want you to be my stunt coordinator.' Obviously, I was saddened for Bennie, but I was very excited about being Walter's stunt coordinator. So I said yes and he said, 'Well, you better come out and do *Johnny Handsome*.' I said, 'I'm ready!' But I told him one thing: 'Walter, we've been friends for a long time, and if there's anything I do that you don't like, or if you don't think I'm doing a good enough job, then just let me go away and be a stuntman and we'll still be friends.' And he said, 'Absolutely I'll tell you!' Well, he never had to tell me because I think I did such a great job for him that he appreciated it and kept me as his stunt coordinator on many movies after *Johnny Handsome*."

As if stepping up to the new task of coordinating a stunt-heavy movie wasn't enough, Graf was also given the task of second unit director. "I always had ambitions to be a director when I was doing stunts," Graf says. "On every show that I worked on I would spend a lot of time talking to the cameraman because I'd be curious and ask them why they are using certain lenses and speeds, why they are doing this and that. I would pick their brains and they never minded telling me about it. Walter was aware of my interest and that's how I came to be the second unit director on *Johnny Handsome*. I was working with Mickey Rourke, Ellen Barkin, Elizabeth McGovern, Forest Whitaker, and Morgan Freeman! He won the Academy Award for *Driving Miss Daisy* right after *Johnny Handsome*. These are the caliber of actors that Walter would cast. And aside from working behind the scenes, I also played Bob LeMoyne, a villain who gets killed during the opening heist sequence. So, I was busy on *Johnny Handsome*, but it was a great time. Walter and I would have a lot of fun on the set. I remember one day he said to me, 'Hey, I'm going to hit you and when I do, go down on the ground.' So he would come up and start hitting me and then there'd be people crowding around us freaking out. Another thing we would do is go into the motor home and start rocking it and screaming like we're having a fight. We just loved to do stupid things like that, we've had so much fun over the years."

Despite the tortured years in Development Hell, as well as the unfortunate indifference that faced *Johnny Handsome* upon release, Friedman considers the film among the very best that he has worked on. The writer duly applauds Hill's understanding of the material and the cinematic context within which the story would work most appropriately. Hill's discernment and sophisticated knowledge of film and literary genre storytelling meant for a great accord between the writer and the director, allowing for the best possible version of Friedman's script to make it to the screen:

"I thought that Walter did an outstanding job with this film. It is still hip and has aged very well. I think it would have performed better financially if it had been advertised and promoted to the audience that we specifically had in mind for this film rather than being aimed at the audience that the production company wanted to bring in. If you know you are going to see a film noir, then you are ready to accept a journey which can be dark and cynical, but if you are being advertised and promised a rousing heist movie or revenge action movie, then you may look at it a different way. It certainly had the right cast to be promoted. I don't know if the production company were disappointed that it wasn't a different kind of movie. As skillful and entertaining as it might be, if you try to promote a film as something that it's not, then it is a recipe for disappointment. Walter said in an interview that it should have been called 'The Tragedy of Johnny Handsome' so that it would have been seen as a film noir. Audiences understand genres. There's kind of agreement when you go in to see a genre film, whether it's a western or a crime melodrama or a musical, about how things work in that world and in the context of how that particular genre functions. In a musical, characters can stop the story and sing their feelings, and audiences accept that as part of that genre. It doesn't mean you don't have a rooting interest or can't get invested in *My Fair Lady* or *West Side Story*.

"Walter has a philosophy and an overarching theme throughout his career: his characters have a sense of professionalism within a dark world, and they are driven and have set rules of behavior, whether they are criminal or not, and that often predates the beginning of the movie. His characters are searching, there is something they've got to do. In the case of Johnny Handsome, he has an agenda against life. There's an inner anger there because he has been fucked over royally, so he is trying to prove something, that he is a human being and has value. Johnny is going to go out and sell his worth. A lot of Walter's characters come in with a chip on their shoulder for one reason or another and they get on a mission very quickly; sometimes those missions take on a more fatalist noir trajectory and sometimes they become a more heroic mission. It develops very quickly because these characters need to prove something, they need to be somebody, and Walter is attracted to that because it suits the genres that he likes to work in; it's the perfect kind of setup for films noir and westerns."

Following *Johnny Handsome*, Hill and Roven were handed another project in a big-screen adaptation of the beloved sixties television series *The Fugitive*. The plan was for Hill to direct and Roven to produce, with Friedman working with them on the script and Alec Baldwin in line to star as the wrongly accused Dr. Richard Kimble. Hill's would have been a starker vision for the story than what ended up on cinema screens in 1993, one in which the themes of the story would be focused on redemption and truth. Again, Friedman's vision aligned with Hill's. "They hired me to do a couple of drafts and we worked for quite a bit of time on it," Friedman recalls. "Both Walter and I wanted to do something more in the mood of the television show within the context of a revenge story with this doctor and a crooked drug company. It came up in conversation the question of why a highly educated, heroic, well-meaning, surgical genius like Harrison Ford's character did not defend himself in court and let himself be convicted for a crime he didn't commit. Well, the answer was his wife is an alcoholic, he hated his marriage, she was childish, he couldn't stand to be in the house with her, so he would volunteer for every night shift and work 20 hours a day because he couldn't bear to be home with this hysteric and alcoholic. And one of those nights when he should have been at home but wasn't there was a home invasion during which she is killed by this one-armed man, and so the guilt he feels is why he doesn't defend himself. He feels that he should be punished, and the train wreck and his survival is an act of God. Then the question becomes 'how does he seek redemption for the death of his wife?' and he wanders Christ-like through Americana helping despondent housewives. It became obvious pretty quickly that the studio wanted something different which didn't have the potential for depth. We developed a terrific script and there is about 23 minutes in the Andrew Davis-Harrison Ford film which are from the scripts that I developed with Walter and Chuck; it is the segment from when he is on the bus going to death row to where he is in the storm drain telling Gerard that he didn't do it and Gerard says, 'I don't care!' Although it was set at Niagara Falls in our script. That whole section of the movie derives from the work I did on the script with Walter. But what happens to the doctor in search of the one-armed man is completely different to what I wrote."

The Fugitive would eventually be made rather excellently by Chicago filmmaker Andrew Davis and become a massive commercial success for Warner Bros., and while it is tantalizing to think of what could have been had Hill directed the chase thriller, one can be thankful that following *Johnny Handsome* the director would instead return to Paramount, if somewhat hesitantly, for a sequel to his own greatest commercial creation. Eight years after *48 Hrs.* exploded onto screens during Christmas of 1982, the studio decided it was about time to bring back the dynamic duo of Nick Nolte and Eddie Murphy. The latter was no longer the fresh-faced stand-up comedian dabbling in the cinematic arts, but was by now one of the biggest film stars in America and guaranteed to draw big crowds to the theaters for *Another 48 Hrs.*

This time around troubled San Francisco police inspector Jack Cates (Nick Nolte) is under an internal affairs investigation for manslaughter after a police sting to bust drug kingpin The Iceman goes awry. A gangster ends up dead in a shootout with Cates, but the criminal's weapon cannot be found, leading to accusations of police negligence and his facing prosecution for third-degree manslaughter. In the interim, Cates discovers that The Iceman has put a price on the head of Reggie Hammond (Eddie Murphy), whose release from prison is imminent, and so Cates uses this as an opportunity to enlist Hammond to help him nail the criminal overlord and thus clear his name. However, Hammond hasn't forgotten about the $500,000 that Cates promised to hold for him at the end of the first film, money that Cates won't hand over unless Hammond helps him out. And so the pair reach an impasse, with Hammond refusing to cooperate—that is until the county corrections bus carrying him to freedom is attacked by two bikers, Richard "Cherry" Ganz and Willie Hickok, who are hell-bent on vengeance. If the Ganz name is familiar to viewers it is because Cherry is the brother of Albert Ganz, the former associate of Hammond's who ended up being killed by Cates in the original film's dénouement. After Cates is wounded by Ganz in a botched assassination attempt and with Hammond recovering from the bus attack, Cates signs Hammond out of the hospital and into his custody, leaving the former convict no choice but to reluctantly partner up with the cop to bring down the Iceman outfit altogether.

Not one for repeating himself or looking back at his pictures from the past, the idea of directing a sequel to *48 Hrs.* wasn't something on the agenda at this stage, or any stage, in Hill's career, but Paramount knew that they had a property that was too lucrative to ignore. "I was very wary about going into *Another 48 Hrs.*," Hill admits, "because sequels are usual considered to be a dip in quality from their original. In a lot of ways, I didn't want to do it, but at the same it was going to get made and I didn't want somebody else to do it. It was going to get made whether or not I did it, and I thought I'd better do it." By 1990, Hollywood had two major assets that Hill could lay claim to having introduced to the industry with *48 Hrs.*: Eddie Murphy and the mismatched buddy-cop genre. With the odd exception (namely *Best Defense* from 1984), Murphy struck gold all throughout the eighties with *Trading Places* (1983), *Beverly Hills Cop* (1984), *The Golden Child* (1986), *Beverly Hills Cop II* (1987), *Coming to America* (1988), *Harlem Nights* (1989), and, with his comedy career reaching commercial and cultural peak, with the 1987 stand-up concert film *Eddie Murphy: Raw*. By the time Paramount felt it was right for the return of Jack Cates and Reggie Hammond, Murphy's position as a Hollywood power player was firmly established, meaning there was a different dynamic at play when it came to producing *Another 48 Hrs.* "Eddie had become a gigantic star by that time and was living a rather complicated life," Hill says, while producer Larry Gordon elaborates on the industry politics at play behind the scenes: "*Another 48 Hrs.* came about eight years later basically because the studio and Eddie's manager screwed us over. They took Eddie away from us to go make *Beverly Hills Cop*, which meant we had to wait a long time before we could make the sequel. By the time he came back around to making *Another 48 Hrs.*, he had become a big star and he wasn't quite as easy to work with as he was on *48 Hrs.* But we eventually made the sequel and it was a modest hit, but it isn't as fondly remembered as the first film and that is simply because it wasn't as good a movie."

"I think *Another 48 Hrs.* is more interesting than most people give it credit for," Hill says, "but we were really scrambling because it all came together very quickly. The studio said, 'Okay, we've got to get the movie out by the middle of summer.' Then when we were in the middle of finishing the movie the studio said they were moving the release dates up even earlier. Christ, we had three editors working. It was around-the-clock stuff."

Larry Gross, who had cowritten the first film, returned for the sequel only to discover a production that struggled to be bigger than its star and accompanying baggage. "Eddie Murphy was a huge institution by this point," Gross says, "and to be perfectly honest I remember that we were under a certain pressure to service Eddie's stardom and that kind of hampered the film in some ways. He was absolutely no trouble, but there was handlers around him all the time, he carried a whole entourage with him. It was like he was insulated. He was a totally likeable and nice person, but a little bit removed." Despite being a crucial part of the writing of the first film, Gross was initially overlooked by Murphy in favor of up-and-comers Jeb Stuart and John Fasano. Stuart was making a name for himself with high-profile mainstream action pictures like *Die Hard*, *Next of Kin*, and *Lock Up*, while Fasano came from the world of B-movie horror. However, Gross was brought onto the production the day before shooting started, having been put on alert by Hill that he would be sure to receive a call to come in and save the day. True to his word, the director called. "Eddie Murphy wanted to work with several other writers," Gross recalls, "not out of insult to me but because they were very hot action writers and he was keen to work with them. So they were hired and wrote a couple of drafts, but Walter had contacted me at an early stage and said, 'I can't bring you into this process yet, but 99 chances out of a hundred, by a certain date in this process I will be able to do whatever I want to fix this script and you will be called.' He speculated a date when this would happen. That's when I understood entirely Walter's absolute integrity. When he said, 'I can't use you now,' I knew that there was a political reason for that. He said, 'I've got to use these other guys, but between you and me, I'll be very surprised if what they come up with satisfies me, satisfies Eddie, and satisfies the studio. And the day they turn to me and tell me to do whatever I have to do to fix this, you will get a call.' And on that very day at 9:00 a.m. I got the call. The job was mine. I wanted to kiss him, not just for getting the job but for him being totally a man of his word. That was pure Walter Hill integrity and professional clarity. So, I worked with Walter and a guy named John Fasano, who was very talented but who has sadly passed away."

"I brought Larry Gross in before we started shooting," Hill says, "and he was with us when we went up to the Stockton area where we shot the motorcycle scenes out on the highways, and the bus crash. Then we shut down for Christmas and started up again after the holidays. My younger daughter was born in that period. But Larry Gross and Fasano had a rather nervous relationship. I would give them both different assignments."

"John and I worked through it," Gross confirms, "but there were certain things that weren't good enough in the script. We had some ambivalences about the characters of the bad guys that we revised and we found a way to sort of redo the country and western bar scene, which I thought was pretty good. Then it became obvious that we were making a western, especially with that whole thing with the brothers who are motorcyclists." Indeed, the film does contain notable nods to the western genre, its iconography, and its myth—the masterful opening sequence in which aged outlaw biker Malcolm Price awaits the arrival of his two-wheeled horsemen, Ganz and Hickok, is a classic piece of quiet slow-burning montage in the vein of Sergio Leone. Wide angles combine with extreme close-ups as the tension mounts with their arrival to the lonesome saloon, a cold beer haven amid the dusty desert roads out of which the menacing pair of bikers emerge. At one point in the film Malcolm Price delivers a barstool declamation about the Wild West that conveys a message evocative of the speech delivered by William Sadler in Hill's debut episode of *Tales from the Crypt*. "You want to be an outlaw, but you want to play by rules," Price says, continuing, "There ain't no rules. We're the only real Americans left. We believe in freedom. We live the way folks used to, back before there were big cities, and lawyers, and computers with your names in them. Free. The rest of you are just a bunch of fucking slaves." Further allusions to western mythology are present in the name of villain Willie Hickok, surely a Hillian evocation of Wild Bill Hickok, the man about whom the director would make a wonderful eponymous film five years later.

Another 48 Hrs. excitingly raises the bar for the kind of thundering action-film mayhem that Hill would become celebrated for. The violence that ensues is not of a cinema of verisimilitude; rather one would argue that it is a director engaging an audience who are more than aware that they are experiencing a cinema of excess. Everything about *Another 48 Hrs.* is a heightened version of the original, and that notably includes the choreography of the action set pieces and the visual style of the cinematography. It is here, for example, that we see Hill's first use of the exaggerated stunt work involved in his shootouts, where bodies are blown back through windows as if by cannon rather than pistol. With all the elements at work, *Another 48 Hrs.* proves to be one of Hill's most thrilling action films, a sequel that I would dare suggest bests its predecessor in every respect. Its slick photography is stylishly provided by cinematographer Matthew Leonetti, who recalls Hill's unique approach to covering the action. "In the shootouts, when somebody got hit with gunfire, Walter wanted three different sizes on the actors," Leonetti recalls. "He wanted belly, chest, and close. We had to practically stack cameras on top of each other, and in those days cameras were six, eight, or ten inches wide and to do that was a bit of a trick, but that's what he wanted and that's what he got. That's the way it worked with Walter, he would say, 'This is what I want. Make it happen.'"

Second unit director, as well as actor and stunt coordinator, Allan Graf recalls the effort made in making *Another 48 Hrs.* quite literally a more explosive film than any which came before it:

"*Another 48 Hrs.* is a standout film for me, it was just awesome. I directed all of the second unit and we did a lot of new stuff on it. And you have to remember, Wayne, there was no CGI on that, it was all in-camera stunt work and live effects. We had double or triple the action in that film than what was in the first one and I got to direct all of that action, it was so sweet. With Walter you know there is going to be a lot of action, you know there will be big second unit work, and a lot of stunt people are going to get hired. We hired over 200 stunt people on *Another 48 Hrs.* and that's a lot of stunt people. Walter liked my ingenuity and my creativity. I would do stuff most people wouldn't do, stretching the boundaries on stunts, on the action, and on the camera. No matter what movie it was, energy was key to what I was getting. At the climax of the film there's a shootout in the bar and Eddie Murphy knocks a guy out a window who then lands on a water truck parked on the street below. I filmed him falling and landing in all this water, an awesome shot because you can actually see him falling. There is no airbag to catch his fall because we used a decelerator cable. Normally you would have to cut to another angle before the stunt guy hits an airbag, but the decelerator allowed me to film the fall from above. I also put a camera inside the water truck so that we could see the dummy hitting it. I rigged it with air cannons so when the dummy lands it blows the water on impact. I thought it was one of the most creative shots I've ever done. I tried to do stuff on that film that you don't see being done anymore. We had the motorcycles jumping through the theater screen, landing among the audience and riding up through the aisles—they ride right through the porno movie being projected on the screen, right through the woman's chest. I think Walter appreciated the fact that every time I shot something I was trying to make it new and innovative. He lets you do your job and I got to direct these great second units in which he allowed me to put my own stamp on it."

In a remarkable set piece, Hammond is being escorted back to civilian life when the prison bus carrying him is besieged by Ganz and Hickok in their quest to assassinate the ex-con. Graf plays the bus driver and performs the daring stunt that required the tires of the bus to be shot out for the vehicle to flip and roll down the highway on its side. Graf recalls the planning for the memorable scene:

"I've done some great stunts for Walter over the years but flipping the bus was one of the most memorable. When we were prepping that scene, Walter told me that he didn't want to use these pipe ramps like the ones that we use all the time in TV. We used those on *The A-Team* all the time. Walter said, 'Get me something big, something dynamic.' And we did just that! I went to our effects guy with this idea to flip the bus using pipe cannons, and I know that they had used pipe cannons on car rolls before, but they had never done it with a 40-foot bus going 60 miles an hour. For something like this you had to put two cannons in it. So, our effects people went all around Hollywood talking to other effects guys to gauge whether this is something that could be possible with such a big vehicle. Eventually, we came to the conclusion that we could do it. So, I told Walter we're going to do something that no one else has done and we're going to kick butt on it and it will be spectacular, and he's like, 'Oh yeah, sure, okay,' because he likes to give me a hard time. We were going to be the first to ever flip a bus using a cannon, which is a telephone poll encased in steel and which we attached to the frame of the bus. We figured that we need two cannons: one in the front and one in the back of the bus, one of them right behind me. There is a carving on the top of the cannons where we fit a bomb that would require the maximum amount of eight ounces of black powder, which is like a pound of TNT. When those bombs go off, they push the cannons down and raise the bus.

"And this is something that can never be prepped. You can't flip the bus in advance to test the whole thing out because you would ruin it. So we prepped this thing as much as we could. We went up to a place called Magic Mountain, which had a big parking lot where I could slide this bus. I was telling them I wanted to go faster and never want to slow down, I want to slide it and pop it. So we got the sliding down with toggle switches and Hudson Sprayers releasing oil on the back because I only wanted to slide on two wheels instead of four. So, the day comes and I'm a mile from the set because I want to get the bus up to speed at 60 miles per hour without slowing down. So they tell me to get ready and I'm strapped in to the point where I can barely touch the steering wheel, and then the effects guy comes in and says, 'I'm not going to make those bombs hot until you sign this!' And I'm like, 'Sign what?!' 'Sign this release so that if you blow yourself up your family can't sue me.' You don't do that to someone who is sitting there ready go on a stunt that's never been done before. Even his own guys were like, 'Why would you do that to Allan?' A lot of unpleasant things came out of my mouth in that moment. I said to this guy, 'Are you nuts?! Why didn't you do this three months ago when we were prepping this? Am I just going to

Actor and stunt coordinator Allan Graf appears in *Another 48 Hrs.* (1990).

The daring bus flip, successfully coordinated and performed by Graf in *Another 48 Hrs.* (1990).

blow myself up now? I'm here ready to go and you wait until now to have me sign this thing?' I was going crazy and told him to get hell out of here. And then I hear, 'Allan, we're waiting for you!' So I say, 'Okay, let's go!' Then, 'Action!' Boom, I hit the gas and the rest of it is there on film. It went great. When it landed I had to get out and call my wife on the cell phone that they had waiting for me. She wanted to make sure that I was okay. And then the effects guy comes down to me and he's like, 'I didn't want to do that, Allan, but they're suing us all the time and I didn't know what would happen!' 'You didn't know what would happen?! Thanks. We've been prepping this for three months!' He was a nice guy though. But I did it, I flipped the bus and it's a great scene."

"On the bus stunt we had to line up at least four or five cameras," Leonetti recalls, "and these were unoperated cameras that we'd put on the ground so the bus would go over them or by them. We had that scene well-covered. But it all goes back to having good crew, having good camera operators, and good second unit guys like Allan. Those guys are so good at their job that there's no worry of having to do take two of a scene like that."

"Cinematically and visually, I think it's better than the first," Gross says. "I think the action sequences are very exciting and incredibly well staged. It is made with an aggressive visual style that's very impressive. Everything that is fundamentally characteristic of Walter's work is in there. Walter was ready for it, and he wanted the film to be successful and it was fairly successful, although some people's fees complicated that. There are things in *Another 48 Hrs.* that I really like. I was there every day watching Walter Hill direct it, and that was a joy on every conceivable level. Walter is extraordinary to watch on set. In several respects there are things I observed that make him unlike other people."

"A lot of the photography of *Another 48 Hrs.* was intuitively felt," Leonetti says. "Walter and I could discuss without discussing. We didn't have to say a whole lot to each other; it was almost telepathic. Walter already had the movie in his mind. We would shoot the day's work and then he would show us the scene and say what he'd like and we would go about our business putting on the screen what he wanted to see. Walter is smart. He has the movie already cut in his head before he starts making it, so he always knows what he's looking for, he's not guessing, and that's obviously a great attribute to making movies. I remember coming home from shooting the scene in the gymnasium of the prison. Walter said, 'I know how we're going to cut this: we're going to have this close-up here and that shot there, and that's how that scene is going to be laid out.' He had it all figured out before we shot it. That is, in a nutshell, how Walter approaches filmmaking. And he was pretty open when it came to the lighting of the film. If he didn't like something he would say so, but usually he would go along with what we did. I could do things such as arbitrarily and for no good reason placing huge beams of light in the background of the nighttime exteriors. I got a couple of searchlights like they used for movie premieres years ago and I put them down the end of the street or a couple of blocks away, turned them on, and threw a little smoke in front of them so there was enough atmosphere in the air that you could see the beam of light."

Another 48 Hrs. garnered sizable box office returns (against an admittedly sizable budget) as audiences showed their support in droves. The film narrowly missed out on making the top 10 highest-grossing films at the US box office in 1990, trailing behind *Days of Thunder* (Tony Scott), *Presumed Innocent* (Alan J. Pakula), and *Back to the Future III* (Robert Zemeckis) but wildly overshadowed by Paramount's other hits of the year, *Ghost* (Jerry Zucker) and *The Hunt for Red October* (John McTiernan). But despite selling as many tickets as it did, the film remains one of the most critically mauled of Hill's career. Such criticism is somewhat baffling, especially when the original—which the sequel is identical to in many ways—is held aloft in high acclaim. Much of the snarky response feels reactionary, perhaps a snide riposte by the media to reports of the ostentatious production, including Murphy's inflated salary. A misreading of the film's use of comedy and action seems to have been another misstep by critics of the time; yes, humor and violence are uneasy bedfellows in the wrong hands, especially when the devastation of death and destruction is undermined by a casual and ironic temperament—something that the imitators of Quentin Tarantino's brand of filmmaking could certainly be accused of indulging in and exploiting. But at no point in the film are we under the illusion that Hill is presenting anything other than a deliberately stylized, highly aestheticized, heightened action film punctuated with comic book levels of absurd violence underscored with a considerable sense of fun and humor. "*Another 48 Hrs.* is much darker than *48 Hrs.*," Gross says, "and even though the humor is there, I have always felt that some of it seems to have gone missing in the final cut. Walter's humor is very apparent in it but it's very hard to explain. It's a very wry sense of humor and a lot of irony goes into it. He's not always letting you know he's being funny."

"The general feeling is the film is a tired sequel to an exciting movie," Hill says. "I thought in some ways the relationship between the two leads lacks the bounce of the first one, but is in a couple of ways more thoughtful. And the action sequences are pretty good."

Five

Tales for Television and Way Out West

After informing much of his cinematic work with subtle aesthetic allusions to the distinct formalism of comic books, Walter Hill's most affectionate and unabashed indulgence in such was his involvement in HBO horror anthology series *Tales from the Crypt*. Based on William Gaines and Al Feldstein's popular and controversial EC Comics of the 1950s, the show is hosted by The Cryptkeeper, a rather lively rotting corpse who delights in spinning spooky stories that deliver poetic-justice payoffs to protagonists who dare to navigate the world according to their own macabre moral code. The comic book run lasted between 1950 and 1955, during which time it attracted considerable negative attention for publisher-editor Gaines. The demise of the property was instigated by the United States Senate Subcommittee on Juvenile Delinquency at which Gaines volunteered to testify in opposition to the censorship of comic books by conservative moral arbiters. Despite some serious and important themes being addressed within the lurid pages of the EC publishing empire, some community spokespeople, including parents, teachers, and clergy, just couldn't see past Feldstein's ghastly panels. *Back to the Future* screenwriter and producer Bob Gale notes that this most problematic of pop-culture pariahs was perfect for one of Hollywood's most maverick of moviemakers: "I love the fact these comic books were banned in America in the 1950s," Gale says, "that our Congress actually sat down to suppress them and even put EC out of business, and yet the people who were influenced by them turned out to be some of America's greatest filmmakers, including Walter Hill."

Indeed, Hill was one of five powerhouse filmmakers who would executive-produce the series, a considerable quintet consisting of Hill, Richard Donner, David Giler, Joel Silver, and Robert Zemeckis. Combining their industry clout and influence, they introduced this cult comic classic to a whole new generation of horror fans. While Hill has alluded to the influence of comic books on his previous cinematic work, this project would prove an opportunity for him to explicitly draw upon the previously much-maligned medium to inform his storytelling and aesthetics. The director recalls the influence of EC Comics and their chilling tales. "It was absolutely my love of comics and graphic art that influenced me to go into *Tales from the Crypt*, no question," Hill states. "I was always a fan of comic books as a kid, but it wasn't so much Marvel or any of that, it was more the EC Comics and stories with detectives and cops and crooks. That kind of business and the horror stuff is what I really liked."

The 1980s had not been kind to the big-screen horror anthology. Some notable entries appeared throughout the decade, including *Creepshow*, *Creepshow 2*, *Twilight Zone: The Movie*, *Cat's Eye*, and *Two Evil Eyes*. But anthologies weren't natural box office attractions. They were often marred by commercial and cultural indifference, flailing in the shadows of spectacular sequels to readily identifiable horror franchises that sold on the familiar logos of Freddy Krueger, Jason Vorhees, and Michael Myers. Rather, the format appeared to thrive on television, where that style of storytelling was far more suited to being spread out across several seasons instead of being shoehorned into a truncated two-hour cinematic endeavor. Thus there was a proliferation of horror anthologies appearing on network and cable TV, giving employment to many genre writers and directors between their feature films, including *Freddy's Nightmares*, *Friday the 13th: The Series*, *The New Twilight Zone*, *Tales from the Darkside*, *Monsters*, *The New Alfred Hitchcock Presents*, and *The Ray Bradbury Theater*. And so when it came time for a screen adaptation of *Tales from the Crypt*, it ultimately made better business sense that Hill and his writing-producing partner David Giler to take their project to the smaller of the screens, though that wasn't the initial intention. Hill says, "My producing partner, David Giler, wanted to do an anthology movie and Universal acquired the rights but a couple of anthology movies came out at that time, but didn't do well, so the studio lost interest. We got a chance to do it as a series and we formed partnerships, but if you want to know the truth, I just said I'd do mine; Dick and Joel ran with the ball and got it set up. My deal was basically 'nobody tells me what to do and I'll do it on budget.' I directed three of them."

And those that he did were the excellent pilot, "The Man Who Was Death," and Season 2's "Cutting Cards" and Season 3's "Deadline." With the opening episode Hill exquisitely sets the tone for the series with this morality tale of a misfit man who loves his profession as state executioner so much that he would rather continue the role unpaid and unofficially than find a new job. William Sadler plays Niles Talbot, who loses his beloved position in the penitentiary after the death penalty is abolished and then duly sets out about fixing what he sees as failures of the bureaucratic liberal justice system. "Let me tell you something," Talbot says, "if they put executions on TV it would be the highest-rated show of all time. It'd be Nielsens through the roof. The other networks would start killing people just to compete. Pretty soon, Geraldo Rivera would be pulling that switch." Talbot's twisted vision is reinforced by his barman Vic (Roy Brocksmith), who tells the freshly unemployed and contemplative Talbot that "I hate to see talent go to waste. It's a fucking shame," while reiterating and supporting his customer's extreme views on capital punishment. Talbot's gallows humor emerges when Vic notes that media commentators, whom he disparagingly refers to as "ACLU types," always make the point that the majority of people who get the chair are minorities. Talbot dryly replies, "They're all pretty dark when I get done with them, Vic." A witty remark that highly amuses the prejudiced booze slinger.

These feelings of resentment and disillusionment, coupled with high-profile miscarriages of justice that sees killers let free by the courts on technicalities, encourage Talbot to go freelance and take it upon himself to mete out the judgment and punishment the criminals deserved but eluded. He sits inconspicuously at the back of the courtroom and watches silently as the guilty are set free; little do those depraved defendants realize that the real judge in this court is he that sits behind them, not the officially garbed and appointed one before them. Talbot begins to fill his void and regain his purpose by taking out these dregs of society, beginning with a hoodlum biker who is let off a murder charge on a clerical error. A former hog man himself, Talbot commends the culture to which the thug belongs, but condemns him to death in the same breath: "Bikers believe in freedom. They don't want anybody to lean on them and they don't give a good goddamn what polite society thinks of them. They figure they're throwbacks to real Americans. You know, what the country was about before it all went to hell, with big-city lawyers and computers, corporations, and time clocks and what all. There's a lot to be said for that. Those ain't bad ideas. But this biker, Jimmy Flood, now he went way out of line and he ought to pay." This monologue on bikers being the successors to the outlaws of the Old West, representative of a nobler version of America, is a sentiment that would be reiterated by Ted Markland's villainous biker, Malcolm Price, in *Another 48 Hrs*. And in a neat nod to the Walter Hill movie universe, Ry Cooder's rendition of Link Wray's "Rumble" is applied as a musical theme to score the appearance of the leather-clad men and their motors, just as it did in *Streets of Fire*.

Having Talbot directly addressing the camera is a novel stylistic touch, the character breaking the fourth wall even as he is surrounded by other people within the diegetic world of the story. Sadler effectively recites Talbot's righteous speeches as if delivering an impassioned sermon backed by the blues of Cooder's choir, preaching poetically to the pro-penalty pariahs whose voice he is there to represent. "See those two junkies?" Talbot asks the audience rhetorically. "Pitiful bastards, ain't they? I'll tell you something though: in a way I respect them. They're honest, they spend all the money they can get just to shoot a little Death into their arms, just for a thrill, just to get a little taste of the grave. They know Death is coming; they tease it. I like that. Of course, at the same time junkies are shits. Two-bit criminals." Talbot's quest of vengeance doesn't discriminate. He is judge, jury, and executioner to criminals of all classes, white collar or no collar, from wealthy scoundrels to beggarly go-go dancers, all of whom share the guilt of having gotten away with murder. The ultimate irony and poetic justice of the piece is rendered in Talbot being caught by police and receiving his comeuppance when the state legislature reinstates the death penalty; in the end, this strident proponent of capital punishment becomes its latest casualty. This is a perfect example of Gaines's "just deserts" twists that were a feature of *Tales of the Crypt*, in which the lead character will meet their fate in the same manner of malevolence that they had been inflicting upon others with impunity. "It's my job," Talbot pleads as he is wired up for electrocution. "That's why I did it, because it's my job. If a man ain't good at his job, then what the hell is he good for? What's anything good for?" But leave it to The Cryptkeeper to deliver a final trademark pun in honor of Talbot: "It just goes to show what happens when you get too caught up in your work. Don't worry, though. I'm sure he never knew 'watt' hit him."

By the time he was cast as Talbot, William Sadler had been an acclaimed stage actor and familiar face from television, having appeared in popular shows such as *Roseanne*, *St. Elsewhere*, and *Murphy Brown*. When he auditioned for *Tales from the Crypt*, it was for a minor role, but casting director Karen Rea saw something in the actor's skill and ambition that encouraged her to offer him the chance to read for the lead. Sadler recalls the casting session: "When I auditioned for 'The Man Who Was Death' I hadn't really done much on film before that, but I had done 11 years of theater in New York City. I went in to audition for the cop who arrests Niles Talbot at the end of the episode and the only line he has is, 'Mr. Talbot, you have the right to remain silent…' He just says the Miranda rights and that's what I read for Karen Rea. She said, 'Thank you,' and I asked, 'What's up with the role of Talbot?' So she told me that they needed a star, a big name for this lead character like John Malkovich or someone of that level. I said okay and I left, but I got halfway across the parking lot and she stuck her head out the window of the office and said, 'Bill, come back!' and she handed me the sides for Talbot and said, 'Get here on Monday and I'll put you on tape.' So I went back on Monday and in the audition they handed me this page-and-a-half opening monologue in which Talbot talks about executing these tough guys who all cry on their way to the chair. I came up with these things for the character, making him this Okie with the southern drawl who would talk about electricity and how much he liked it. And that's when Walter Hill cast me."

William Sadler plays eccentric electricity and execution enthusiast Niles Talbot in *The Man Who Was Death* (1990).

Sadler continues, "I was not a name, I was not what they were looking for, but Walter chose me and all of a sudden I was working for these major filmmakers: Dick Donner, Robert Zemeckis, Joel Silver, David Giler, and Walter. It took a week to shoot and I got paid something like $1,700 to play the lead role of this executioner who looks directly into the camera and says how much fun it is to kill people; he has these big, long monologues right into the camera and I was thrilled about that. Back in New York I won an Obie Award for a 40-minute monologue onstage, so this wasn't new stuff for me. When we were filming I would come in to work and Walter would be sitting there writing in longhand another monologue, he kept adding monologues, and he would tell me to read it and 20 minutes later we're shooting it. I think he really enjoyed this character that we created and he decided to take full advantage of it, so he was constantly doing little rewrites and adding things. Walter was just wonderful to work for. However, he is not effusive in his praise and I was very insecure. When we were shooting Talbot being executed, I'm kicking and screaming and I left my heart out on the floor doing that, so when I'd hear, 'Cut! That's it, we're on the wrong set,' I kept looking to him waiting to say something like 'Good job!' or 'That's great, that's what I wanted!' or any kind of approval, but he was just like, 'Yep, we got it.' He was already gone to the next set. I was not good working to a camera yet, it was still strange to me, but he was just a terrific teacher in that regard; he would tell me to do less and he would explain that all you have to do in the close-ups is let the penny drop in your head and the audience will get it as clear as day."

The episode is laced with pitch-black humor and sets a suitably seedy stage for Hill to craft his ghastly tale of terror, all of which is augmented by the presence of his regular composer, Ry Cooder, who opens proceedings with an amusing carnival-esque score that heralds the surreal and absurdist story to follow. The famed musician also brings in some tasty guitar and piano blues licks to underscore the gritty, hard-living milieu of Talbot and his fellow barstool cronies. Meanwhile the director's erstwhile camera operator John Leonetti (*Red Heat, Johnny Handsome, Another 48 Hrs.*) steps up to cinematography duties and does a terrific job in creating a neon-drenched film noir world for our cynical antihero to wander. Leonetti's stylish camerawork and vivid lighting contributes significantly to establishing the comic-book-style panel framing that feels authentic to its graphic art origins. "I was always interested in graphic art and the influence on my work is not simply the lurid, but the efficiency of storytelling in a brisk and formalized way," Hill says. "Comic books are a great lesson in artistic economy and that is perhaps the greatest influence they have had on me, although the lurid and graphic qualities have had an undeniable influence as well."

"There was this wonderful dark humor to all of it," Sadler admits. "Walter and I both locked into it and made it fun. It wasn't just like 'look how cool it is to execute people,' it was tongue-in-cheek. When he is executing the first guy and he says, 'Electricity is so fast that the prisoner never feels a thing,' then he pulls the switch and he looks right at the camera and says, 'I hope that isn't true!' and he pulls the switch again, zapping the guy, it's cruel and it's funny. Walter has a great, evil sense of humor and he was responsible for the style of it all, including bringing in Ry

Cooder, whose music made it like some crazy carnival atmosphere. The episode was very successful, it was up for a Cable ACE Award and it also brought me to the attention of a half-dozen other people who hired me for the next 10 years. Frank Darabont was one of the writers on *Tales from the Crypt* and he came up to me on the set and said, 'I'm doing a movie called *Rita Hayworth and Shawshank Redemption* and I'd like you to be in it.' Joel Silver's next movie was *Die Hard 2* and he hired me to play the villain in that, and I went on to work with Zemeckis and Dick Donner as well, so having Walter Hill trusting his instincts about this actor who he had never heard of before really launched my career, which was sputtering along up to that point. There's a hundred projects that I've done and that I never would have had the opportunity to do if it weren't for Walter and that initial engagement in casting me for that first little half-hour episode. It just kicked so many doors open and I give Walter full credit, as well as Karen Rae, for shouting out the window after me and saying, 'Let's give Bill a shot!'"

Hill's second episode, *Cutting Cards*, is a nifty riff on the classic 1960s episode of *Alfred Hitchcock Presents* called *Man from the South*, which was originally written by Roald Dahl for *Collier's* magazine in 1948. This oft-imitated tale tells of two rival gamblers, Reno Crevice (Lance Henriksen) and Sam Forney (Kevin Tighe), a pair of punters of ill repute and fierce rivalry who engage in the most dangerous game of their lives, wagering body parts for pride and glory. They are so obsessed in this game of one-upmanship that they eventually run out of limbs to chance, and in the grisly though hilarious dénouement we see them reduced to boughless bodies bobbing awkwardly above a checkerboard and using their noses to shuffle the pieces about. Bob Gale was impressed that Hill not only had the temerity to evoke the wicked ingenuity of Hitchcock but to go one further in delivering a truly twisted and hilariously macabre finale. "Walter's episode 'Cutting Cards' is a classic," Gale says, "and it is something that Hitchcock did so well before, so it's like, 'This is Hitchcock, are you really going to go there?' and Walter did go there and he put images on-screen that Hitchcock daren't do. That episode is an example of how great a director Walter is." In contrast to Ry Cooder's atmospheric blues of Hill's previous episode, the director brings in the electronic tones of celebrated composer James Horner for "Cutting Cards." Horner had memorably scored *48 Hrs.* and its sequel, as well as *Red Heat*, and once again he is working with synthesized instrumentation to draw us into the den of iniquity in which Crevice and Forney play out their demented games.

Hill's final directorial entry in the series is "Deadline," a cautionary tale of infidelity and tabloid journalism taken too far. Inveterate alcoholic newspaperman Charles McKenzie (Richard Jordan) has thrown his career away in a haze of booze, but after embarking on an affair with a young woman who proves a sobering influence, he is afforded one more chance on the condition that he deliver a major scoop. When the grisly murder of a diner proprietor provides McKenzie with sensational headline material, his potential for personal and professional redemption is compromised when he discovers the dead man's wife is the very woman whose indiscretion has instigated his recovery. It is the least-remarkable episode of the three, lacking the rich aesthetic inventiveness and clever audio-visual palettes of the previous two entries, though remaining an entertaining tale regardless.

The producers of *Tales from the Crypt* wisely drafted in some of the biggest and best names in horror cinema to helm episodes and in doing so also allowed them to deliver some of the most playfully wicked and imaginative work of their careers. Some of those who contributed their talent include Tom Holland (*Fright Night*), Mary Lambert (*Pet Sematary*), Fred Dekker (*The Monster Squad*), Jack Sholder (*A Nightmare on Elm Street 2: Freddy's Revenge*), Tobe Hooper (*The Texas Chainsaw Massacre*), William Malone (*Creature*), and Mick Garris (*Critters 2*). Coming off another controversial horror anthology, *Freddy's Nightmares*, producer Gil Adler joined the series in 1991 for Season 3 and would work on the big-screen spinoff, *Tales from the Crypt: Demon Knight*, and later return to produce and direct on *Perversions of Science*, the television adaptation of William Gaines's other EC Comics property, *Weird Science*. Inspired by the creative freedom that the show afforded its filmmakers, some of the most recognizable movie stars of the time were attracted to get behind the camera and call the shots, such as Arnold Schwarzenegger, Tom Hanks, Michael J. Fox, and Bob Hoskins. Indeed, it was a playground for visionary artists to play in a highly creative milieu, and the opportunity wasn't lost on Hill's *Trespass* screenwriter and producer, Bob Gale, who was given the chance to direct the Season 5 episode "House of Horrors."

"I have to credit Walter for my work on *Tales from the Crypt*," Gale admits. "He was really an advocate for me, even more so than Bob Zemeckis was, believe it or not. I had been on-set with Walter when we were filming *Trespass* and there were times when I would see him puzzled about how a scene should be done, so I would step over to him politely and say, 'What if you did this' and 'What if you did that.' Walter would look at me and say, 'Gale, you should be a director!' So we already had a good working relationship established and when he saw that I wanted to direct an episode of *Tales from the Crypt*, he backed me all the way and said, 'Absolutely, Gale will be fine.'"

Hill would retain his executive producer role for the various film spinoffs of the series, as well as further television excursions into the EC Comics universe. The big-screen tales of *Demon Knight* (1995) and *Bordello of Blood* (1996) are largely successful in keeping within the tone of the series, while the third entry, *Ritual* (2002), fails to carry over the style and charm of what made the show and the previous two films so loveable; in some commercial territories, *Ritual* was released minus The Cryptkeeper's humorous prologue and epilogue, thus eliminating all references to it being a *Tales from the Crypt* property. In doing so it functions even less effectively as a mere run-of-the-mill low-budget horror picture. William Sadler was once again brought into The Cryptkeeper's realm as the star of *Demon Knight*, playing a war veteran drifter named Frank Brayker who is in possession of an artifact that was one of seven keys that allowed dark forces to wield great power over the universe until God banished them out of existence. However, one key remains that contains the blood of Jesus Christ and which in the wrong hands has the power to unlock the ancient evil and open the Gates of Hell; those wrong hands belong to The Collector (Billy Zane), a demon who desires the key for his own sinister means. Brayker takes refuge in an old church now functioning as a boarding house, which becomes under siege from The Collector and his demonic minions as they attempt to reclaim the key to regain a dark hold over the universe.

The Cryptkeeper (voiced by actor John Kassir) calls the shots in *Tales from the Crypt: Demon Knight* (1995).

The instantly recognizable and iconic EC Comics cover art makes an appearance in *Tales from the Crypt: Demon Knight* (1995).

Sadler recalls the modest production: "*Demon Knight* had the same cluster of producers, and it has the same sense of humor and that dark murderous tone to it, but the film was pretty inexpensive. They built the sets and shot it in an old airplane hangar in Sherman Oaks, California; it wasn't even on a soundstage! There were pigeons up in the rafters and before every take you had to shut them up somehow, just dozens of pigeons up there cooing and making all this noise. So, before they yelled 'Action!' they were trying all kinds of things to shut them up and finally what they settled on was someone took a shotgun loaded with blanks and they fired it up there so the pigeons would all scatter; then they would say 'Action!' You would have a couple of minutes before they would come back and start courting each other again. In some ways my character in it, Frank Brayker, is the same kind of guy as Niles Talbot. He is this dangerous loner, so there's some continuity there with 'The Man Who Was Death' in my casting and in the kind of character I played. When I look at *Demon Knight* now, I think that you could never get that group of people together again for love nor money. Billy Zane steals the movie, and you have CCH Pounder, Thomas Haden Church, and Jada Pinkett, but we shot the whole thing for a dollar ninety-eight!"

Perversions of Science, which adapted stories from EC sci-fi comics *Weird Science* and *Weird Fantasy*, was a doomed television series that met an unceremonious early demise that recalled the apathetic public reaction to its source material in failing to capitalize on youth market appetites in the way that its beloved horror predecessor did so successfully. Neither *Weird Science* nor *Weird Fantasy* could live up to the popularity of *Tales from the Crypt*, despite containing great stories and wonderful artwork in the EC tradition, and unfortunately for Hill and his co-executive producers, the small-screen iteration of those texts similarly couldn't capture interests, of neither network executives nor audiences, and it duly failed to launch in 1997. The 10 episodes produced in its first season are directed by *Tales from the Crypt* alumni, including William Malone, Gil Adler, Tobe Hooper, Russell Mulcahy, and, of course, Walter Hill, who once again set the tone for the series in helming the pilot episode, "Dream of Doom." In it, Keith Carradine plays troubled professor Arthur Bristol, who is caught in an endless cycle of dream paralysis; every time he wakes up from one dream, it seems as though he has entered another. The surface theme suggests that Arthur is a middle-aged man stuck in a rut; he is divorced and childless, and it is alluded to that his wife desperately wanted children, but he demurred, which may have sounded the death knell of their marriage. We also learn he has some health issues, which could be interpreted as being the catalyst for this surreal nightmare of the mind: Are these the dreams of a dying man, or the terrifying lucid torment of a coma patient?

Despite the obvious budgetary limitations of the series, Hill's episode is stunningly shot by his longtime cinematographer, Lloyd Ahern, who brings a wonderfully skewed sense of surrealism to the dreamlike illogic of the episode. It remains easily the best entry of the short-lived series, perhaps benefiting from the fact that this particular story does not rely on digital visual effects to support its narrative; instead it utilizes skillful editing and photography to heighten the illusive nature of the confusion and anxiety of the character and his Kafkaesque quandary. "*Perversions of Science* was based on the EC *Weird Science* comics," Hill says, "but HBO decided not to pick it up and go with it, but I thought my episode, 'Dream of Doom,' which had Keith Carradine and Lolita Davidovich, was as good as any of the three that I did for *Tales from the Crypt*. Maybe better."

Whether critical or commercial success was gained or eluded throughout his time working within the EC universe, the one thing that Hill and his fellow filmmakers can claim with certainty is that their vision of *Tales from the Crypt* is as faithful an adaptation of EC's beloved comic books as is possible to achieve. Tonally, aesthetically, and literarily, Hill's own trio of terror within the first three seasons are classic examples of how to adapt source material to the screen while maintaining the spirit of the initial texts and staying true to all of the elements that made them so special in the first instance.

Walter Hill's surprising but successful detour into television as the executive producer and occasional director of *Tales from the Crypt* wouldn't keep him from his big-screen duties for long. Enter Bob Gale. The Saint Louis native had just experienced huge success as the co-screenwriter and producer of the *Back to the Future* trilogy when the opportunity to work with Walter Hill came about. On the suggestion of his producing partner and former Hill assistant, Neil Canton, Gale dug out an old script gathering dust in his drawer that he deemed ideal to become the next film in the Walter Hill oeuvre, an urban western entitled *The Looters*, which Gale had cowritten with his friend and collaborator, Robert Zemeckis. Though released on Christmas Day 1992, and ultimately renamed *Trespass*, the roots of this troubled project go all the way back to the mid-'70s, the result of influences as varied as John Boorman's *Deliverance*, John Huston's *The Treasure of the Sierra Madre*, and an *Esquire* article entitled *The Savage Skulls*.

The film tells the tale of two Arkansas firemen, Vince (Bill Paxton) and Don (Bill Sadler), who are handed a potentially lucrative piece of information while trying to save the life of an old man who perishes in a deadly blaze the duo are battling. In a moment of guilt-ridden redemption, the elderly man, a former criminal, prays for forgiveness and bequeaths to them a map that sketchily details the location of a haul of gold that was stolen from a church years ago and is now buried in an abandoned industrial facility in crime-ridden East Saint Louis. Hit with the financial pressures of ex-wives and multiple mortgage payments, the opportunistic Don hatches a plan to claim the pot of gold, bringing a reluctant Vince along with him. What the two naive outsiders don't realize is that the decrepit building harboring the haul is also the site for local gangster kingpin King James (Ice-T) and his posse to conduct their deadly business deals. A tense standoff ensues after Vince is witness to a gangland execution by the James gang, which includes James's half brother, Lucky (De'voreaux White)—so named because "bullets fly through him"—and henchmen Savon (Ice Cube), Cletus (Tommy Lister, Jr.), and Wickey (Stoney Jackson). Vince and Don have a potential savior in a vagrant named Bradlee (Art Evans), who squats at the building unaware he is sleeping on a gold mine. Bradlee knows the layout of the building intimately, information that could benefit the panicking out-of-towners greatly, but the Arkansas men are wisely suspicious of the vociferous derelict. "I don't know what this stuff is anymore," Don contemplates as he realizes the quagmire he is in, "our gold. God's gold. Fool's gold."

According to Gale, "Bob Zemeckis and I wrote the first draft of the script in 1976. We had the idea to take *Deliverance* and turn it inside out: instead of having city guys going out into the rural sticks, we would have some guys going from Vermont to the South Bronx looking for this treasure. Of course, *The Treasure of the Sierra Madre* was another major influence on it. There is definitely a bit of Bogart's Dobbs in Don. At one point we also had three characters, as there are in that film, and on a certain level you can compare Bradlee to Walter Huston, as the old guy that knows what's going on. The *Esquire* article that we read, *The Savage Skulls*, was also the inspiration for the film *Fort Apache, The Bronx*, and it was about a neighborhood in the South Bronx that was so vicious and savage and degenerate that the cops didn't want to go in there. We needed a reason for the characters to want to go there and the treasure made the most sense for us."

Neil Canton recalls that "Bob [Gale] and Bob [Zemeckis] had the script for *Trespass* written since the seventies and after the *Back to the Future* trilogy the three of us were looking for another movie to do together. I asked them if they had anything that they were interested in making and they showed me the script for *Trespass*, which at the time was called 'The Looters.' I read that script and asked if either one of them wanted to direct it, but neither of them felt like they wanted to, so I said if I could get Walter to direct it would they be okay with that. I knew Bob and Bob were fans of Walter's and I was hoping they would say yes to the idea, and they did so enthusiastically. Even though they had written it, I couldn't imagine Bob Zemeckis directing it; he is a fantastic director, one of the greats, but it was just hard to imagine him doing such a gritty urban tale. As soon as I read it I immediately thought Walter should do this because it was kind of an urban retelling of *The Treasure of the Sierra Madre* and I knew Walter liked that film. I also knew how adept he was at making urban films and that it was the kind of rough, tough story that Walter would like to tell. It was set in a confined space, and I thought that would appeal to him on a dramatic level."

If Canton's plan came to fruition, he would serve as producer, with Zemeckis and Gale executive producing, and Walter Hill would direct. Canton called the director posthaste to tell him about the script and, wasting no time, he proceeded to drop it by the Hill house on his way home. By that evening, *Trespass* had its director. Hill immediately informed Canton of his interest in the script and would later tell Gale that the moment that sold him on the script was the scene in which Vince and Don accidentally find the treasure in the ceiling, hidden above their heads the entire time. "Walter said when he read that scene the movie just jumped five levels higher than it was before," Gale says. Having Hill officially on board meant the momentum was provided for the trio to endeavor to set it up at a studio. However, the duo's script would prove somewhat sensitive as racial tensions were boiling over in certain American cities. As Gale and Zemeckis didn't pull any punches with the racial aspects of the script, they were duly advised by their agent to reconsider shopping it around. "When our agent read it he told us we were completely insane to think that any studio would even consider making a movie like that," Gale recalls, "and he was right! At the time that was absolutely correct, but one of the things that helped it was a film called *New Jack City*, which had Ice-T in it. When I saw that I thought, 'Oh man, they're going there!' This is no-holds-barred, no-punches-pulled, real urban stuff. Bob and I thought the time was right for *Trespass*. It wasn't called *Trespass* back then; first it was called 'Three White Men,' because it was three white guys from Vermont going into the South Bronx; then we changed it to 'White City Volunteers,' named after a town in Vermont and their volunteer fire department. So, even after we pulled the script out of mothballs and did a polish, it was still too hot to handle."

However, at this time Robert Zemeckis had an overall deal with Universal

Pictures and was contractually obliged to offer his next potential project to that studio before shopping it elsewhere. Surprisingly, Universal said yes, and thus a deal was made to make the movie. "It surprised us that Universal wanted to do it," Canton says, "because we weren't quite sure that they would be interested in it, but we were happy that they were, and we went about setting it up."

"The executives at Universal then were Nina Jacobson and Jim Jacks," Gale recalls, "and we were worried what Nina was going to think of this pretty hard-edged thing, but she loved it, she totally embraced it. Walter then did another draft of the script and he improved it a great deal, but it was still the core story."

"The film is very much the script that Bob and Bob had written decades ago," Canton says, "except for some dialogue changes to accommodate the casting of Ice-T and Ice Cube; they would tell us that there were certain things they would never say, so they would inform us how they would say it and Bob Gale put those alterations into the script."

Another reason for bringing *The Looters* up to date with multiple revisions is that *Fort Apache, The Bronx* had already been released in 1981 and so the location would have to be changed to avoid overbearing similarity to that film. With Gale hailing from Saint Louis, he knew all too well how much the neighboring city across the Mississippi River, East Saint Louis, bore much of the same social issues as the South Bronx, as well as sharing a cosmetic resemblance. Gale said of the hometown inspiration: "Having grown up in Saint Louis I knew that East Saint Louis was just as bad of a place as the South Bronx was, nobody in their right mind would ever go there. So, we changed the location, did a polish, then gave it to Walter and he absolutely loved it. But we never actually shot anything in Saint Louis. The footage you see of Saint Louis, including the bridge across the Mississippi River and the Gateway Arch, is actually B-roll footage from a Universal film called *White Palace*. We knew we had to get some establishing shots of downtown Saint Louis and I knew that *White Palace* was shot on location there, so I found that footage myself when I went into the stock-footage library at Universal. I looked at a bunch of stuff and I chose those shots from *White Palace* and I sent them over to Walter."

When it came to casting, Hill would bring in some familiar faces from previous projects, including William Sadler, whose career Hill had given a major boost by casting him in the lead role for the pilot episode of *Tales from the Crypt*. Bill Paxton and Stoney Jackson both appeared in *Streets of Fire*, while the considerable physical presence of Tommy Lister, Jr., could be seen previously in *Extreme Prejudice* and the Hill-produced *Blue City*. As Universal wanted to keep costs down, the casting of major-name actors was out of the question, which suited Hill perfectly as it was the kind of situation in which he could cast actors such as Paxton and Sadler, reliable actors whom Hill liked personally and who could deliver the goods while not commanding the kind of salary that would have executives balk. According to Canton, "Both Bills—Sadler and Paxton—were great guys and were ideal to be cast here because they had to be believable as two guys who were foolish enough to go do this thing and they were indeed believable. I mean this in the best possible way, but Bill Paxton had the ability to play an everyman who would do all the wrong things. A really smart person would have read the article and said, 'Yeah, I'm not going there!'

but you are able to believe that Paxton would go, 'Yeah, this is a good idea, let's do it!' He was such a wonderful actor, but he was sort of anti-intellectual, so you could see how he could be talked into going through with this really bad idea. He always had this happy-go-lucky demeanor and had that quality as an actor to make you believe that he was naive or gullible enough to be talked into doing something idiotic and dangerous. And you believed that Bill Sadler could talk him into doing it. Walter had cast Bill Sadler before and really liked him. Sadler has kind of a tough-guy bully quality about him and you could see how he would be able to manipulate or force Paxton to go along on this crazy pursuit."

While it is hard to imagine anyone else embodying the characters as those who were cast do, Gale reveals some tantalizing alternative casting choices that were being mooted: "One of our first choices for the part of Vince was Brad Pitt, but he turned it down. I don't think he wanted to be in a movie where the word 'nigger' was used so frequently; it was more than he wanted to deal with at that point in his career. So, Bill Paxton was cast and he brought so much to the part. We lost Paxton way too early; may he rest in peace. Bill Sadler came in on a casting call and we saw that he had some of that Humphrey Bogart quality that was ideal for Don, and so we cast him. The real surprise, however, was Art Evans, who played Bradlee. We were going to go with Samuel L. Jackson but then Art came in and did a reading that knocked everybody's socks off. We just said, 'This is the guy! It's gotta be him!'"

The fractured friendship of Vince and Don becomes increasingly strained as the greed for gold is intensified by the volatile situation that they find themselves mired in, and so the casting of the two characters would benefit from real natural chemistry and mutual respect between the actors, but nobody expected that some genuine tension would emerge and play a part in the on-screen action. Sadler recalls some particularly, and unintentionally, tense moments that inadvertently led to the on-screen fighting being more authentic than expected: "By the time we were making *Trespass*, Walter and I had a kind of shorthand going," Sadler reveals, "and one of the things that I love about him is that he does like to work with the same people over and over again because you don't have to go through the getting-to-know-you process, he can say two or three words to you and you go, 'Aha! Got it.' I would get simple directions from him like, 'Bill, make him bigger,' or 'Make him angrier.' Just these little directions and it was never subtle stuff. I was doing a fight scene with Bill Paxton on the set one day where our characters have a big blowup, and we choreographed this whole enormous fight on a Friday afternoon with Paxton holding the gun and I'm trying to grab it out of his hand. So, I reach down and come across his face with a big sweeping punch and he spins around and goes down. That was what we choreographed. Then we did a take and Walter said, 'No. Harder, Bill.' And I go again: wham! 'No, again!' Wham! Still not right, and Walter says, 'Just let him fucking have it!' After doing it 10 times, on the last take, either I got out of position or Paxton got out of position, but when I came up and swept my hand across him I caught his jaw, his head spun around, and he went down in a pile on the ground. That was it. 'Cut!' And I'm sure that is the take that is in the movie."

Sadler continues, "They had to take Paxton to the hospital and have his jaw

The Treasure of East St. Louis: Vince (Bill Paxton, left), Bradlee (Art Evans, center), and Don (William Sadler) argue over the gold while under siege from "King" James and company in *Trespass* (1992).

x-rayed. I didn't mean to hit him; I have never intentionally hurt anybody, and I have done fight scenes my whole life. It's always a dance and you make it look as violent as you can, but you are always super careful, whether it's swords or guns or knives or whatever is involved. But I really clocked Bill Paxton across the face, and he was convinced that I had done it on purpose, which was really unfortunate, and I kept apologizing to him. But he came in the following Monday, and he was okay, I didn't break anything. But then we had to shoot the other half of the fight scene and in that part of the scene his character knees me in the balls and then gives me an elbow to the bridge of my nose, and I just knew, somewhere in my reptile brain, that he was going to land those blows 'by accident.' So, I went to the stunt guys and said, 'Give me the biggest cup you have,' and they gave me this football helmet to wear as protection down below; sure enough, when it got to the third or fourth take, Bill's knee lifted me off the ground and as I crease over he hits me on the bridge of my nose with his elbow. Both of them connected and that was the take they ended up using. I guess somehow, we were even. I liked Bill, I always liked him; he was fun to work with and a good actor. But he took offense to me, thinking that I had hit him on purpose, and I hadn't."

One of the biggest selling points of the film would be the casting of Ice-T and Ice Cube in the villain roles of King James and his trigger-happy cohort, Savon, with both actors parlaying their careers as preeminent rappers into a cross-promotional soundtrack album released by Warner Bros. But it wasn't just their eminence in the music industry that made them appealing to the studio executives, as Canton recalls that casting his lead villains became easier thanks to the success of two recent urban films that signaled to Universal that Ice-T and Ice Cube would make bank for the studio as rising film stars:

"Once Walter agreed to it, we began to go through the regular processes with the studio, so we got to the usual question of 'Who is going to play the two leads?' There was some heat with Ice Cube from *Boyz n the Hood* and with Ice-T from *New Jack City*, so the executives asked if we could get those guys for this picture. We said we could try, and we did, we got them because they were eager to work on a Walter Hill film as they were both fans of his, particularly of *The Warriors*. The studio thought that having Ice-T and Ice Cube on board would help in terms of cross-promotion, given the success of their music careers and how that could be used to their advantage for releasing a soundtrack, but their casting really came down to the sense of realism that they brought. Ice Cube has really great presence on-screen, he is very powerful, and you just can't take your eyes off of him; the same with Ice-T. We had the benefit of them being really great actors. But they came from a musical background which is tied to this world, so it made sense to just go with them, they brought a sense of urban credibility to the film. After that, Reuben Cannon cast the movie and brought in all these great actors to round out the cast and it was just a case of fitting all the pieces together to give some authenticity to it feeling like a real group of guys who worked together. Stoney Jackson was another early casting choice, and De'voreaux White, who had been in *Die Hard*, came in on a casting call and he was fantastic; it all came together very quickly once Ice Cube and Ice-T were cast."

"Ice-T was certainly a major act, he was a big deal at the time," Gale says. "I'm not sure that Ice Cube was considered bankable, but he had credibility. He had done *Boyz n the Hood* and was looking for something that would push him up a level and this was it. But certainly, the combination of Ice-T and Ice Cube together was irresistible. They were both big Walter Hill fans and over the moon at the chance to be in a movie of his."

"*Trespass* was an exciting experience," says costume designer Dan Moore, "but it was all pretty much down to the bone; there was a designer and two costumers, and we didn't have much extra help, which was made more difficult by it being a lot of hard work out on location. We shot partially in Memphis and partially in Atlanta and a lot of it was just being out there on the set making it work. My bailiwick was always story, and in costume design if there is a spectrum between fashion and story, then I'm way more on the story side, sometimes to a fault. Walter was always pretty happy with that because story is his business and I was always in his ballpark, it wasn't like he had to be dragged into my ballpark. There is no dragging of Walter. It was a raucous bunch of guys on that production but the good thing about working on a Walter Hill film is that there is never any question about who is boss; if I express to the actors that Walter is on board with an idea, then there would be less discussion about it. If you look at Ice-T, we have him in dress shirts, braces, and I had a little gold ring made for him, because to his character, King James, it's all about business and the perception he has of himself as being a businessman. So, the clothing and accessories add a richness to his character. It was a lot of fun working with Ice-T and Ice Cube."

Once the cast was in place and the filmmakers and studio were in accord on a satisfactory budget, they were off to make the movie; it was just a case of figuring out where to shoot it. For Hill and company, it could never be a Hollywood soundstage. They needed to find a suitably grungy location for the grimy, abandoned East Saint Louis warehouse. Unable to find a single place that suited both interior and exterior shooting, Hill suggested a combination of Memphis and Atlanta, filming interiors in the former and exteriors in the latter. Ultimately, two different derelict buildings in two different cities would stand in as the single fictional location. Movie magic? To some degree, indeed. Laborious logistical planning? Absolutely.

"It really was a case of breaking down the logistics of it all," Canton says, "getting things prepped to make sure things were happening in the two cities, all those logistical movie nightmares. But it all made sense once Walter said, 'Let's shoot interiors here and exteriors there.' After that it was just about figuring out how to shoot scenes in one location that match with scenes from another location from a lighting standpoint, and working on which actors were working in which places, all those kinds of technical things that movies have been doing forever and it is a wonderful thing: you can shoot a reaction shot in one town and you can shoot the reverse angle in some totally different location and yet it is made seamless. But it all came down to us not being able to decide upon a single place that we wanted to shoot at and Walter just saying, 'Let's use them both!' It was a great solution, rather than making ourselves crazy trying to make changes to accommodate something that wasn't really totally working."

Sadler is amused at the illusory practices that took place in making the disparate locations appear seamlessly matched. "*Trespass* contains one of the great moments in American Cinema and it is the scene when we're being shot at and I grab the hostage, then I dive through the doorway; well, I make the leap in Atlanta and land in Memphis. I remember Walter talking about the continuity, which is always kind of a bugaboo with filmmakers, and younger filmmakers especially. They are very particular about the specifics of continuity: 'He has to come down the stairs this direction and into the door that direction…' But because we were in this strange warehouse/factory place, Walter deliberately ignored that. If we started paying attention to that we're dead; nobody cares which room you just came out of or which hallway you just ran down, or which door just got the shit shot out of it. He deliberately muddied all of that so that the audience was just as confused as we were in this mayhem."

"The annex room was the dividing line between the set in Memphis and the set in Atlanta," recalls cinematographer Lloyd Ahern. "We were working on the fifth floor of this building in Atlanta and that was brutal, but we had to be high up so we could get those shots of the characters looking down and seeing the activity below in the yard and the cops coming in. We eventually had to have an elevator company come in and put in a new elevator because there was no elevator when we began. It was very tough, and it was extremely cold in Atlanta that winter; we were really cold in this damp place so once we got all the good shots that we needed from the height of the fifth floor, we moved down to the second floor. Being on the fifth floor was highly impractical but we just had to get those point-of-view shots from that angle; it wasn't the kind point of view that you could just shoot from anywhere."

"The Atlanta location was very gritty," camera operator Bobby LaBonge concurs. "We were in a warehouse in the middle of winter, and everything about it was rough-and-tumble. I live in Malibu, so when you gotta go to a filthy dirty, cold, 37-degrees warehouse in the middle of beat-up downtown Atlanta, I would rather be at home on the beach. But that hardship made you part of the process; you were cold, you were damp, you were wet, and you were tired, but you and everyone else were feeling that you were there for the same goal of making the movie, and that is important. When everybody is in the same boat it makes for a better process, and that includes Walter. He was also there bundled up trying to keep warm, he wasn't doing it remotely."

"Oh my God, it was so depressing to be there," Gale says. "I was there at the start of shooting in Memphis and when the company moved to Atlanta I went there for about three or four weeks. You do some shows and it's a joy to go to work every day because you are on a wonderful location and you're outside, like on *Back to the Future Part III*; we were outdoors in the beautiful countryside of Central and Northern California for much of that film and we couldn't wait to go to work every day. But the location in Atlanta on *Trespass* was an abandoned factory or warehouse and it was filthy; if people got lung disease from working in there I wouldn't be surprised."

Despite the genuine grittiness of the location, Lloyd Ahern and production designer Jon Hutman decided to make it even less salubrious for the screen. "I had a lot of time to prepare those locations," Ahern recalls. I had a great production designer, and we got a standby painter to spray the window glass this nicotine color to give the effect of this place having been populated for years by many people who smoked. Depending on the contrast of the day and how much light was coming through, I would have him put a little bit or a little more on the windows. On the days where we had a lot of sunlight coming through, I would get him to double up and spray a lot of it on. It gave the background look of that warehouse a lot of character, a lived-in old-fashioned look. It was all part of a grittier lighting style that I went for on this picture."

"Walter was about rolling your sleeves up and getting dirty on this one," Sadler says. "We had a lot of practical stuff being done right there on the set; you have to remember that this was in the years before digital special effects came in and took over. We had a guy there who used to be a member of the CIA, a really big heavy-set guy, and he sat right next to the camera lens with this air rifle, and he would shoot a variety of things depending on what was needed for the shot. He would shoot squibs, dust hits for if you were running across a wooden floor, zirconium hits which made sparks, and he would shoot ball bearings if we needed to break something. He chased me and Bill around again and again. We would dive behind a table and the hits from this guy would be landing all around us. There is a wonderful shot where Bill is looking out of the window when he gets faked out by a police car pulling up and he thinks we're rescued, the whole point being that the gangsters were tricking us so that we would show ourselves and they would take us out. So the shot is of Bill looking out of the window when he sees the car and then he turns his head to yell for me, but in the split second that he turns away this man with the air rifle puts a shot through the piece of glass right in the spot between Bill's eyes; then he turns back around and you see that it would have taken him out right between the eyes and I tackle him out of the shot and the window starts exploding with gunshots. Another thing Walter used to love doing was to shoot a lot of blanks, because there was a lot of gunfire in this film, and he insisted that we used full loads, which means they are loud as hell and your ears are ringing after it; Walter liked that because it wakes everybody up on the set. When one of those things goes off, it says, 'No, we're not kidding!'"

Limiting any unnecessary time at the unfortunate location for his cast and crew, Hill was able to parlay his editorial nous into an economy on the set, as Sadler recalls:

"Walter worked like an editor. There were moments when he knew precisely what he wanted or what he needed to get on film in order to edit the scene together; he would say, 'Bill, take a hold of the doorknob, and now look to your left ... that's it! Got it!' And that little piece of connective tissue was what he knew he would need to make the scene work. He is editing the movie in his head as he is directing it, so there wasn't much wasted and it meant we wouldn't have to shoot whole scenes over and over again; once he had the pieces that he knew he was going to use, he would just say, 'Okay, we're on the wrong set!' which meant he got what he needed and it's time to move on. Walter did one of the smartest things I've ever seen: the scenes with Ice-T and Ice Cube would be just riddled with curse words. He would have us do the scenes in which there is a lot of cursing and as soon he shot the scene the way he wanted it, he would say, 'Let's go back and do a clean version,' and he would have us do the same scene again while the actors were still hot and everybody knew all the lines, while the lighting was perfect and the camera was right; so we would do it all again but this time leaving out all the curse words. What Walter was doing there is planning ahead, because later on you have to go and replace all of those lines in a recording studio and loop that stuff with something like 'you sugar-footed barnstormer!' and that's the version that ends up being shown on TV or on airplanes. That's what happens, they always bring the actors back to record TV-friendly words over those scenes. Every time you said 'shit!' you have to dub it with 'ah shoot!' But Walter did it right there on the set, so he already had his clean version done so he didn't have to go back and do that stupid dance that everybody has to do when they make a movie. He is economical and that is a hallmark of someone who had been in this business and at this game for a long time."

In a photographic sense, *Trespass* begins elegantly enough in the tradition one would expect from a major studio production, though as the film progresses the style and aesthetics of the camerawork become something bolder and edgier, reflecting the rising tensions of the siege and the drama unfolding. Lloyd Ahern was able to bring this stylistic ingenuity to the film with the help of his brilliant camera operator, Bobby LaBonge, whose dynamic camerawork keeps the film alive with a nervous energy that visually reiterates the anxiety of the characters. LaBonge had operated on several prior Hill productions, including *Extreme Prejudice*, which meant he was well-versed in the director's hard-edged approach in making the best action cinema. He recalls how the unique camerawork on the film translates to the film's restless resolve:

"Walter and I were really attached at the hip on that one. The first shot that we did in that movie was handheld and as soon as we got that shot, Walter said, 'We're going to do this whole movie handheld!' There was a certain energy because of the handheld camerawork that he liked, and it was definitely the right call in making it a better movie, even though as the camera operator it meant the camera was going to be on my shoulder for the next 10 weeks. But we all do what we must do to make it work as best as possible and *Trespass* is a great-looking high-drama movie. Walter was famous for using long lenses and because we were shooting in tight areas on this movie, we were using wide-angle lenses at minimum focus to get a whole different in-your-face feeling. This is something I can't stress enough as a camera operator: nowadays the director is often in Video Village the next stage over along with the writers, producers, actors, and whoever else, but Walter's process was to be right alongside the camera, right underneath the lens; I could practically kick him if I wasn't careful, that's how close to me he would be. If we got the shot the way he wanted, he would turn over his shoulder and ask me if it was okay technically, if it was in frame and in focus, and I would say, 'It looks good here, sir!' and he would say, 'Okay, let's move on.' Walter is a very present director. That really helps the process and ensures that we get what he wants with a lot less bullshit. He might turn to the dolly grip and say, 'When that actor turns and looks back, I want you to start to push in at about 10 miles an hour, don't do it too fast, just cruise in.'"

When Lloyd Ahern took on the mantle of Hill's director of photography, he was stepping into a position previously held by some of the best in the business: Andrew Lazslo, Ric Waite, Matthew Leonetti. Ahern brought a bold new style to the proceedings, something that would continue to be showcased throughout his ensuing work with Hill. However, their association didn't begin on *Trespass*, it goes all the way back to the very beginnings of their respective careers. "Lloyd and I have been friends for years," Hill states. "I met him when we were first working on *Gunsmoke*. He was second assistant camera and I was a production assistant and we became friends. Years later I became a director and Lloyd became a camera operator and worked on several of my movies. We always stayed in touch and always said we would work together whenever we had the opportunity. When I was going to do this low-budget movie I called Lloyd up and said, 'Okay, Lloyd, if we're going to do it, then we better start,' and he said, 'Let's go.' That was *Trespass*. It worked out very well, but sometimes working with old friends isn't always a good thing because you have a relationship based on a different set of values than a work relationship, but I was pleased with the results on *Trespass*, it wasn't an easy movie to make, and I thought Lloyd did a great job under tough conditions. I asked if he wanted to do my next movie, which was *Geronimo*, and he said, 'Of course!' After that, I've been stuck with him. He likes to move it along and I don't like to do a lot of takes, I like things to move briskly, shall we say. Once I have a scene rehearsed, I could talk it out with him in two minutes and then we go to work. He is a very high-quality photography cameraman and that's really what it's all about finally."

Ahern is quick to acknowledge Hill's disregard of conventional Hollywood thinking as playing a part in his hiring: "Walter's previous director of photography was Matt Leonetti, who is a friend of mine, we went to the same high school, and Walter had a deal which was like an unwritten rule whereby if you shot his last film and he liked you then you were instantly invited to shoot the next film. But when *Trespass* came up Matt already had another job and was completely committed to that, so Walter called me. That's how I got started as Walter's director of photography. I had not shot any movies, only television, and so Walter was taking a big chance as far as my track record. In fact, there was no track record! I got promoted on *Simon & Simon* and from there went out and shot some pilots, but it was all television work. The movie business is so typecast-oriented, as in if you worked in television, then you were considered a television guy and if you work on movies, then you are a movie guy. So, typical Walter, he didn't care about that kind of conventional thinking, he just did what he wanted to do, and it was the beginning of a great relationship."

One of the most striking aesthetic elements that Ahern incorporated is the use of VHS footage that is spliced into the picture, offering a subjective perspective from the gang, whose crimes are being filmed by the aptly named Video (T.E. Russell). The inspiration behind this novel aesthetic was a real-life case of criminals filming their crimes, which was noticed by Gale and Hill as a potentially ingenious narrative device. "The black-and-white VHS footage was based on a news story that I read which defied logic," Hill recalls. "There was a street gang in either Baltimore or Washington, DC, and a member of the gang had a camcorder, and he was recording all of their activities, most of which, of course, were illegal. So, when they got busted by the cops, they had a treasure trove of evidence. It made you wonder about how dumb someone could be that they recorded their own misdeeds, but it was true. I was looking for something visual to get us beyond the normal style, making it different by introducing the camcorder footage."

When Gale saw the news story he immediately integrated it into the script, but the ingenious visual and narrative device also served an economical function for production. "That device was useful in several ways," Gale admits. "Having one of the gang videotaping everything and shooting scenes from the POV of the video camera became useful for the story and for making the movie because it meant we could work faster. It allowed Walter to get back on schedule whenever he realized he was running out of time or was falling behind, because it took less time to set up and shoot those." Bobby LaBonge applauds the unique idea to adopt the grainy, potentially uncinematic camcorder footage into the film's visual palette: "At that time the idea of using a black-and-white camcorder was a gutsy move; in fact it's unbelievable thinking about it now," says the cameraman. "It is something you see a lot of these days but at that time it hadn't been done before, and we also did it again in *Wild Bill*, where we incorporated videotape for the black-and-white dream sequences. There were people saying, 'What are you doing? You can't be doing this!' to Walter and Lloyd, but they just kept marching to the beat of their own drum. It's what they wanted, and they were going to make it work. It was the right call."

Ahern says, "We certainly took some chances on *Trespass*, particularly in using the camcorder footage. There is a character named Video in the film and he is one of the gang members, and as his name suggests, he likes to video things and I don't know where Walter got the idea, but he is always really bold in taking chances. I never shot on video before and we were literally using a camcorder for those scenes, and a consumer camcorder at that, there were no big fancy professional video cameras that you could hand-hold. Walter never even tested it; he just went for it. The character of Video is always shooting with his camcorder and Walter wanted to use that footage as the character's subjective point of view and to cut back and forth between that video footage and the film footage of the same scene. Then we started looking at the dailies when we were in Atlanta, and I would see this stuff and it was really cooking; once we saw how it looked when it was transferred to film and knew that it was good enough to be shown on the big screen, we started shooting full scenes using just video."

Ahern continues, "When we started shooting those video scenes, Walter said rather than shooting it conventionally with coverage, why don't we just follow the character in one shot; this was unconventional because we would normally have the camera getting different angles and different-size frames on the characters. It had its own look to begin with, so I knew I could get a bit raunchier with it. Sometimes it would be all without any cuts, just moving the camera around the room. I would have to go back and see how those scenes are edited because Walter was an unbelievable man for changing things in postproduction; he could seamlessly match things that weren't supposed to be matched and change the story around in editing. Technically, that camcorder stuff was all easy to shoot and it was an artistic decision rather than an economic decision; it was a very revolutionary and off-the-wall idea to incorporate that footage the way he did. I didn't do any tests on it in advance, we were flying blind on that one. After that we did tests on everything, but the one we should have done the tests on, we didn't. But considering the way Walter does things, it wouldn't have made any difference. He would have just gone and done it anyway. As time went on, we just kept doing more because we loved the frenetic style of it and the craziness of the gang."

"The idea to use the camcorder footage was a later addition to the script,"

Cinematographer Lloyd Ahern's VHS camerawork in *Trespass* (1992) gives the film a grainy, immediate aesthetic. Framed in action are villains "King" James (Ice-T, left) and Wickey (Stoney Jackson).

Canton says. "How we got that was we had read an article about incidents that were occurring in Washington, DC, where these gang members were videotaping robberies they were committing or a beat down they were giving, and it just sounded like an interesting thing to incorporate into the film. So, Walter asked our cinematographer, Lloyd Ahern, if we could do this and what the impact would be, and Lloyd said it would actually be easier on the shoot because we needed less lighting time. It also brought a sense of energy and realism as to what was going on, so it was a great device, but then we began thinking, 'Are we using it too much?' or 'Are we not using it enough?' Then we would consider scenes that weren't written as camcorder scenes to be shot as camcorder scenes, because we were getting excited about it, there was an immediacy and at that time it was a very different way to go. But that all came out of Walter and Lloyd talking about how to make a scene more realistic and not just staying back with long lenses and doing the usual kind of thing, instead it was giving it a real sense of energy. It's one of those things that is ahead of its time because the use of found footage and camcorder imagery became more heavily used in recent years."

Bringing even more action expertise and experience to *Trespass* is longtime Hill collaborator Allan Graf, here working behind the scenes as the second unit director and stunt coordinator. Graf proved himself to be a premier stuntman after performing jaw-dropping stunt work throughout many Hill films and here he is instrumental in crafting the thrilling action sequences that punctuate the tense narrative, even earning himself an "Ice"-themed moniker along the way for his efforts. "Because we had these famous rappers in there with those names, Ice-T and Ice Cube, they gave me an Ice name too; they called me 'Ice-Berg' because I was a big guy," Graf amusingly recalls. "I directed a lot of stuff in *Trespass*. The one thing I thought to myself when I started in this business is that I don't want to duplicate things, I want to be able to bring something new to the plate, if they can afford it that is; a lot of stuff is expensive to pull off, but we got away with some great stuff. And if you are going to work with Walter, you have to know how to do action. We had a scene in there where a guy goes over the railing and falls 80 feet, going down through those electrical wires and creating all the sparks. I have cameras on different levels of the building following him all the way down and that was a high freefall, there was no cables on him, it was one hell of a stunt."

Trespass would be the victim of unfortunate timing. For five days across April and May in 1992, the city of Los Angeles erupted in a blaze of racial tension after video footage captured the beating of parolee Rodney King by five LAPD officers, the violent culmination of an attempted traffic stop gone sour. After the footage of the excessive force emerged, a national scandal ensued. A trial was set in motion but, controversially, four of the charged police officers were acquitted. The reaction was devastating and led to one of the darkest moments in the history of Los Angeles. From April 29 to May 4, the city burned. Stores were looted, innocent passersby were beaten; arson and assault reigned in the streets. Thus, for a film entitled *The Looters*, in which white heroes square off against black antagonists as both sides fight for instant financial gain, the path to release was a pretty rocky one. The film would ultimately be tainted goods in the eyes of Universal, the studio fearful of thematic association with the real-life tragedy of the Los Angeles riots and all the sociological allusions that could be applied to readings of the film.

"Making *Trespass* was smooth sailing until the tragedy of the Rodney King situation," Canton admits. "At that time the film was called *The Looters* and because there were all these headlines with the word 'looters' across them, we knew we couldn't use that title. Then the studio got cold feet about the release of the movie because they thought it was too risky for the company and for their name to be attached to it. As well as that, around that same time Ice-T's band Body Count had come out with his song called 'Cop Killer,' so it became a touchy situation where real-life events got in the way of the studio's enthusiasm for the project. When Universal thought we were making a simple *New Jack City/Boyz n the Hood* kind of story, they were very supportive, but then the real world entered our world; the studio thought it was a bad image for them to come out with a movie called *The Looters* while there is all this looting going on in the city, not to mention one of the lead stars having a song out called 'Cop Killer.' So that is where we came up against some issues."

"We had shot the movie under title of *The Looters* and then the Rodney King riots happened," Gale recalls, "and then Universal said they wouldn't release a film with that title. We were told we would have to come up with a different title. *Trespass* was the one that worked the best. But Ice-T and Ice Cube had already cut a song called 'Looters' and we had to go back to them and tell them they would have to do a new song and it would have to be called 'Trespass.' Our first preview we had in South Pasadena and in that version of the movie was the original ending, in which Don kills Ice Cube. The audience was incensed that Ice Cube got killed that way; it was a 75 percent majority black audience and three-quarters of them screamed at the screen and then got up and left before the movie was over. Meanwhile, here we are: a bunch of white guys and other studio executives sitting in the back of the theater and thinking, 'Oh shit, they're going to kick our asses!' But we had them up until that point, they were totally with the movie, but after that we knew we had to revise the ending. So, Walter, Bob, and I brainstormed over a couple of days and came up with the idea that it should be Raymond and Ice Cube that do each other in and that would be acceptable. I think at one point in the various drafts Vince got away with one or two artifacts from the church, but then we decided that Bradlee should get everything. We shot that ending on stage at Universal, about a two-day shoot, and it was hellacious with all the fire that was in that sequence, it was pretty dangerous actually; but we put that ending together and the movie worked great."

Canton says, "Once the studio became scared because of all these real-world occurrences it became obvious that we would have to take a look at some things in the movie, and one of the things we changed was the ending. We reshot it so that Sadler and Ice-T kill each other, so it wasn't just a white guy shooting a black guy. And we also made it that Art Evans's character, Bradlee, ends up with the stolen goods, so it's not like Bill Paxton gets away with it, the white guy didn't get to 'loot.' It was sort of a poetic climax to have the homeless guy, or the squatter, ending up with the money; it made it less racially contentious."

Despite the concessions made in providing the film with a less-controversial denouement for release in the volatile sociopolitical atmosphere of the period, it wasn't enough to make Universal treat the film with any more respect or encourage them to look upon it as a more audience-friendly, commercially viable product. And so in an ill-conceived, counterintuitive move, the studio was happy to have *Trespass* quietly creep into theaters on Christmas Day 1992. "The studio hated the movie," Hill admits. "I don't think they were too keen on it under any circumstance. It was in the aftermath of the riots here and they were scared to death of the racial politics and situations, so they just wanted to get rid of it. They gave it a minimal release, opening on Christmas Day, and it wasn't exactly a Christmas movie."

"Nothing we did satisfied the studio," Gale states. "Despite reshooting the ending they still weren't happy with the title of *The Looters* and they just could not come to terms with its subject matter in the wake of the Rodney King riots. And then, Tom Pollock, the president of Universal, decided to release the film on Christmas Day, a decision that I consider to be one of the stupidest moves of counterprogramming in the history of motion pictures. He could have waited three weeks and released it on Martin Luther King Day and that definitely would have been a better time to release it, but instead he released it at Christmastime. Zemeckis and I were thinking, 'What's the tagline going to be? 'Merry Christmas, Motherfucker!' But Tom was dead set on that release date, so it opened on Christmas Day and it didn't do very well. I think it grossed around $10 million or $12 million in its US domestic run, which was not even the negative costs of the picture. Either way it disappointed."

"Walter would say the film went down without a bubble," Sadler says, "and it certainly wasn't launched and it wasn't received in the way that it should have been. But there was so much about *Trespass* that was cool. Walter was in his element; he had all the toys in the world on this great shoot-'em-up movie. So it is unfortunate that the release of the movie was as awful as it was."

Had the film been released into a cultural milieu less fraught with civil and racial unrest, and with the backing of a more supportive studio, *Trespass* might have ended up a more well-remembered film than it is. The film is as deserving of pop-cultural discourse as *The Warriors* or *48 Hrs.*, but despite being one of Hill's finest, *Trespass* remains largely unsung. Here, Hill has surrounded himself with collaborators who contributed to making the film one of the director's most immediate, original, and exciting contributions to the action cinema canon. While it may not have lingered long in the cinematic consciousness, it is justly remembered by those who made it at an important moment in their careers. For Sadler, working with Hill meant an opportunity to experience a tradition of filmmaking that goes back to the early days of the masters of American Cinema. "I really enjoyed making *Trespass*," the actor states. "Working with Walter felt like I was working with someone like John Ford, or John Huston, or one of the greats from the old westerns. He is a craftsman. He doesn't hold himself out as anything special, he just has a vision of what he wants and gets it. Walter told me about how he worked in the days before there was video playback, when if he wanted to see what the camera was catching, he would stand with his head right next to the camera and watch the scene and watch the actors. If he felt that the whole thing lifted off the page and it felt real to him, then he would then turn to the camera operator and ask, 'Was that in focus?' and if they said yes, then he would say, 'That's the one! Let's go, we're on the wrong set.' That was the world he grew up in, where you trust your instincts and you hire people whose instincts you also trust, and you give them free enough rein to bring everything they've got to the story."

"I think *Trespass* is a terrific movie, but most people haven't seen it or even know about it, which is a shame," Canton says. "It just got lost in the craziness of Rodney King and the craziness of the real world that was happening around it. The film hasn't found a cult audience in the way *The Warriors* has, but when I was teaching at the AFI I would have students from all over the world who wanted to talk about *Trespass*. They really liked the film and wanted to know about what happened, and you have to put it in context for them."

"I love *Trespass* and I love Walter," Gale admits. "I think he did a fabulous job with it. I don't think anybody could have made a better movie out of our script than Walter did. I don't see him that often but every now and then the three of us—Walter, Neil, and I—meet for lunch. So, I do have a lot of fondness for that movie."

As Walter Hill and producer Neil Canton were coming to the end of production on *Trespass*, the pair had been discussing what potential films lay ahead. Hill mentioned his desire to bring to the screen a long-gestating project, a western based on the life and exploits of famed Apache warrior Geronimo. Canton was familiar with the script that Hill had gotten filmmaker John Milius to write several years prior, with Hill having sought the producer's feedback on the property as a potential project. Canton was naturally drawn to the material, having been fascinated by the myth of Geronimo ever since seeing John Ford's *Fort Apache* as a child, and was therefore keen to get the project off the ground to make it his and Hill's next collaboration. Hill wondered if they would be able to find an appropriately supportive home for the project, so Canton endeavored to get the film set up at a studio, and it didn't take long for the producer to find an intrepid Columbia Pictures ready to work with the duo. The Milius script had taken the form of a temporally all-encompassing biographical film, but a comprehensive account of the warrior's life is not what Hill had in mind to direct. Rather he was interested in presenting a harrowing look at the conflict that took place between the United States Cavalry and the Chiricahua Apache tribe. With Milius long gone from the project, Hill rewrote the script; his revised drafts retained the essential structure of the original screenplay, but embellishments Hill made ultimately deconstructed the biographical form of Milius's initial version as he crafted a chronicle of war. Several months before filming was due to begin, *48 Hrs.* and *Streets of Fire* co-screenwriter Larry Gross joined the *Geronimo* camp to assist in what would become the final draft of the script, specifically adding further elements of character and nuance.

The film is framed from the viewpoint of Second Lieutenant Britton Davis (Matt Damon), who joins First Lieutenant Charles Gatewood (Jason Patric) and Chief of Scouts Al Sieber (Robert Duvall) as they track the titular Apache leader, Geronimo (Wes Studi), after he absconds from a reservation on which the US government expected the Apache Indians to dwell. This settlement is under the command of Brigadier General George Crook (Gene Hackman), a respectful admirer of Geronimo's fierce fighting resolve in the face of such oppression. Despite surrendering,

Geronimo's nomadic spirit cannot remain on such a limited piece of land. It is not in his nor his people's nature to accept this false idea of "home" as decreed by the White-Eye, and so he flees. In the aftermath of Geronimo's escape, General Crook resigns from the army and is succeeded by the autocratic Brigadier General Nelson A. Miles (Kevin Tighe), who sets out his troops in place of scouts to bring Geronimo back to the reservation. A blood-soaked pursuit ensues and results in another, ultimate, surrender by Geronimo.

For Hill, the story of the Apache wars with the American army contained far more complex social implications than the traditional western format of old was capable of conveying with any kind of subtlety. It would have been easier to take the conflict between the two sides and make a western of simple black-and-white morality, of "good and bad," as many of the more generic and less-contemplative westerns had in the golden eras of the genre. But that wouldn't be acceptable in the 1990s. This film needed to be more considerate of the details of the characters and to translate that into a dramatically interesting and commercially viable property. *Geronimo: An American Legend* eschews the popular sentimental approach of its western peers in favor of a typically tough, no-nonsense narrative that one would expect from Hill. As pretty as the film is on an aesthetic level, with its painterly mise-en-scène and richly expressive colors, there is a starkness to the proceedings; as with *The Long Riders,* Hill is tasked with maintaining truth in his depiction of real-life characters and even though there are moments of justified violence, the director never makes a claim for heroics—these are men who are struggling to maintain dignity in a changing landscape, facing the adversity of oppression and despotism. "With *Geronimo* we stuck to the history pretty well," Hill says, "but we conflated certain things. The film really should have been called *The Geronimo War* because when you call it *Geronimo* it sounds like you are doing a biopic of the man and that was not the idea. It was a story about the tragedy of the last time they broke off a reservation and went down to Mexico and almost starved to death. I was struck by the memoirs of so many of the soldiers and how many of them were sympathetic to their opponent, not all of them,

Geronimo (Wes Studi, left) and Charles B. Gatewood (Jason Patric) survey a hostile landscape in *Geronimo: An American Legend* **(1993).**

but many. The army wasn't so much the enemy of the Native Americans as it was the settlers, and they were insatiable in their demands. Look, everybody, including the Native Americans, had many transgressions too, but it was not an equal fight."

Gross recalls, "Walter certainly saw it as a war film. We had a conversation over dinner one night after I got the *48 Hrs.* job and he explained that he approaches every project from the standpoint of *The Iliad*; everything is about the Greeks and the Trojans, and to me *Geronimo* is the most monumental of the Greeks and Trojans movies that Walter has made. He said that the Greeks knew everything that everybody has ever known about how to construct drama, and all we're doing is footnotes to Sophocles and Homer, and that's what I like about westerns, they are Homeric. When we would have discussions about film history, Walter would say, 'There are two ways to go: there is social and psychological realism and there is the road of myth and archetype, and I'm more interested in myth and archetype, with the appropriate amount of social and psychological realism that is necessary to the story.' The dialectic of those two are more complex in *Geronimo* than most of his films. There is the literal historical accuracy, which on one level you feel as part of the experience, and the other element present is the archetypal battle, the myth, and I think both things are there and make the film incredibly complex and rich. There are big statements about big concerns, and I just felt lucky to be along for the ride."

Gross reveals that it was Hill's encyclopedic knowledge of the subject that provided him with all the research he needed to craft his part of the story. "People ask me if I did a lot of research on Apache folklore and culture when I was working on the script, but I did none," the screenwriter admits. "I just asked Walter questions. He read dozens of books on the subject and knew all the facts of the story in such detail. I think it is safe to say it is the most historically accurate depiction of the Cavalry-Indian wars. Everything in the script is a little bit off from the facts, but it's like six inches off; we have three guys but there were actually five guys. Everything in the film is based on something that happened and is close to the real events, and I'm very proud of that aspect of the film. But it wasn't my talent or my knowledge, it was working with Walter. I ended up going out to the set to Moab with him for the first two or three weeks of production and I was also very involved in the editing and writing of the voiceover narration by Matt Damon's character. That character was not really in Milius's script, so I wrote several scenes between Matt Damon and Jason Patric and a number of scenes with Robert Duvall. There were things about the characters that we worked on, trying to enrich them and make them more detailed. One of the things we were very, very pleased with was Jason Patric's performance. We thought he was great and we really hoped it would make him a star, but it didn't have the impact that we had hoped for. It's not a consoling character."

A stellar cast abounds, all uniformly excellent, but so powerful is Wes Studi in the lead that one can never look at previous renderings of the warrior-leader in the same way again. Studi brings his character to life with such impact and conviction that it will mercifully erase all memory of Chuck Connors as the titular character in Arnold Laven's unfortunate 1962 western, *Geronimo*. Robert Duvall also deserves special praise for his performance of the conflicted scout, Al Sieber; in one of the film's finest moments, the actor's portrayal of Sieber's death is a feat of subtlety. "Duvall is a brilliant actor because he is such a minimalist," Canton says. "He is doing all these wonderful things, but you don't actually see them as he is doing them; he is so subtle, but it is there on the screen. Duvall achieved the moment of Al Sieber's death so economically—he says, 'I'm just going to go to sleep for a few minutes,' and he closes his eyes and he is gone."

Hill concurs, "Bob Duvall is very good in his death scene. We did it in one take and I said, 'I think we got it,' and he was very pleased because he doesn't like doing a lot of takes. But he said, 'Maybe we should just do one more,' and so we did one more. He did it exactly the same and we used the first take. I think that whole sequence is one of the best I've ever shot."

Canton continues, "That scene is also a perfect example of Walter's storytelling. Duvall didn't want to do a movie where he died, so that scene wasn't in the original script, but as we were telling the story we felt that he needed to die and so Walter came up with that scene and Duvall agreed to do it. When we shot the first take, Walter said, 'Print!' It was a fantastic take and Walter turned to me and said, 'We don't need to do another take,' and I replied, 'We have to do another take, what if something happens in the lab? What if the negative tears? What if something goes wrong and we lose the footage? We need to have a second take.' So, Walter agreed to do another one exactly the same and that was it. It was like you were watching absolute perfection in performance, direction, and cinematography. *Geronimo* has some of my favorite scenes of any film I've made, such as when Robert Duvall and Gene Hackman say goodbye, it is just total respect; or the scene on the train at the end where the Apache are being transported to what is really their death, and an acknowledgment that their way of life is now over. It is an incredibly moving scene."

Of all the striking elements of *Geronimo: An American Legend*, one of the most wondrous things is the cinematography. The film brings together the talents of two excellent directors of photography: Lloyd Ahern and Michael D. O'Shea, the former being the film's chief cinematographer and the latter lensing the second unit photography. The skillful eye of each man results in a visual feast, perhaps Hill's grandest canvas of all. "We shot it in 1.85 and we went anamorphic," Ahern affirms. "We had a great production designer named Joe Alves and we built and designed all the sets east-west. Everything we shot was based off which way is east and which way is west. I shot everything in backlight, so we shot east in the morning when the sun is on the back and on the rim of your hat from behind, and in the afternoon we shot everything going towards the West; we designed the whole fort that way. There are very few shots where you see a cross-light situation; we always moved the actor and put them in another spot if we needed to follow where the sun was and cheat the background. Walter has a saying which I have made famous all over town, which is 'the audience knows what we tell them.' We cheat the geography of a set in order to get the best shot; if the audience were to stand on a set and look around they would think they know where the shots should be set up because they would see the geography and think, 'This is how it has to be,' but the geography is what we tell the audience it is. If I like another part of a set because it gives us a better shot, then we'll just move the actors and change something in the background to match up. People call it 'cheating' but I call it 'creating a better image.'"

Geronimo would be the third film on which Bobby LaBonge operated the camera for Hill, and here with Ahern he creates a dynamic and beautifully framed cinematic experience. "*Geronimo* is incredibly cinematic," LaBonge says. "It was shot with an anamorphic lens around the magnificent mountain ranges near Moab, Utah. I was so proud of working on it that I rented a movie theater in Westwood and invited around 80 or 90 of my family and friends to see this movie at noon on a Sunday and they all walked out of that theater stunned. They could not help but be awed by the visuals. Lloyd did a wonderful job with the photography on this film."

"Another reason that picture looks so good is because I put tobacco filters in there, which gives it a tinge that makes it look different," Ahern states. "I put those tobacco filters in the whole movie; I was really taking a chance with that. When it came to dailies, I was thinking, 'I like it, but I wonder if everybody else likes it,' and I wasn't so sure if they did, but I do know that if they hated it, they would have said that they hated it. I would ask Walter if he heard anything back about the filters, and he would say, 'All I hear is that they think I found some young genius cinematographer. Don't worry about it.' But I do know some people didn't like it or were scared of us using it, so that was always in the back of my head. One of the important things you do in life is when you've got half a doubt in your mind about something, but you still go ahead with it, that is a big moment in terms of the breakthrough in who you become as a person; you've got to confront your fears like mad and plow through them. That's what I was doing the whole time on that movie; I had the confidence that what I was doing was good. Even when people questioned it, I would say, 'No, it's fantastic! If they don't like it they can change it in postproduction.'"

Adding to the incredible pedigree of talent on the film is Michael D. O'Shea, shooting second unit cinematography, while Allan Graf directs those portions of the film. Like Hill and Ahern, O'Shea came up through television westerns such as *Gunsmoke* and *Death Valley Days* as an assistant cameraman before making his way into feature films as camera operator on the likes of *Cannonball Run II*, *City Heat*, *The Goonies*, *The Lost Boys*, *The Burbs*, and Hill's *Extreme Prejudice*. He would later become Mel Brooks's cinematographer of choice before putting his unique visual

The glorious Moab, Utah, captured beautifully in *Geronimo: An American Legend* (1993).

stamp on television shows such as *Doogie Howser, M.D.* and *CSI: Miami.* "Another reason why the photography is so good in *Geronimo* is because we had Mike O'Shea as our second unit director of photography," Ahern applauds. "Mike and I grew up in the business together shooting westerns, so we knew how to go out into the desert and shoot because we had been doing it all of our lives. Mike shot a lot of great scenes where he waited until the sun was just perfect."

"Working on *Geronimo* never felt like I was going to work, I felt like I was going to make art," O'Shea states. "My job was to get to the locations that they picked and find the right light and to find the combination of filters that Lloyd liked. It kind of made me look like a hero at times but I got all my information from Walter and Lloyd, and that translated to Allan, who brought his own expertise. Physically, the locations could be hard, but I never felt like there was a lot of pressure; when you went back to the hotel at night you really felt like you had captured something special. Lloyd set the look on that movie; as the second unit director of photography I conferred with Lloyd a lot, and Lloyd conferred with Walter, but they gave us a lot of freedom. Walter is a quiet guy but he likes to have fun too and he keeps guys around him who are like that. Lloyd and Allan are the same way. They have been friends with Walter forever, and even though I only worked on a few films with him, I feel like I've known him forever, he makes you feel like that."

"Sometimes the director or the first unit cameraman doesn't really want to let their movie go to a second unit," LaBonge says, "but Walter is such a respectful person that he would hire Allan Graf, who is an excellent second unit director, and will tell him to go out and make a great fucking movie. He will say, 'Go shoot what I'm asking for, but if you see something you like, shoot it!' He empowers you in the process of making a movie. Beautiful things happen because you've got horses, dust, and a sunrise, and everything comes together as you expected, but then you see another angle that you didn't think about beforehand but on the day it looks great. Walter gives you that freedom, so if you see something that you think looks great cinematically, you can shoot it and he will also acknowledge your contribution, which is again not typical of every director. He will let you know that you have dazzled him, and he will thank you for getting a great shot. Sometimes a second unit can be a little more nimble, you can get around a bit quicker than with the crew size of a first unit, and sometimes you are able to capture things you weren't planning for, and Walter gives you the credit and honors you if you have done something that he likes."

"Allan Graf is a marvelous second unit director," O'Shea states. "I know Allan from way back when he was an extra and then when I shot second unit for him on a football movie called *Necessary Roughness*. At that time he didn't have a lot of experience as a second unit director, though he knew exactly what he wanted in the football stuff and that is what we shot. On *Geronimo* it was fantastic to see him and Walter working together and laying it all out. Walter and Allan have an amazing rapport, they are both big USC guys and Allan played there. Watching them two communicate and witnessing the banter they have made it a lot of fun to be on that set."

"We filmed for three months on second unit," Graff recalls. "It was a lot of work, but we did a hell of a job on it. The cameramen used to love that I would push them to their limits and their work speaks for itself, the photography is majestic on that film. Some of the stunt work we did on that film was unbelievable. There were a lot of stunts on horseback as well as some scenes where we were up 200 feet on the sides of cliffs shooting gunfights. We got some shots where I couldn't see the cavalry from where I was unless I looked through the camera; we used 1,600 millimeters, which gave us some beautiful shots, and Lloyd was using tobacco filters, which gives the film a real unique look. It's one of the best westerns of the time; between the cinematography, the music, and the action, it adds up to a beautiful film. When Walter and I went out to Moab, Utah, it felt like we were out in the old John Ford movies. Neil [Canton] and I would have dinner with Walter a lot out there and we would just talk about how happy we were to be there in that part of the country making a western. We just thought, 'This is real moviemaking!'"

Indeed, being out in John Ford country meant for a spiritual connection to the great cinematic history of the Old Hollywood master. Having just shot the gritty *Trespass* for Hill, Ahern brought majesty and an epic scope to *Geronimo* that evoked the sublime vistas of Ford's films. "All my life I have watched John Ford westerns and marveled at Monument Valley," Ahern reveals, "and when we went out on location I said, 'This is an open invitation to steal.'" Costume designer Dan Moore believes that stepping out into Ford's canvas allowed Hill to indulge in his recurring themes: "When you see Walter out there in the desert directing his movie in John Ford's country, it makes you think about how much it means to him. Walter is always singing the same song, his movies are all about destiny and character, that's one of the themes that runs across all of his films, and it is something that went from John Ford right into Walter's bloodstream. Walter has a great respect for the past, he might have been born a little late in life. You see in *Geronimo* that he has a great respect for the Apaches and he has a great respect for the Cavalry, and to hold those things in tension is really important; he gives everybody his due in that film.'"

Once again, acclaimed musician Ry Cooder was brought in to provide the film with a scintillating score to complement Ahern's stunning visuals, though Cooder wasn't the only notable musician to work on the picture. Legendary composer Van Dyke Parks recalls coming aboard: "Wayne, there is a thing called 'social provenance': who meets whom through whom in what sequential order. I wouldn't have gotten to work on Walter's films if it wasn't for the fact that Ry Cooder was the idol of Walter's eye for his uniquely singular stamp that he brought to the guitar and the attitudes he brought out of the guitar that Walter thought would be a great signature for the Wild West. It's very interesting that Ry did that, and not only in the context of the Wild West but in all of the work that he has done which is not orchestral in intent. The reason we are speaking right now is because at one point during *Geronimo*, Ry was inconvenienced and did not want to work. There was an infinitely long battle scene, an endless montage of blood and guts with Injuns and honkies hammering it out on the battlefield, and Ry didn't want to do this stuff because it was five minutes of ho-hum. He didn't want to continue doing the picture and I don't blame him at all, it is a herculean task, and it is a discipline to stay transparent. So, Ry called me in and I had fun picking on the cellos. I remember recording one cue for this battle scene that I'm referencing and the first cellist held aloft his bow with a white bandanna on it. He was saying 'I surrender!' because it was so lengthy and complex. But I want to mark my gratitude to Ry."

"The music played a big part in that film," LaBonge says. "Walter was using Ry Cooder's music as well as some historical Indian pieces and famous calvary marching songs, all of which really added to the whole authenticity of the experience."

A big-budget western would have been considered a risky move for any studio to undertake in the early nineties, after the genre spent a decade out of favor in Hollywood. The *Heaven's Gate* debacle had appeared to seal the fate of the western upon its disastrous release in 1980, thus not many high-profile studio westerns made their way to the big screen throughout that decade. Those that did offered subversions or deviations, rather than sincere adherence to traditions of the genre. Lawrence Kasdan's *Silverado* is a nicely photographed adventure but it largely functions through a prism of postmodernism, a nostalgic baby boomer evocation of the grand-scale westerns of their youth. Clint Eastwood's *Pale Rider*, surprisingly the highest-grossing western of the decade, was far from traditional with its brooding atmosphere and dark fantasy elements, a vision not unlike Eastwood's previous surrealist western, *High Plains Drifter*. Despite the financial success of these high-profile studio westerns, it wasn't enough to encourage Hollywood to reinvest in the genre with any grand effort. Many of the films of the decade that evoked the traditional western style were made for television and often cast country music stars, and so we had Kenny Rogers, Willie Nelson, Kris Kristofferson, Johnny Cash, and Waylon Jennings headlining titles such as *The Tracker, Where the Hell's That Gold?, Stagecoach*, and *Wild Horses*. Elsewhere, filmmakers continued to evoke the mythological and iconographic elements of the genre with contemporary, comedic, futuristic, and even horror interpretations of the western, which appeared in the form of Steve Carver's *Lone Wolf McQuade*, Peter Hyams's *Outland*, Kathryn Bigelow's *Near Dark*, Paul Bartel's *Lust in the Dust*, John Landis's *Three Amigos*, and Hugh Wilson's *Rustler's Rhapsody* (produced by David Giler and Walter Hill). Notably successful was Christopher Cain's self-conscious Brat Pack bonanza, *Young Guns*, written by *Crossroads* screenwriter John Fusco.

And while this trend of calculatedly aware, genre-bending films continued into the nineties, there was a brief revival of the more sincere, nay traditional, western in the first half of the decade, which instilled enough confidence in some studio executives to bankroll an epic of the genre like *Geronimo: An American Legend*. Success stories such as *Dances with Wolves, Unforgiven, Last of the Mohicans, Tombstone*, and the attendant accolades heaped upon them may have pointed to the western film coming back in vogue after a decade of uncertainty, but there were financial failures afoot, namely *Wyatt Earp, Bad Girls, The Quick and the Dead*, and Hill's own *Wild Bill*, which meant that studios remained cautious, resulting in the western once again receding from production slates and popular culture. Indeed, given the elaborate nature of their production, greenlighting a western was an expensive gamble for any company, as Columbia Pictures was to find out with the apathetic reception that would greet their Hill-helmed picture.

"It is an incredibly beautiful movie," Canton says. "I love everything about it, except I wish it would have done more at the box office. Time has been good to it, but when it came out it didn't get its due. Ted Turner was doing a series on Native Americans on TNT and one of the episodes he did was on Geronimo, and that version aired 10 days before our movie came out. I had relatives call me and say, 'We just saw your movie on television!' and I had to tell them we hadn't even opened yet. So, I think that hurt us a little bit."

"Turner had put out a Geronimo film on his channel the week before we came out," Hill says, "and he kind of rode our publicity and their film was a huge hit on TV, so I think most people who were interested in it had thought they had seen it, so we didn't do well. But I thought there was a lot of good material in the movie."

"We hoped it would do better," Gross affirms, "and it did get some spectacular reviews, but I think people had enough ethnic suffering. As it turned out, the annihilation of the Indians is not something people wanted to be reminded of. There were two other ethnic films that year, including one that I very much respect, *The Joy Luck Club*, and the other is *Schindler's List*. Evidently, *Schindler's List* was the holocaust that people did want to see, while *Geronimo* was the holocaust that people didn't want to see. Columbia had made it because of the success of *Dances with Wolves*, and that is a wonderful film in many ways, but it's just not interesting. It tells the story from the standpoint of the Indians' survival, which is partly a true story, but it omits a tremendous amount of the negative part of the story. Nobody gets sick with consumption in *Dances with Wolves* and that's what killed 90 percent of the Indians. There are things that film just doesn't want to look at, and it contrives a fake win for the Indians over the cavalry at the end, which is completely misleading. With *Geronimo*, I felt Walter really let the complexity, the seriousness, and the ambitions of it out of the closet, if you will, and there is a grandeur and a starkness to the film that is very impressive and durable. The other thing is that the film is so unsentimentally straightforward about a disaster in American history, and people have a hard time with that I think."

As with *Heaven's Gate*, a studio's loss was cinema's gain. In making *Geronimo: An American Legend*, Walter Hill created not just one of his finest works but one of the best American films of the last 30 years. Hill made a western that was sincere, soulful, and solemn, just as irony, camp, comedy, and self-reflexivity were all creeping into the genre. The action sequences are thrillingly and stylishly cut, with brief but brilliant use of canted angles and slow motion to emphasize moments of tragedy amid the chaos; elsewhere it is poetic and majestic, stately even. The film holds a special place in the heart of those who worked on it and knew they were collaborating with a filmmaker at the top of his game. For Lloyd Ahern, it remains a touchstone in his career as director of photography: "*Geronimo* is the film I am most proud of in terms of the work that I did on it. There was a wonderful scene with Bob Duvall that I would say is the best thing I have ever shot in my life, but it's not in the movie. It was this beautiful funeral scene where he sings and we shot it with every camera we could get off the truck and we even brought in a couple more cameras; at that time of year the sun went down at seven thirty and we had 10 soldiers, Bob Duvall, and some graves and we were going to shoot the whole scene with Bob singing a song while he is all bandaged up. We put ourselves under the gun to get this big scene in the perfect light within those three hours. So we started at four thirty, probably didn't begin shooting until five thirty, which is when the sun started getting low, and we shot everything again between six thirty and seven thirty. So we had this massive amount of film shot in this great light and then they cut the goddamn scene out of the movie."

Dan Moore recalls a particularly special moment from the production: "One day we were shooting the scene where Geronimo comes into the fort and everybody was there, all the main cast. Gene Hackman had just come in because he was cast late. They kept trying to cast somebody cheaper but it got to the point that we were well into shooting and they still hadn't cast General Crook, so eventually they said, 'Screw it, we need somebody to help carry the movie,' and so they brought Hackman in. So, we were filming the scene with all of the Apaches and all the cavalry there, which means Wes Studi is working, Bob Duvall is working, as is Gene Hackman, Jason Patric, Matt Damon, and around 300 extras. It was a big, exhausting day and it was also my birthday, and someone said to me, 'Gee, Dan, I'm so sorry you had to work so hard on your birthday,' and I said, 'Work hard? This is the most alive I've ever been!' Making that film was an amazing experience."

"*Geronimo* is my second-favorite Walter Hill film," Gross states. "It just happened to be one that I worked on. I don't want to exaggerate or to sound pretentious but I think of Rossellini when I think of that film. There is an objectivity to it which makes it unmelodramatic. It's not pleading to the Apache, and it's not turning a blind eye to the devastating unfairness in the way that the Apaches are treated. The right characters are sympathetic but at the same time they are trapped, they are in an untenable position. It's a very intelligent film that asks you to be intelligent along with it because it makes you think about what you're seeing and what you're watching. I think it's extraordinary."

"I'm incredibly proud of *Geronimo*," Canton affirms. "It was a great story, a great script, and I think we put together a fantastic cast, from Gene Hackman to Robert Duvall, from Matt Damon to Jason Patric to Wes Studi. We told an honest interpretation of the American West, that there was good and bad on both sides, it was not one-sided either way. These people were trying to find out if they could live in harmony or not, but one side was always going to win and we ultimately know who that was. I've seen it a couple of times since its release and I noticed how incredible the sound is and I think Lloyd did a great job; the production design is brilliant, and the acting is fantastic; it's all just so good. Making westerns is one of those wonderful things about making movies. You can never experience a western town with steam trains, people on horseback, and Native Americans unless you are making a movie, because that part of America no longer exists, But if you are lucky enough to be a filmmaker and you are fortunate enough to have somebody finance it, you can find yourself standing amongst a hundred Native Americans and horses in Monument Valley. In a way it's like being a time traveler, which is an idea I really like, and for me, *Geronimo* was really like that. I had the same feeling on *Back to the Future Part III*. It was an amazing experience. I think it is one of Walter's best movies and that is hard to say because he has so many movies that are favorites."

Walter Hill's third western proper is yet another that is partly based in myth and partly based in truth. In the film, Charley Prince (John Hurt) tells the tall tale of the titular "Wild Bill" Hickok and his final days in Deadwood. We first meet Bill in 1867 Nebraska, when he takes shelter from a snowstorm in a saloon; moments later Bill is forced to display his pistolero prowess after an aggressive bar patron dares to touch his hat—"You ought to understand, you ever touch a man's hat." After witnessing just how wild this Bill can get, Prince takes us to the incident that leads to the lawman hanging up his badge: a fateful night in Abilene, Texas, when a barroom melee spills out onto the dark, rain-sodden street where Bill accidentally shoots his deputy. In the ensuing period, Bill moves east to join his friend Buffalo Bill in performing a stage show called *Scouts of the Plain*. However, his time in the spotlight is short-lived as he is plagued by vision issues and is ultimately diagnosed with glaucoma by a Kansas City doctor, after which he soon becomes addicted to "whiskey, cards, and the wastrel's life." Bill takes a brief sojourn to Cheyenne, where he engages in a showdown with an old rival, the wheelchair-bound Will Plummer (Bruce Dern), who calls out Bill as "a coward and a wife stealer." From there Bill continues on through the Dakota Territory and lands in Deadwood, where "get rich quick" is in the air after gold was discovered there. This is where Bill will spend his final days in the company of Calamity Jane (Ellen Barkin) and fighting off the unwanted attention of a youthful drifter with a grudge, Jack McCall (David Arquette).

The film is based upon two texts: Pete Dexter's *Deadwood* and Thomas Babe's *Fathers and Sons*, the latter of which had been adapted for the Broadway stage in the late seventies. After seeing a performance of the play, Hill—who had been considering making a film on Hickok—thought the story contained the right elements for a film and duly purchased the screen rights from the author so as to set about writing a script. But before he could get the film off the ground, Hill was approached by the production team of Richard and Lili Zanuck, who had a deal at MGM and pursued Hill to direct a script they had that was written by Pete Dexter based on his own book. Ultimately, it would be the combination of both Babe's and Dexter's source material that Hill would use to fashion his own script and to make a deal with the Zanucks for what would become *Wild Bill*. Cinematographer Lloyd Ahern was busy filming reshoots of *The Next Karate Kid* at Sony when he received an urgent voice mail from Hill.

"I checked my answering machine," Ahern recalls, "and it said, 'This is Walter, call me right away!' That's all that was on the tape, so I called him and he told me that Dick Zanuck sent him a script and he wrote back to Dick saying he loved it but that he already had his own Wild Bill script. But he thought, 'You know what, if I ever make this thing, Dick might think that I stole this from him,' so he told his secretary, 'Carol, take this script, write a note, and messenger it over to Dick Zanuck so he knows I didn't write this thing overnight.' He wanted Dick to know that he had this already written because everybody steals everything in Hollywood, it is worse than you know, but Walter is an incredibly honorable man. And then Zanuck calls him and says, 'Hell, this is perfect! We'll take your script and we'll take my script we'll put them together. You love parts of mine and I love parts of yours, so let's rewrite it with the best of both of them and go make this thing. And let's do it fast!' So, Walter said they are going to start right away over at Goldwyn and he will be rewriting the script as they roll into production. Walter and I always have around three discussions before we start a film; from the time we get the script we bash everything around about what the film is going to look like, but I didn't really have that luxury with *Wild Bill*. It was the fastest I have ever seen a movie begin production in Hollywood."

And so began the assembling of cast and crew, including many returning collaborators such as Ahern, camera operator Bobby LaBonge, editor Freeman Davies, costume designer Dan Moore, and second unit director Allan Graf. The titular role would go to Jeff Bridges, who leads a fine cast that includes Bruce Dern and Ellen Barkin, as well as a fresh-faced David Arquette. "I think Jeff is very good in it," Hill applauds. "When we were filming that scene on the street where Bill shoots the Texan in the montage of action, we were standing by the camera watching and Lloyd leaned over to talk to me—I don't look at a monitor, I hate the monitors, I like to stand on an apple box next to the camera—and he said, 'Oh Christ, I'm worried that he's playing it too mean. He's supposed to be our hero but he's too mean.' And I said, 'Shit, I'm worried he's not tough enough.' And he just said, 'Yeah, well, that's you!' But the point is Jeff was smarter than both of us, he played it not too mean while remaining plenty tough; he made it agreeable to a viewer with that balance. He is a wonderful actor."

While the screenplay is credited to Hill, Larry Gross also joined the production for uncredited contributions to the script. Gross finds the project to be "one of the movies where Walter comes out of the closet as an intellectual." He elaborates: "I think it is one of the movies where there is a subconsciousness operating here that he does not always allow into his work and that complicates and enriches this film. It's ironic in an unbelievably sophisticated way, and if you know Walter you know how smart he is, but if you don't know him you might think he's masqueraded all these years as a primitive entertainer when in fact he is incredibly cultivated. He comes out as a sophisticate with *Wild Bill* in a way, which is one of the reasons I love the film so much. I can see aspects of Walter in it that are harder to see or are concealed in other films. They're more emphatic here."

"On *Wild Bill* I don't think my intentions were terribly clear because I don't think people knew the character of Bill as well as I did," Hill says. "I wanted to take everything fictional that was said about him as well as the hard truth and I wanted to do a mix. The movie is often criticized for being inaccurate about Bill's life, and, well, yes, it is inaccurate but it is not inaccurate about the myth of Wild Bill, the mytho-poetic. The central core of it is you have a man who has the choice of living up to his own legend or living a reasonably normal life and he chooses the legend. I think that was true of Hickok, the real Hickok. So, I say that the movie is vastly more accurate than any film that has been made about Hickok."

Marking a break in the run of scores provided by Ry Cooder was the hiring of celebrated songwriter and composer Van Dyke Parks, here returning from a stint working on *Geronimo: An American Legend*. Arranging songs and parlaying the kind of haunting, reverberating piano tones that he brought to the mystical moments of *Crossroads*, Parks brings an element of authenticity and an askew musicality to accompany the often experimental proceedings. "I knew Van Dyke from Ry," Hill says, "and they knew each other from back in the Warner Bros. Records

Wild Bill (Jeff Bridges) "evens the odds" as he is strapped in for an unusual showdown on the streets of Cheyenne in *Wild Bill* (1995).

Bill's handicapped nemesis is old foe Will Plummer (Bruce Dern) in *Wild Bill* (1995).

days. Van Dyke did a lot of music for us on various scores for my movies. That magic piano music in *Crossroads* is Van Dyke, and he also came in and did some things on the *Geronimo* score. And, of course, the music on *Broken Trail* was very much Van Dyke along with David Mansfield. Van Dyke has a very open personality and he is a million laughs. He is a great storyteller and a very good positive force. A wonderful guy to be around."

Gross was particularly happy with Parks in the composer's seat, as he recalls that "Walter was thinking about the music in a deeply fundamental way on *Wild*

Bill. It is profound, and I felt it was even more profound when I saw the film with the cut footage, but I can honestly say that it's the interaction of the music within the action that is to me the single most successful and powerful thing about the movie. The music is so important."

Parks recalls the challenges of scoring an entire picture for an auteur filmmaker while working within the hierarchal corporate constraints of a major studio:

"To work on a picture like *Wild Bill* is to be out of the box for sure, it is beyond the ho-hum of the present tense and I think it is a highly meditative process as well. And that is without losing a beat and in terms of being inferential. Working on *Wild Bill* was a musical challenge and I am reminded of something that the composer Jerry Goldsmith confided a long time ago; he said, 'When you're watching a man on a galloping horse, don't score the hooves; score the mind of the man.' In Walter, you have a director who is eminently sympathetic and understanding and learned, and I don't think Walter was reduced to a conversation with me when preparing the score for *Wild Bill*, or at least in any such depth or detail; he is not that dogmatic a man ... but I did get some clear instruction from the hierarchal superiority of a 'music supervisor,' which I believe is what she was called. Bunny Andrews was her name. There was, in this particular situation, and as there are in any, a standard ordinary procedure in that the composer will arrive and a temp track is in place. So the temp track becomes a directive and I always try to consider that very carefully and think, 'Should I not be creative? Should I just stand there and that's all?' And also, you have to think about how to reconfigure the temp track, or whether to just reject it entirely. That is a very hyper-disciplinary consideration for every composer no matter what his bravado is with a bottleneck or anything else, because you are up against a hierarchal superior and that's the person who oversees what's beyond the moat at its castle of authority; that's who guards the gate. But it used to be the other way around! It used to be that the composer was the intellectual property; before they flounce the belly they should have kept the brain. But it was another era when the composer was considered an intellectual property, and it does happen occasionally these days, but I confess to you that my job on *Wild Bill* was highly reactive and just to get it done required a supernal talent and patience and I'm so proud of the fact that I did that. I did not bring originality to it."

Parks's score was set to some of the most avant-garde imagery of Hill's career, as here the director juxtaposes a mixture of the rich, sumptuous color film stock with the fuzzy, washed-out video footage of the psychedelic flashback sequences. Ahern had embraced this contrast of style previously on *Trespass* and here he incorporates a similar creative approach to amplify the illusory nature of the narrative. The film's opium-induced dream sequences inform the film with a surrealist edge that is unusual in the realm of the western. With its degraded, not entirely decipherable imagery, variety of inventive camera angles, and manipulations of color, this experimental aesthetic allows *Wild Bill* to break from western genre tradition, which is to say the film is much looser and more playful than the standard western picture that usually keeps within the boundaries of diegetic reality. "*Wild Bill* was a very experimental movie," Hill says, "an unusual film in many respects; unusual in structure and unusual in its content. Several people have accused me of making a movie about myself. I had a lot of fun doing it."

To shoot the flashback and dream sequences, cinematographer Ahern bought three consumer camcorders, each costing $500 and far from professional grade. Ahern gave each of his operators a camera and told them to just film anything to get use to the technology and handling of the devices. After the footage came back looking decent enough to use, they set about shooting the required sequences that would utilize the video footage.

"*Wild Bill* was fun to shoot," Ahern says. "We got to do some interesting things on it, visually speaking. The first day of shooting was with these lousy camcorders up in the Angeles Crest Highway forest, we were up about 40,000 feet in May and we were shooting one of the flashback scenes which is covered in snow. The studio had already been there for days laying that snow down; they had these snow machines making it and laying it as far as you can see, if you look at those scenes you will see that the snow goes off into the horizon. This was the first week in May and it could have gone either way because of the Southern Californian weather, it could be very hot or very cold and it happened to be very cold so the snow stuck. But I was nervous as hell that something is going to happen and the snow will start melting or something. I wanted to make sure we were rolling and that everything was good to go because we weren't coming back to shoot here again; we had the snow machines in place and all these hotels were booked for everyone, so it was a big financial undertaking. We were shooting these scenes all on video, we were not shooting any film for the whole three days we were there. So because we were going to be shooting for three days with just camcorders, I showed these tests that we did to Dick Zanuck, the head of the studio. I wanted them to know how it was going to look when we switch to the black-and-white scenes. But when Lili Zanuck, Dick's wife, saw it she flipped out; I didn't realize she had to know about it because she was a producer in name only. But Dick Zanuck was a smart, cool guy and very easygoing, but you didn't want to screw with this guy because you knew he made a lot of great movies. So he liked the look of it and approved of the idea.

"The whole thing was very chancy and very revolutionary. One day Walter said, 'Well, what are we going to do if something goes wrong?' and I said, 'We'll have technology save us,' which was a good answer because I didn't know what we were going to do if something did go wrong. We were gutsy and confident but at the same time we were always anticipating the worst-case scenario. We were smart enough to know that something could go wrong, and sure enough something happened on one of the scenes that we shot on video. It was Bill's dream where he is with Diane Lane in the mental institution and we were shooting over in the Veterans Administration Building and in setting up the scene I went completely against my training. There was a huge, old-fashioned window that looked like something from the 18th century; the VA was built in the thirties or forties. So we were shooting her from over his back, it's his point of view looking down on her, a beautiful image of her with this blown-out window and I shot it with the camcorder, we didn't back it up with film or anything. Then one day I was at home in Malibu and Walter calls me up and says, 'You better get in here!' When we shot it we looked back at it on the camcorder instead of seeing it blown up on a screen in dailies; when we looked at it on the camcorder we were confident that we handled it. But I arrived down to Goldwyn and they said, 'Look at this…' and they roll it. And then I see the problem: there's no head in the shot, you can't see Diane's head. She is so blown out by the window that her head is gone. The lousy dynamic range of those camcorders could not handle the window. If it was film, of course it would have been a very beautiful shot, and if it was these days, a digital camcorder would have been able to handle it because they have better dynamic range; what they have now is phenomenal compared to what it used to be on analog. But Walter was like, 'What did you do?' and he is a very funny guy because he can take something that he categorically made a decision on and turn it around on you and make you defend it. It's like, 'Walter, it was your idea!' But it wasn't, it was all of us and I was the one who shot it with the window blown out like that. And Walter says, 'Well, I hope your technology will save us!' So the movie is shut down, it's over, because we don't have a scene because we can't find her head in the shots; we've wrapped. But they found it! They found her head. They somehow put it all back together and if you look at the scene now it is really beautiful in a crazy way."

It is this kind of unique creative input and vision of artists like Ahern who contribute massively to what ultimately gets credited as being a director's own formal film style. In this case, such distinctive choices by Ahern do not undermine Hill's authorship. Rather they help bring his director's singular vision to the fore, drawing attention to the kind of fluidity with which Hill can work. In tracing Hill's filmography, no two films look the same, yet there is no mistaking them for the work of any other filmmaker. Hill's well-chosen collaborators have helped translate Hill's written words to an identifiable form of screen grammar that has over time allowed the director's work to be immediately recognized as a Walter Hill film. "Collaboration is not the antithesis of authorship," Larry Gross says, "it is the way the highest level of authorship is achieved, by being able to absorb into your vision the capabilities of the greatest collaborator. Walter is very eloquent on this subject of collaboration and auteurism, as I found out after I made an off-topic remark about how Woody Allen had only become a real director since he met the cinematographer Gordon Willis, who was a gigantic talent who added a visual element to his movies that hadn't been there before. Walter said, 'Yeah, but don't get the wrong idea. You're wrong if you think somehow it's Gordon Willis that enabled Woody Allen to be Woody Allen; it's Woody Allen that's making you see Gordon Willis's contribution to Woody Allen.'"

"Walter encourages a sense of creativity on his sets and that makes everything better," Ahern affirms. "That sense of fun and boldness is very contagious because it gets crew members involved. A lot of the time people are afraid to speak up and express an idea because they expect someone will say, 'No, you idiot, we can't do that!' Well, there is no stupid idea in movies. If you hear two ideas that don't work, then someone will come up with a third idea that does work, and they mightn't have reached that good idea if they hadn't heard the two ideas that didn't work. If the director and the cinematographer want to be the smartest people on the set, then you are going to have stagnation because the crew's brain stops working. I learned as a camera operator and camera assistant that when directors or cinematographers try to be the smartest guys on the set, I check out emotionally and intellectually; it's like, 'Okay, I'm not going to help you.' But then you have guys who love getting creative ideas from other people. I don't mean everybody is going around lining up shots and telling you what to do, but it's people quietly relating ideas they have which they think might make something better. It's very easy to read the room and feel when people are behind you, when they are neutral, or if they are with you or against you. On *Wild Bill*, as on every film, Walter was constantly coming up with ideas and also bringing out the creativity of those that he chose to work with. It was a collaborative effort and the results of that are there on the screen."

"*Wild Bill* is my favorite film of Walter's that I've worked on," Gross admits. "I worked on it uncredited, but I had a fair amount to do with writing the voiceover narration. It's a movie that is so full of rich elements, the supporting actors are fantastic—you have John Hurt, Ellen Barkin, Bruce Dern, and obviously Jeff Bridges, and it's one of the best casts of any of Walter's movies. I think it is a great film which is very idiosyncratic in all sorts of ways. Walter told me the divinity behind that film was going to be Orson Welles and I think it's a profoundly Wellsian film. Walter spent a lot of time editing and re-editing; there were terrific things that aren't in the finished version. There was a whole lot more in the original script and film about the theatrical production of Wild Bill, the traveling circus show, and that's something I missed very much in the final version of the movie. But with that being said, I do think the choices that he made were the right ones."

Hill would return to the South Dakota town of ill repute when he directed the pilot episode of David Milch's *Deadwood*, which premiered on HBO in 2004. Throughout its three-season run, the show would feature many faces from the Hill filmography, including Keith Carradine, Allan Graf, William Sanderson, and Powers Boothe. The first episode was shot by Lloyd Ahern and edited by Freeman Davies, making this much more than a "guest director" slot for Hill. That year's Emmy Award for Outstanding Directing would be bestowed upon him for his efforts, though by this point Hill had exited the show amid postproduction disagreements. And while it is tantalizing to consider what kind of quality Hill would have brought to the show as it progressed, his big-screen sojourn to Deadwood means *Wild Bill* remains his definitive moment in the company of Hickok and Co.

Hill's next period opus is also one of his most misunderstood films. *Last Man Standing* is a brooding crime thriller that boasts a big star in Bruce Willis, here playing John Smith, a mysterious drifter driving across the Texas plains in his Ford Model A coupe as he makes his way to Mexico, where he "needs some time to hide out." You see, Smith has spent much of his life getting away from trouble, but trouble soon finds him. Smith meets a fork in the road and lets fate decide which path he will take—"You go one way so you can try to live with yourself. You can go the other and still be walking around but your dead and you don't know it." Unfortunately for Smith, a spin of the bottle points him in the direction of Jericho, a border town torn between two rival bootleggers who are locking horns over control of the local booze rackets. One mob is Irish and the other is Italian, and both vie for Smith's allegiance and skill with two pistols. Without loyalty to either faction, Smith manipulates the situation for his own gain and plays them off against each other.

With an undefined past, Smith emerges mysteriously out of the shimmering sunshine of the Southwest landscape, a lone Ronin in a waistcoat, and by the end of our time spent with him, he disappears once again into the dust. The character shares similarities to Charles Bronson's Chaney from *Hard Times* in that both men are spectral, stoic figures who enter the lives of those engaged in illicit financial gain (bootlegging, bareknuckle boxing), put themselves through pain and brutality, experience a fleeting moment of romance, and then they retreat back into themselves and onto the road to nowhere. *Last Man Standing* is a legitimate adaptation of Akira Kurosawa's 1961 samurai film, *Yojimbo*, credited as it is to Kurosawa and Ryūzō Kikushima, transposing the story from post-feudal Japan to Prohibition-era America. Of course, *Yojimbo* was remade before, unofficially so by Sergio Leone in 1964 with *A Fistful of Dollars*. If *Last Man Standing* takes anything from the Leone film, it is in Bruce Willis's taciturn rendering of John Smith, who carries himself in the same vein of Clint Eastwood's similarly tight-lipped "The Man with No Name." Of course, John Smith, as the name suggests, is a Nobody. Another notable influence on all three filmmakers—Kurosawa, Leone, and Hill—may have been Dashiel Hammett's 1929 novel, *Red Harvest*. In fact, it is *Red Harvest* to which *Last Man Standing* feels most in harmony with, given that Hammett's novel is also set in the Prohibition era and deals with bootlegging gangsters, rather than 17th-century swordfighters or 19th-century gunslingers. Ultimately, *Last Man Standing* is unlike any previous incarnations of the story, distinguishing itself with a gorgeously rendered vision of the American Southwest of the 1930s that juxtaposes explosions of extreme violence with moments and moods that are contemplative, poetic, and even melancholic.

"You're right, there was a great deal of melancholy in it," Hill says, "and I think that's why I'm happy to say Mr. Kurosawa liked the movie, because it attempted to add a perspective on the heroism and there was a kind of conscience to it that separated itself from his film. I wasn't doing a remake. I was doing an adaptation. The only reasons that I was doing the movie really is because when I had been sent the possibility of redoing *Yojimbo*, I said, 'No, I'm not going to do that. I'm not nuts. Never remake a good movie.' So, they came back to me and the Kurosawa family said they approved me. I said, "I will do a script and it will be a very loose adaptation, it will not be a remake, but I'm not going to commit to it as a director." So I did the script and it met with Mr. Kurosawa's approval and the family approval, so at that point the walls were closing in and it seemed like an unseemly gesture to turn down my own script. I kept saying, until the day I finished postproduction, 'This is an adaptation, not a remake!' And of course the film comes out and every fucking review says, "Walter Hill's remake of Akira Kurosawa's *Yojimbo*..." and I'm like, "What the fuck!"

Yes, *Last Man Standing* shares the structural modeling of its preceding films, but that is all. While Kurosawa retains a serious manner throughout his film, and Leone displayed a flamboyant formalism in his spaghetti western take, Hill's approach is neither as sober as the former nor as absurdist as the latter. It is a singular film with a unique style all its own. The clothing, artillery, and automobiles on display are identifiably those of the urban crime picture of the 1930s, but Hill transplants them to a dusty southwestern setting, the kind that we are more used to seeing being populated with ponchos and pistols rather than tailored suits and tommy guns. Hill plays with and blurs the iconography of both genres to further the dreamlike atmosphere of the film; it is a thrilling combination that results in what could be called a Wild West mob movie. But unlike most gangster pictures and westerns, both of which are rooted in a mythologized form of social realism, *Last Man Standing* remains a deceptively surrealist picture that feels like it exists in its own comic-book-like universe untouched by external concerns or character histories; without explicitly saying it—as *Streets of Fire* does—John Smith's journey to Jericho feels like a trip to "another time, another place." Ry Cooder's ethereal score alerts us to the dreamlike tone in the opening frames before introducing a hard-edged blues guitar riff as John Smith's theme; much of the film is led by the composer's beautiful ambient pieces that convey a lyrical beauty as well as a depth of emotion that is never uttered by its characters. Accompanying Lloyd Ahern's sumptuous monochromatic cinematography, Cooder's haunting music makes the film feel like a fleeting illusory vision.

"I do like working with Ry," Hill says. "I'm not consistent on this but generally I don't want big, full scores or that kind of thing, and I don't want to underline the drama. I want something that surrounds the atmosphere of the film and Ry is very good at that. I'm not one for big musical stings, though there are exceptions. The scores for *48 Hrs.* and *Extreme Prejudice* are big, full orchestral scores."

Last Man Standing is one of Walter Hill's most beautifully photographed works, courtesy of the ever-reliable Lloyd Ahern. As drenched in the southwestern sun as it is cast in the long shadows of chiaroscuro lighting, Ahern manages to bring the greatest visual qualities of the western genre and film noir together, tasked as he is with a setting that suggests both the late 19th century and early 20th century, an era of the horse and the horseless carriage, of cowboys and bootleggers. "I shot *Last Man Standing* with as much of a film noir look as I could," Ahern discloses. "Everything was hard light with deep shadows and we had the costumes of the period. We shot it all in extreme light conditions and we shot it fast. Walter likes to shoot fast; he doesn't like to screw around. It was all down to planning and a real good assistant director. We had an east-west street and it was the same street that we shot *Wild Bill* on; the town we shot it in was the Deadwood set just redesigned to be 1939. The benefit of shooting on an east-west street is that you shoot one way in the morning and one way in the afternoon, and you can time your shots so that you are not sacrificing anything; in fact, by doing it this way you are moving faster, and knowing what you are doing ahead of time means you get so much more work done."

Ahern's camera operator on the film was Bobby LaBonge, who was also responsible for some stunningly dynamic visuals on previous Hill films such as *Geronimo: An American Legend* and *Trespass*. "*Last Man Standing* is a gorgeous movie, I think it's one of the best-looking films of Lloyd's career," LaBonge says. "It was lit for that time period, which was a dark time in America. This film is a great example of Walter's style—it is majestic, cinematic, gritty, and gutsy. Walter's movies are in your face."

Last Man Standing offers little respite from its solemn tone, and it is all the better for it. It is a beautifully stark picture, tough and serious yet infused with great

Cinematographer Lloyd Ahern's beautiful photography captures the climactic carnage of *Last Man Standing* (1996). John Smith (Bruce Willis, standing, left) and Joe Monday (William Sanderson, standing, right) survive the climactic standoff with Hickey (Christopher Walken) and Doyle (David Patrick Kelly).

beauty courtesy of its aesthetic approach. When it is violent it is indeed violent; there is little of the slow-motion frames that Hill lovingly intercuts with regular speed as in the action scenes of *The Long Riders*, *Geronimo: An American Legend*, or *Southern Comfort*; here, the violence is swift and brutal. "When I think of working with Walter I think of guns, a lot of guns," LaBonge recalls, "and a lot of very loud guns in particular! There was a lot of that on *Last Man Standing*, I can tell you. Being there felt as close to being in war without actually being in war: it's loud and it smells and there's all this blood coming from the squibs that the actors are wearing; it always looks so authentic." As with any self-respecting gangster-western hybrid (not that there are many), the film is loaded with kinetic action sequences that called for the expertise of Allan Graf, who once again pulled triple duties as stunt coordinator, actor, and second unit director. It is Graf's flair for spectacular action cinema that makes the film so thrilling and effective in its explosive set pieces.

"We did a lot of second unit on *Last Man Standing*," Graf recalls. "We filmed out in El Paso and we also filmed a lot of it here in LA, and I shot the hell out of everybody on that one. I directed the scene where Bruce comes in and shoots all the guys who are sitting around having dinner, a big action scene. There's another sequence where a guy gets shot and is blown back out of this building and lands on the street. I used this big old stunt guy who weighed about 240 pounds, and he flew 20 feet in an instant. I told that guy, 'When you land and stop, don't move because you're supposed to be dead,' and he says, 'Okay!' So, 'Action!' Boom! I ratcheted him back so fast that he gets blown back, hits this car in the background, and I see blood everywhere. I was freaking out! I'm thinking, 'Fuck, I killed this guy!' I run up to him and I'm like, 'David! David, are you okay?' And he says, 'Yeah, I'm all right. You told me not to talk or move!' The squibs went off and there was fake blood everywhere, but I thought we did him in for real. All of the crew are going nuts because they couldn't believe the stunt, and that is the beauty of doing stunts for real, it gets your adrenaline pumping. But you have to prepare the best you can because a lot of people's lives are my responsibility; I have to do my homework and talk to everybody, and I have to make sure what I'm saying is correct because whatever I tell them they have to believe me. But what other director would allow a second unit director to shoot big sequences like that? A lot of second unit directors fail because they try to make their own movie, they don't stick with what the director wants in his vision. But what I do is stick to what the director wants and stick to the style of shooting that the cameraman has set for the film. Walter and Lloyd had a lot of confidence in me and they were very excited about the footage I was getting."

"Walter likes real stunts," Ahern says. "He wanted the stunts to be shot through the camera, not done later in postproduction. Back in our day we didn't have visual effects and in many ways that was good for us because Walter isn't big into that kind of stuff. You have these Marvel movies coming out these days and they just look like a cartoon, they are nothing but visual effects, but on *Last Man Standing* we shot the stunts for real and that's what made it exciting and gives it the kind of energy which translates to great action cinema. I've asked Walter if he ever regretted not using more effects in his films and he goes, 'No, I prefer the fact that we did it all for real and in-camera.' It put pressure on us, but the result is worth it."

"Everybody who works on Walter's movies are of a very high caliber," LaBonge says, "they are all top-tier experienced filmmakers. To be in that group you are at the top of your game and you are bringing you're A game. We're all working for Walter to make it a better film. He gets the best out of everyone. I will always remember the utmost respect that he gave me as a filmmaker. You know, Wayne, the word 'love' gets thrown around a lot, but all of us who are Walter's soldiers not only think he is wonderful filmmaker but we have a great love for the guy. Moviemaking is a team sport. John Huston once said something to the effect of: 'You write the best script you can, you hire the best cameraman, you hire the best production designer, you hire the right actors, and then you stay out of their way.' You hire the best and you let them do what they do. That's Walter Hill."

Last Man Standing marked Hill's first time to work with Robert Shaye's fledgling production company, New Line Cinema, colloquially known as "The House That Freddy Built" in reference to the fact that Wes Craven's 1984 low-budget horror film *A Nightmare on Elm Street* changed the company's fortunes forever. By the time Hill would join them in making *Last Man Standing*, the company was still a few years away from the mammoth *Lord of the Rings* franchise and was still thinking in the kind of low-budget terms on which it had started out. "The relationship I had with New Line varied between nervous and poor," Hill recalls. "They were very new to making big movies. The producer Arthur Sarkissian was very smart about the whole thing, he worked at New Line before." Reflecting its status within Hollywood as an emerging industry powerhouse, New Line took the gamble on bringing some star power to what was originally conceived and developed as a modest production. Fresh off two box office hits with *Die Hard with a Vengeance* and *Twelve Monkeys*, Bruce Willis trades in his wiseass cynicism for something more dejected and low-key, notably downplaying his normally amiable screen persona. At first it is jarring, as gone is his considerable personality that fueled his most memorable and beloved characters of David Addison in *Moonlighting* and John McClane in *Die Hard*. The film's tone is heralded immediately by the star's subdued voiceover and taciturn performance. With his flat delivery and a gruff low-register voiceover, he is quite obviously channeling the Humphrey Bogart and Robert Mitchum film noir protagonists that the character is indebted to.

"Originally we didn't think we were going to have an actor at Bruce's level," Hill says. "We cast him at the pinnacle of his stardom. The original idea was to keep the movie small and cast an unknown or a relative unknown in the lead role. I was fine with that. But then the studio said they needed a name. So I sent it to Bruce and I got a call saying Bruce is interested in the script, but he is in Idaho and can't leave for whatever reason. I was told to go to the airport, there will be an airplane waiting for you to fly up to Idaho to discuss the script with Bruce. So I flew up there and went to his winter home outside of Ketchum, Idaho. We talked pleasantries for a little while and then he said, 'As far as I can see you want me to play this like Robert Mitchum.' And I said, 'Yeah, that'd be fine!' And that was the entirety of the script discussion. We just talked football after that, then I went back to the airport and flew home and had dinner."

Ahern recalls working with the star:

"Someone told me that Bruce is a very dominant person on the set, but in my experience, if he likes what's going on, thinks it's sufficient, and he looks good, then he is happy. That's the good Bruce. Now, when things are going badly, he is the bad Bruce, and he can be just as bad as he can be good, and both are extremes. Bruce had a toupee at the time and he had this hairdresser with him named Bunny, and you would think with a name like Bunny that she would be a lightweight; well, she was no lightweight, she ruled the roost, she took care of his toupee and if you got approved by Bunny then you were approved by Bruce. After every rehearsal I would ask, 'Bruce, is this going to be a hat or no hat?' And Bruce might say, 'It's going to be no hat.' I knew that this toupee was important and one of the lucky things was the film noir look that I was bringing to the movie meant a lot of shadow. But the movie is also very action oriented, meaning Bruce would be moving around a lot,

Battered and beaten, John Smith (Bruce Willis) remains the *Last Man Standing* (1996).

but Bruce can hit a mark in a gunfight like no other person; some actors couldn't hit a mark if you painted a crucifix down on the ground in yellow, but Bruce can hit a mark like you couldn't believe. I told him, 'Hitting your mark in this movie is especially important because we're going to put a stick through the main light on your face because it's going to put a shadow across your toupee, so you are going to have to hit your marks perfectly as we don't want to see that thing,' and he said, 'Very good, you're catching on.' Before each take I would have five grips, five spots, and they all have the C-stand, and then Bruce would hit his mark and look at himself in the mirror of the camera—it became a mirror because we had a diffusion filter in there to knock the edge off and give it an older look—and the grips would just move the C-stand up and down so Bruce could see where he was being hit with that shadow. So in every shot in which Bruce doesn't have a hat on you will notice how frenetically it is edited; if you freeze-frame it or slow it right down you can see these guys adjusting the sticks, because Bruce is coming in and hitting his mark but he is also moving around ducking bullets. If Bruce wasn't in the mood to go through all of that he would just wear a hat. But having to do what we did to mask the toupee meant it enhanced the film noir look because it added more shadow in the lighting. By the third day of filming, Bruce knew every grip's name, which was unbelievable."

"Bruce has a similar action cinema screen presence to Arnold and Sly but has more range as an actor than those two guys," Hill says. "He came with a reputation of being a real director killer, but I liked him, though he was distant. As long as you are professional you can usually get along fine with these guys because they don't

Walter Hill directs David Patrick Kelly (right) et al. on the set of *Last Man Standing* (1996) (Photofest).

want to waste their time, they just want to get it done." Hill continues, "We all have our own style of directing, everybody's different. I'm a movie director, I'm not an acting coach. There are directors who were acting coaches, and they sometimes do wonderful things; Elia Kazan is probably the most obvious example. I think Kazan changed everything. For years movie directors were all about getting the shot, but Kazan was such a different kind of director working in Hollywood. There are legendary stories about Ford, or Walsh, or Hitchcock, or Wyler, about their refusal to discuss anything with an actor. It was 'get your ass in there and do it!" I'm in the traditional school of "discuss the script ahead of time before you start shooting and then after that keep it brief."

Last Man Standing is quintessential Hill, an unsung masterpiece. Much maligned and rarely discussed in cinematic discourse since its 1996 theatrical release, the film is ripe for reappraisal as one of the toughest and most stylish pictures of the mid-'90s movie milieu. Disappointingly for New Line Cinema and everyone involved, *Last Man Standing* failed at the box office. There may have been a misconception of this being another good-time Bruce Willis vehicle wherein audiences believed they could find the same kind of wisecracks and repercussion-free action that marked Willis pictures such as *The Last Boy Scout*, *Hudson Hawk*, and the *Die Hard* films. But they were in for a shock, as the tone of *Last Man Standing* is neither celebratory nor heroic, it is melancholic and sorrowful; some may even say it is cynical and depressing, but that would be to misunderstand the timbre of the piece.

"When you alter the personality of a movie star sometimes it's tough on an audience," Hill says, "and they were used to Bruce as a more gregarious personality than he played in *Last Man Standing*. The movie was chosen to be the closing-night film at the Venice Film Festival and we had a good screening. The movie did well in Europe. The domestic marketing of the movie was a travesty."

"Not a lot of people understood the film the way you do, Wayne, that it is part film noir gangster picture and part western," Graf says. "You get it. I mean it has the look of both but still not too many people understood that it was playing with elements of both genres. A lot of people were confused by that mix. But I think that is one of the great things about it: that it isn't just a western, it isn't just a gangster movie, and it isn't just big stunts and fight scenes, it is a totally unique experience. That's what makes it an exciting film. And it was certainly never boring going to work on it, because you were always going to be doing something new that day. It's a shame that *Last Man Standing* isn't thought of more highly, because it is a wonderful film. I actually think it is one of Walter's best movies."

"I hope what you are doing with this book will help some of these films gain the recognition they deserve," costume designer Dan Moore says, "because we felt really good about some of these films which aren't so well-remembered, especially a film like *Last Man Standing*."

Hill concludes, "A lot of the time you just go out there and do what you do and it just feels right; I think the most important thing is to not just turn out homogenized, pasteurized product. I like to think that one can bring something of yourself that is distinctly you. Whether they are liked or not, these are ephemeral things. There are movies that are liked in their time that don't hold up very well in the years after, and there are movies that are not liked in their time that take on a greater force. *Out of the Past* is my favorite example. That's a film which is now considered one of the top three noirs but nobody said anything about it for 30 years, and then in the 1970s it began to build in reputation. Time does a funny thing to movies and in ways not predictable. And every filmmaker should know that."

Six

Same Director, Different Hollywood

In perhaps the most unfortunate moment of his career, Walter Hill returned to the realm of the science-fiction horror picture, a genre that he had previously worked in when he and David Giler wrote a draft of *Alien* after Dan O'Bannon and Ronald Shusett took their original story to Brandywine Productions, the company that Hill co-founded with Giler and Gordon Carroll in 1969. Just as that experience had proved a contentious situation, with much verbal and legal fighting throughout the years over the authorship of what ended up on-screen in Ridley Scott's 1979 film, 20 years later *Supernova* would prove an even bigger calamity. The film began life as a script written by horror filmmaker William Malone in the late eighties called *Dead Star*, the idea for which came to him after viewing Philip Noyce's Hitchcockian sea-set thriller, *Dead Calm*.

"I thought that if the premise of that film was set in space it would make a really good science-fiction thriller," Malone says. "So I took that basic idea and changed it quite considerably. My script was about an expedition that had gone out years before to do research near a black hole and nobody had received any word from them, so a rescue ship is sent out and when they arrive to see what's happening there's this crazy guy who has this alien artifact that was actually a machine that could transport you to the world of the dead. When they bring him aboard, all hell breaks loose. The first person I wanted to tap was H.R. Giger. I thought he could add a nice spin to it, and we did a lot of preproduction on it. I went over to him in Switzerland for about 10 days to design various elements of the film. For the first time ever he did a painting of Satan, something he had never done, and it was such a really cool thing."

Malone worked on the project into the early nineties and was set to direct the film, which would be produced by Sunil Shah, with whom Malone had worked on his 1985 film, *Creature*; Shah had a company called Imperial Entertainment that was going to make the film with the view to having one of the major studios pick it up. But that plan didn't work out. "We had an original budget of around $6 million," Malone recalls, "which doesn't sound like a lot these days but it was a reasonable amount of money in 1990 for a high-budget indie movie. We got pretty far into production and then the producers started telling us to make it bigger and bigger, to the point that I was starting to get nervous because I realized they didn't have the money to make it that big, and that is exactly what happened—the project got so large they had to pull the plug. I had a feeling that as the film was getting bigger they were going to bump me out because I hadn't directed a high-budget film before, but they just ended up pulling out of the project altogether around 1991. After that the script did the rounds of Hollywood and was read quite a lot. Many people really liked it and it got very close to being picked up again. But I think what happened was the script got kicked around town for so long it ended up being robbed by various people because elements of it ended up in different films over the years. One particular film was the biggest offender; it lifted major portions from my script. But then after quite a long time, *Dead Star* started garnering attention again and I think the reason for that was because I was doing *The House on Haunted Hill* and that got people excited about my work."

The script was eventually retitled *Supernova* and was picked up by United Artists, who set about making the film with Australian filmmaker Geoffrey Wright, whose previous credits included the controversial *Romper Stomper*. Given his low-budget independent origins, he was a surprising choice of filmmaker for a major studio to hire to direct a big-budget science-fiction spectacle. Not that it mattered, as Wright wouldn't be attached for long. Wright was displeased with the script, rewrote it, and informed the executives at United Artists that this would be the film he was going to make. They disagreed and Wright was taken off the project while the film was deep into preproduction; with a 60-foot spaceship constructed, considerable sets already built, and costumes designed, the studio needed a director fast. Six weeks before shooting was scheduled to begin, filmmaker Jack Sholder received a call from an executive acquaintance at United Artists who wanted him to interview for the job of directing the film. Then, just as Sholder felt poised to take over, United Artists Chairman Frank Mancuso had different ideas.

"It's a very Hollywood story," Sholder says. "But the studio bought the script and decided to make it with a budget of between $40 million and $50 million. This was around 1999 and that was a decent budget for this kind of film; it wasn't a huge amount for a big sci-fi movie but it wasn't small change either. So, I went in for the interview and it went really well as I was the head of production's preferred choice to take over the film, and it would have been the biggest film I had ever done. I normally don't get nervous when making a film. I mean I have had days which were extremely anxiety-producing, but I normally don't get as anxious as I did at the idea of working on *Supernova* because this was a huge production. So, I thought I was going to direct the film, but then I got a call from the executive that I knew and they said, 'Jack, I'm really sorry but the head of the studio, Frank Mancuso, met with Walter Hill—he and Walter have a long relationship and Frank has decided to hire him to direct the film.' This is the guy who wrote *Alien*, his bona fides are pretty good and he has made some very good films, so that was the end of that. Being that I was there just before Walter got hired, I saw what the script was like as he came in, and honestly, it wasn't a great script."

Despite being off the film, Sholder would remain in touch with his acquaintance at United Artists, occasionally inquiring as to the progress of the project; all reports were positive until a year later when he received another call from the studio. They informed Sholder, a former editor, that Hill was no longer on the film and wanted him to take over to recut the footage that Hill had directed to date. "When I came in, Walter had the film scored by The Chemical Brothers, and normally you don't score a film until it is locked, but he had the whole score done. They had a $20 million special effects budget and had Digital Domain, which is Jim Cameron's company, doing a lot of big special effects in the film. They had been editing for about four or five months and this cut was long, around two and a half hours, and slow. Walter's editor, who had cut all of his films, was still there when I came back onto the project but he said to me, 'Look, Walter is off the film and so am I.'"

Amid the bureaucratic problems that Hill endured was the insistence by an inimical United Artists to run the film for a test audience, long before it was ready to be seen by anybody not working on the film. Hill had several scenes that he wanted to reshoot and resisted screening a rough-cut assembly that would never work as a commercially releasable picture, but the studio held firm and would sanction reshoots only if the test numbers came back positive. Despite Hill's abhorrence of the idea, they duly recruited an audience of a hundred people to rate the film. As expected of any unauthorized rough assembly of an unfinished film, the scores were negative. Sholder made plans to reshoot the ending and replace Hill's Chemical Brothers soundtrack with a more traditional score by a Hollywood orchestra. With five days booked to record the score, Sholder was enjoying the process until an unwelcome moment on the second day into recording, when he received yet another phone call from the executive halls of United Artists.

"We were on a lunch break and I got a message from the studio saying, 'Call the editor, he needs to talk to you right away!' So I called him and he said, 'Did you hear?' and I said, 'Hear what?' and he said, 'Francis Ford Coppola is taking over the film! I'm supposed to pack up everything over the weekend and bring it up to Napa Valley so we can edit the film there.' I was just like, 'What?!' So I immediately call up the executive that I had been working with and he said, 'Yeah, I was about to give you a call.' The studio was owned by a guy called Kirk Kerkorian, who was this billionaire who owned hotels in Las Vegas, and he decided he was going to change the management at MGM/UA. So, he got rid of Mancuso and put his own people in, and the person who replaced Mancuso was this guy who had been running hotels in Las Vegas for Kerkorian. He wore these shirts with the lapels, like he was Joe Pesci in *Goodfellas*; he looked like he stepped out of a Martin Scorsese movie. He also brought in this guy who he made the head of production, Chris McGurk, who did have experience in the film business although I had never heard of him. Coppola was on the board of directors at MGM and he finds out they are having a problem with *Supernova*, and Francis says, 'Oh, I can fix it!' So, of course they say, 'Okay, then let's get rid of this Sholder guy and let Coppola fix it!' And that's what happened, Coppola went off and did his thing with it and I doubt anybody ever questioned him along the way."

Longtime Hill friend and frequent cinematographer Lloyd Ahern shot the film and recalls some of the political maneuvering that took place behind the scenes: "Walter cut his version of the film, but there was this woman at MGM, whose name I can't recall, and she had a real problem with it and that's when it became all screwed up. Then they brought in Jack Sholder to re-edit it. There were a lot of creative differences on that film, too many points of view on what they wanted to do in post-production with the story, ideas which were different to the way Walter envisioned it. So it was just mash-mash of story problems."

"The film just got destroyed in Development Hell," Malone says, "So many different people had been sticking their fingers into it over the years that there are not many elements of my script in the final film that became *Supernova*. After Walter, Jack, and Francis worked on it at different stages, and everyone else who had come and gone, very little of the original story remained. But that's the kind of thing that happens in this business. It is heartbreaking, but that's Hollywood."

Supernova as it exists, regardless of authorship, is not without its qualities, and those are largely visual. Lloyd Ahern's photography remains its greatest element. "I'm pleased with the photography on *Supernova*," Ahern admits. "I think it looks good. On a film like *Supernova* there has to be a specific language between the director of photography and special effects coordinator. That is the guy who is putting all of this stuff together and every one of them has their own formula, so you have to adapt to what that this and what they want, not what you want, because those are the guys who have to put this thing together. There is a lot of discussions and planning, you always talk to them ahead of time about what you are going to be doing because you don't come in at the last second with a photographic idea on a special effects movie like this."

"I have a lot of respect for Walter," Sholder affirms, "but those are always strange kinds of situations. You could look at it like this: Walter is a real artist and auteur who was trying to make a film that was different from the usual Hollywood product. But he is being pushed into doing something that he didn't want and so he fought for the film and to preserve his vision, and when push came to shove it was him versus the studio, and the studio had the upper hand because it was their money. I watched the film that Walter put together and, honestly, I thought it was very well done, the look of the film is all him, but I just found it very dark and unfriendly. I think Walter was trying to make it more of an art movie, something that was moody

Captain A.J. Marley (Robert Forster) amuses himself while in the depths of outer space in *Supernova* (2000).

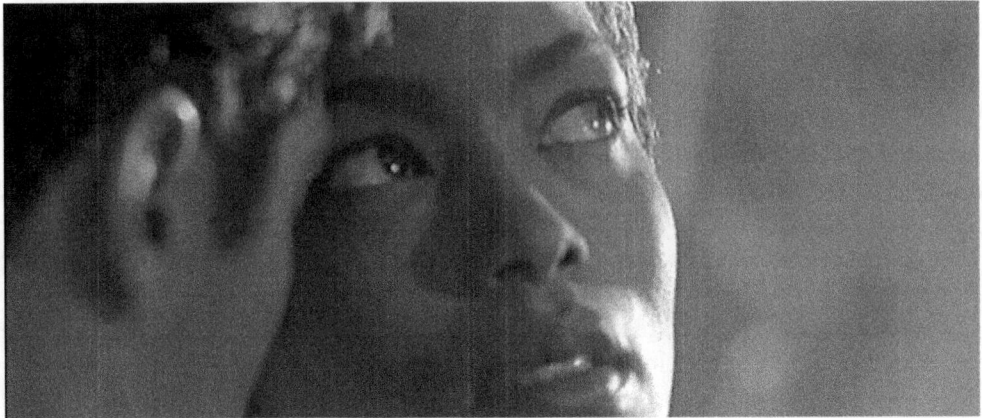

Pilot Nick Vanzant (James Spader) and Dr. Kaela Evers (Angela Bassett) prepare for their journey home in *Supernova* (2000).

and brooding; that was his concept. I think he wanted to make something interesting, a dark and moody sci-fi movie that was Tarkovsky-esque. That's the impression I got. But all of a sudden he has this film that the studio has $50 million invested in and they wanted a movie that was going to make its money back, so when I was brought in I tried to make it more of a commercial movie. I wanted to change the ending to make it little more uplifting or exciting. Through all of this I thought a lot about Walter, and I actually met him one day at a Starbucks and we sat down and talked for about 10 minutes. I don't think it was a talk he was particularly happy to have but he was a gentleman about it because in a way he sort of blamed me, but it wasn't like it was my idea. I was just a guy who came in and did the job. He told me that this was a film he really did have a passion for and he had a clear vision of where he wanted to go but hadn't gotten there at that stage of the editing. He was disappointed about the way things went."

If nothing else, the *Supernova* debacle is a cautionary tale of studio politics gone rampant, a moment of corporate executives meddling so detrimentally with the vision of their artists that a film that has the fingerprints of three distinguished, if disparate, filmmakers such as Hill, Sholder, and Coppola can exist without displaying any signs of authorship at all. The film has been meddled with to the point of being utterly rudderless, an indecipherable mess of a story, and a waste of fine cinematography. "Ultimately, the film had three different points of view," Ahern says, "those of three very different filmmakers, and you can imagine how screwed up that is. When you have a lot of film in the can, you can do a lot with the footage to make a film out of it, so those people had a lot of material to work with. Some directors shoot a film in a certain way that dictates how it has to be cut; it can only be assembled according to the way it was shot because their footage doesn't give you any editorial options. Well, those guys have to be a genius or God, because if they've got a bomb on their hands and people don't like it, they can't fix it. But after Walter left and they brought in Jack Sholder and Francis Ford Coppola, nothing they did was enough to save the film. Everyone was coming at this like they were the film's director, but ultimately it's nobody's film, it's credited to a pseudonym. The version they released is not Walter's film because he took his name off it."

In the aftermath of the dispiriting *Supernova* situation, Hill and his partner David Giler came upon a concept that would take the director back to an edgier and altogether more dramatically interesting milieu that seemed ideal for Hill: prison pugilism. Hill and Giler concocted a scenario that contains some obvious allusions to Mike Tyson's 1992 controversies in its depiction of a champion boxer's legal troubles after having been convicted of a violent sexual assault on a young woman. Hill recalls the moment he and David Giler conceived the project: "My friend and partner—who sadly passed away over a year ago—David Giler and I were having lunch one day and we speculated on the changing things in show business, in the studio system. We thought about how in the old days, as in the thirties and forties, before our time and maybe even during a bit of our time, the studios would seize upon national events and news events and make dramas out of those kinds of things. We were both sports fans, and boxing fans in particular, and we were saying what a great potential story it was that the heavyweight champion of the world had been accused of rape and had been sent to jail. We wondered what this jail would be like if the heavyweight champion showed up. And then what if Sonny Liston, who had been in jail years before, was the champ fighter in the prison. We wondered why the studios don't do things like that anymore. And David said, 'Why don't we do it?' So I wrote the script in about a week and then David and I worked on it together, the way we usually did things."

Undisputed takes us into a hypermasculine world in which heavyweight champion George "The Iceman" Chambers (Ving Rhames) is convicted of statutory rape while facing a civil suit to the tune of $75 million as well as impending tax litigation. His lawyers tell him he is looking at a six-to-eight-year sentence with possible time off for good behavior. If he proves himself a model prisoner he will be eligible for parole in four years. "So it don't matter whether I did it or not?" Chambers incredulously asks his legal team. "It doesn't work that way. Justice and the law are separate issues," his smarmy lawyer informs him. The champ is sent to Sweetwater, a desert prison where he tries to impress upon the population that he is as tough inside as on the outside. Incarcerated mob man and boxing buff Mendy Ripstein (Peter Falk) runs the illegal sporting rackets within the Sweetwater walls and sees a financial opportunity in the tension between Chambers and resident fighting favorite Monroe "Undisputed" Hutchen (Wesley Snipes). If Iceman is to preserve some sense of pride and honor among the prisoner population, which is already predisposed to disliking his wealthy arrogance, he must do so the only way he knows how: to fight. Ripstein ruminates upon the beauty of the brawl when he says, "This is what it's all about: two guys digging to the finish line until one guy is left and it shows he is the better man." However philosophical Ripstein's words may be, Chambers puts it more succinctly: "When you're the champ, everybody wants a piece of you." However, this proves too controversial a scenario for Warden Lipscomb (Denis Arndt), who is more than aware of the public relations nightmare on his hands and duly decides to conveniently take his vacation at the time of the planned main event: "Just my luck he got sent here. Iceman, my ass. He's just another goddamn thug."

Wesley Snipes plays Monroe "Undisputed" Hutchen in *Undisputed* (2002).

"It's a tough little movie," Hill affirms. "It had no interest with a female audience, and it was an all-black movie, which in those days meant it would only fit within the exploitation field. I could have written it where there was another story going on, you know, guys digging a tunnel to get out of the prison or someone having a romance with the warden's daughter, some horseshit like that, but I wanted to keep it very pure. I wanted to make it very linear. I always thought of it as a short story; there's a couple of my movies that I always thought of as short stories. There's much in there that is about the philosophy of fighting, of prize fighting, and prison stuff, about the horror of the modern prison."

With its distinctive Stanley Clarke score, complete with the composer's trademark slap basslines and ambient synth tones, as well as a soundtrack featuring hip-hop stars, the film's aesthetic approach is much in the mold of the urban culture of the period. Even the prefight national anthem rendition gets a hip-hop backing track. The vibrancy of cinematographer Lloyd Ahern's camerawork is the ideal accompaniment to the high-energy sound design, incorporating canted angles and other stylistic techniques as his roving camera observes the pumped-up prison population in the throes of pugilistic fervor. The muted color scheme of the film is occasionally interrupted with kinetic handheld black-and-white flashbacks to Hutchen's boxing days, adding further to the dynamic visual aesthetic. Freeman Davies's and Phil Norden's punchy editing occasionally matches the rhythm of the soundtrack, often creating the illusion of an extended music video, not least in the obligatory training montages.

For his two leads, Hill wanted to cast two black actors, which meant he came up against resistance from potential producers. Only Avi Lerner, of Millennium Films, would dare touch the material as Hill envisioned it, but with the caveat that he would do it only if Wesley Snipes could be cast in one of the starring roles. "Since it was for an all-black cast, nobody wanted to make it," Hill says. "It made sense that the two leads be black because for a long run all the champs were black. The white guys made a comeback in the last 20 years, but for a long time it was mainly black champions. Nowadays I doubt I would be allowed to make the movie because they would want a black director for that kind of material. And that's to do with diversity and this woke society and all of that. But Avi Lerner said he would make it if Wesley Snipes would do it. So, I talked to Wesley and he liked it. Although, the first thing about Wesley is he doesn't look like a heavyweight, he's a smaller man, but he is certainly very athletic. And the Sonny Liston idea kind of went away; the Wesley Snipes role became a different character. Ving Rhames is different than Mike Tyson in many ways too, although his character and Tyson shared a similar predicament. The cast did a terrific job. Everybody knows Wesley is a terrific actor, but Ving is not as well-known and I thought he did very well, he was very good. But they didn't like each other much, so I kept hoping nobody was going to really hit each other. They didn't."

Undisputed proved the unlikely source for a franchise that would be continued by Avi Lerner though without any involvement from Hill. The resulting sequels were produced quickly and cheaply in Eastern Europe, went direct to video, and featured none of the original cast, instead starring Michael Jai White and Scott Adkins, respectively. Indeed, Hill was far more interested in returning to the genre he loved most: the western. However, it would not be for the big screen that Hill would stretch his grand canvas.

Hill's next epic of the American West, *Broken Trail*, began life as a feature film script developed by star Robert Duvall and writer Alan Geoffrion, who approached Hill to direct. However, as westerns were out of favor in the Hollywood of the new millennium, funding proved elusive. On the suggestion of Duvall, Hill agreed to expand the story into a three-hour television film and duly sold it to AMC, which broadcast it across two parts in June 2006. Set in the rugged landscape of late-19th-century Oregon, aging cowboy Prentiss Ritter (Robert Duvall) reconnects with his nephew Tom Harte (Thomas Haden Church) to settle an inheritance issue and to offer him a job assisting in the transportation of 500 horses to Wyoming for sale to the British army. While out on the trail, the pair hire the hand of Irish fiddler Heck Gilpin (Scott Cooper), before running across the conniving Captain Billy Fender (James Remar) and the five Chinese girls he bought as slaves with the

The Iceman (Ving Rhames, left) celebrates being heavyweight champ in Las Vegas in *Undisputed* (2002).

intention of selling them as virgin prostitutes to men of the mining camps. After failing to secure any sexual interest in the women, Fender drugs and robs the three men of their money and horses, then absconds with one of the women. Harte tracks Fender down and hangs him for thievery of the horses and the rape of the Chinese abductee. After saving the girls from a life of shame in a seedy brothel, Ritter builds a bond with them as he takes them en route with the herd of horses. However, the girls were destined for a den of iniquity in an Idaho town that sees its illegal activities run by the local madam, "Big Rump" Kate Becker, who is not pleased that she won't be receiving her inventory. Becker hires merciless killer Ed "Big Ears" Bywaters to track down the girls and bring them back to town for business.

Broken Trail is a stunningly produced piece of television that unfolds in the manner of the grander epics of the western genre. It's a somber and contemplative piece marked with fine performances from all the cast members, but it is the secondary performances that linger longest after the credits have rolled. James Remar's brief screen time leaves a large impression in a scene-stealing performance while, conversely, Chris Mulkey exudes a subtle sense of menace as the chilling hired gun. But it is Hill who must be celebrated for crafting a vast, highly involving story that manages to remain lean and mean, one that doesn't shy away from the more unsettling aspects of life in the American West. "I love *Geronimo* and *Wild Bill*, but I really love *Broken Trail* in particular," composer Van Dyke Parks applauds. "I think it is a picture that was uncomfortable to people because Walter didn't shy away from the incivility of the era, the reality of the west that was won by the gun; that is very uncomfortable for an American audience. But look at what we're up against today, man! This is not the cradle of democracy. Give me a break! There are other solutions than munitions to stop the action and freeze frame."

The music of *Broken Trail* was scored jointly by Parks, returning once again to Hill's western territories, and David Mansfield, the multi-instrumentalist celebrated for his work with Bob Dylan and Bruce Hornsby and the Range and for his exceptional score for Michael Cimino's infamous 1980 epic, *Heaven's Gate*. However, relations between Hill and Duvall had been strained on the making of *Broken Trail* and that chasm remained when it came to deciding upon the music for the picture. While Parks had been an exemplary composer on *Wild Bill* for Hill, Duvall sought Mansfield after he provided a beautiful country score for his 1997 drama, *The Apostle*. In the end, the two men were brought in for a collaboration that resulted in one of the finest scores featured in Hill's oeuvre.

"I had a really good experience with Bobby Duvall on *The Apostle*," Mansfield affirms, "so when it came to *Broken Trail* he wanted me to score it, but Walter wanted Van Dyke Parks. By the time I came on to that picture I found out that Bobby and Walter were at loggerheads all the way through the making of it, from prep onwards. Bobby was a producer on the film and that's why he had some clout and could bring things to a grinding halt if he didn't get his way. Van Dyke used to call it 'Broken Nose,' and it got so bad that they got into a Mexican standoff over it, all the while time was going by and the deadline was looming. So, there was the shock of being on a film where the two principals are fighting, but once I was hired Duvall no longer put up a fuss or became involved, so with all those complications out of the way it was really wonderful, especially being that I was working with such a great filmmaker as Walter and with Van Dyke, who I love and admire."

"It was a set of odd circumstances which brought David and Van Dyke together on *Broken Trail*," Hill recalls, "and this was something that could have been a nightmare situation, but it wasn't, they both did great, they're both gentlemen too."

With the clock ticking, *Broken Trail* proved a different kind of challenge for Parks, who had 10 days to prepare a score and 75 minutes of music to be recorded. "They have an expression at the American Federation of Musicians: 'Do you want it good or do you want it Monday?' In this case, it was both! I told my agent something that my mom told me a long time ago, dear Wayne. She said, 'Van Dyke, do not let your ambition outreach your ability.' She told me that when I was a brunette; I was very young when I heard that from my mother. So I said that to my agent, and I said I'm not that big of a man, I need some coconspirator for this, somebody else with whom we can split the score. And he asked, 'Who would that be?' and I said, 'I will tell you who that would be, that would be David Mansfield.' David played Bach cortinas to my mother when she was ill on the mountains in North Carolina. David and I are perfectly good friends and I respect his music but we had never done a lick of work together, so I said, 'I want to work with David Mansfield on this!'"

"Van Dyke and I have known each other since about 1975 and we said, 'How about we both do it?' At this point, it might even be practical because with the lack of time we could divide up the score, and that worked. Besides being friends we were simpatico enough that nobody could tell who was writing what or anything like that. I don't recall any back-and-forth to say 'this is working but that isn't working.' It seemed to go pretty smoothly. By the time I came on, the film was really at the spotting stage, so we had a spotting session and Bobby wasn't there, it was Walter, Van Dyke, and me. We set everything forth and Walter gave us all the input he felt we needed, so we went off and started working. Once we had that session, he trusted us to work on it and deliver. Being that this was for television and that they had already squandered some time, there was no more time to lose, so we got to work and started sending sketches and cues in. Walter was happy with what he was getting."

While Mansfield had experience in scoring for westerns before, the additional theme of the plight of the young Chinese women brought with it the opportunity to explore the exotic musical styles of the East, which would marry well with those of the West. "I had done a few westerns before," Mansfield says, "including one with my wife, Maggie, *The Ballad of Little Jo*, so I knew what I wanted to bring to it, but the unusual element was the Chinese element and that was fun because I love that music too. I also knew instrumentation-wise and orchestration-wise what Van Dyke liked, so I was thinking of ways to keep us compatible on the sonic palette."

Explains Parks: "*Broken Trail* was a very important picture to me, and I'll tell you something else: David Mansfield has two adopted Chinese daughters and I'm sure he has a phalanx of Chinese indigenous instruments in exotic Brooklyn and beyond in the New York where he hails from. With David it was bang, bang, bang! We traded cues and were having a ball. I was so happy and I really admire him. David made it easy—I don't know how he might have characterized it but it was the easiest job I've ever had. I would call David up and say, 'Do you want to do this next cue or should I?' and I got the one that I loved, which was when they were out on the pasture and it was so beautiful; I got a chance to work with ropes and David was so happy with it, I brought some romanticism to it. Aw, shucks, it was just innocence. I brought music from the Sacred Harp Society of 1886, the '62 Parting Hand.' I did my homework! And I will tell you, Mr. Hill was reduced to tears when he heard it. And do you know why? Because I have the right baggage with me, dammit. I was so thankful that I landed on my feet because part of this whole project was a matter of resource rather than sheer ability; if you look at David Mansfield you will see both. He is resourceful but he is also quite able."

"I did a lot of performing on the cues that I wrote because it was a folk music score," Mansfield affirms, "so we were sending in cues that were in various stages of development but sometimes they were pretty close to what the finished thing was going to be. Van Dyke was working at home in Los Angeles and I was working in New Jersey; I had access to a few really good players for those cues and for the opening of the picture, which had a very Asian hybrid kind of sound to it. It was a great experience. Walter was an encourager. There are directors who work by intimidation and Walter is the opposite of that."

The painterly frames of *Broken Trail* were captured by the ever-reliable eye of Lloyd Ahern, who was blessed once again with a canvas of natural beauty, this time amid the Calgary country landscape.

"When it came to *Broken Trail*, I shot it just like I shot *Geronimo*. Moab is a better location but Calgary is a real close second as a place of amazing beauty. It is one of those great locations where you have a snowcap on the mountains in the morning but by 11 o'clock it is melted off. I would say to the kids who were setting up the cameras, 'If you're looking at something and you think it's pretty, just put the camera on it, and if you are unsure just put the stop on 5.6 to give you some latitude. Just go ahead and shoot it. And if you feel like putting a filter in for something like making the sky a little bluer, do it and shoot it. I want everybody to shoot everything that looks pretty.' We had a ton of wonderful stuff to work with and then they edited it all together to make it look and feel like a big movie. It was made for television but I approached it as I would any film and it looks like a beautiful theatrical release. When it comes to shooting, I have always thought 'you can't have too much.' You don't want to be in the editing room and realize that you don't have that one shot to get you in or out of a sequence, the one shot essential to a scene to make everything work. I used to say to my camera operators, 'Now that we've shot everything the director wanted and that I wanted, let's do the scene with you two guys shooting your own version of the movie.' You can have them grab some extra shots, whether it's a close-up of someone's hand or a shot of someone's face, or something that might come in useful as a transition, little tidbits that you mightn't think much of but which are good to have. Everybody is able use their own creative juices and they may capture something that can save you in the editing room. The actors love it because it's an opportunity to play around and have more little moments to be caught on camera. They already know the dialogue and have the sense of the scene, so just let them go and get one or two takes doing it their own way, maybe don't even stop rolling, do it twice without cutting. And then you bring all of that footage into the editing room and you are able to make a great scene. I used that kind of preparation on *Broken Trail* and it worked out very well because all of that additional footage that I had the cameramen film helped give the movie its sizable breadth."

"The photography of *Broken Trail* is incredible," Parks applauds. "It is the kind of photography that punches up the opportunities for the score. When you cut to these images of the broad sky, you think of Sergio Leone and you get dimension out of it and it offers greatly anecdotal value for the music. Walter's westerns are all heartbreakingly challenging facets of a different, subjective nature. I enjoyed it, I worked hard, and I was in great company. The whole thing was a very civilized project; but then, working for Walter Hill is a very civilized thing."

Second unit director Allan Graf recalls the freedom he was afforded in helping to craft the epic storytelling of the film:

"Walter put a lot of trust in me on that film, as he always does. I filmed all those beautiful sceneries in Calgary, which is great because you've got the Canadian Rockies, you've got all these horses and covered wagons, and you have this amazing backdrop with the snow-capped mountains. We had so many horses on that film, which meant it could be tough to shoot at times. I had to shoot the guys riding and leading the horses. I used an Eyemo quite a lot, which was a crash camera that they used in the war because it could withstand a lot of heavy usage. I would put it on the ground so I could get some great shots of horses running over it. In fact, some people used to call me 'The Eyemo Man' because I would use these cameras to get a lot of extra shots. The editor, Freeman Davies, would say to me, 'If you get me some shots, I'll use them.' So, that's what I did. It was always in the back of my mind that Freeman would be able to cut away to some different shots, something exciting or interesting, if he had the footage. As long as it didn't take any more time or money, I would get as many shots as I could. I remember that Walter wanted a scene with Thomas Haden Church and one of the Chinese girls who likes him a lot, so I had to come up with something and what I did was I shot a scene of them walking along against a lake behind them, a beautiful shot, and I got Thomas Haden to grab a cattail plant and

Prentice Ritter (Robert Duvall) reflects in *Broken Trail* (2006).

hand it to her. It's just a nice moment of two lovers being playful with each other, a little piece of compassion, but Thomas Haden was like, 'What are you doing, Allan? What is this?' And I just said, 'This is what Walter wants.' That's all you have to say. Nobody ever questions you when you say that. And it turned out to be a real good scene in the film. What makes me feel good about my work is that you can't tell which is first or second unit. Walter and I meshed together so well and that made it easy for him to trust me to go and do stuff he needed but didn't want to have to go do. It always felt good when Walter and his editors were excited by the footage that I was getting for them. One time a guy called me 'The Pizza Man' because I deliver. I thought that was pretty good. But I was very proud of the work we did on *Broken Trail*; it is one of my favorite Walter Hill films. It was shown across two nights on TV but it is as beautiful as any movie made for the big screen. It was nominated for a lot of awards and won quite a few, deservedly so."

Indeed, *Broken Trail* was very well-received. It garnered three Golden Globe nominations; won four Emmy awards including one for Outstanding Miniseries; and deservedly obtained an Outstanding Directorial Achievement gong from the Directors Guild of America for Hill. "Duvall and I did not get along so well on *Broken Trail* but he was very good in it," Hill says, "as was Tom and as were the Chinese girls. It won many awards but I wish it had been on the big screen."

It would be another six years before Hill would return to said big screen, and the film that would herald his much-anticipated return was *Bullet to the Head*. A late-career vehicle for Sylvester Stallone, the film sees the inveterate action star play against type as New Orleans hit man Jimmy Bobo, who seeks revenge on corrupt mob-associated property developer Robert Morel (Adewale Akinnuoye-Agbaje) after his partner is killed by Morel's hulking henchman, Keegan (Jason Momoa). In order to bring down the outfit, Bobo joins forces with Detective Taylor Kwon (Sung Kang), whose partner was also killed after getting involved with Morel in various nefarious underworld schemes. The film thrives on the tension and unwitting partnership of the antihero who plays by his own rules, Bobo, and the by-the-book Washington, D.C., lawman, Kwon. Their alliance and grudging respect for each other is cemented as they endeavor to seek vengeance for their fallen partners and save Bobo's daughter from the clutches of the remorseless Keegan.

The film began life as a graphic novel entitled *Du plomb dans la tête* authored by French writer Alexis Nolent, a.k.a. Matz, which was then adapted for the screen by former film critic turned screenwriter and producer Alessandro Camon. Before arriving in Hollywood, Camon worked as a journalist in his native Italy, covering the country's film and rock music scene as well as writing articles on American filmmakers whom he adored. But the writer harbored bigger ambitions: to collaborate with those very artists. And so when Camon arrived in America to attend UCLA, he brought with him a list of directors that he liked and, brazenly, planned to cold-call them. One of those in Camon's sights was Walter Hill, as he recalls: "I would reach out to these directors that I liked and I would say, 'Hi, I am an Italian journalist, I work for this great magazine which is like the Italian *Rolling Stone*.' Which it wasn't, but I would ask if I could interview them for this magazine and most people never returned my call, but Walter did! He was shooting *Another 48 Hrs.* at the time and

When killers collide: Jimmy Bobo (Sylvester Stallone, left) comes face to face with Keegan (Jason Mamoa) in *Bullet to the Head* (2012).

he said, 'Come over to the set and hang out! We can talk between shots.' He was just incredibly generous. I had already liked his work before this but then I liked him personally very much, so I was very happy when he came on to direct *Bullet to the Head*. I'm a huge fan, and it just made sense because it was in the vein of *48 Hrs*."

Bullet to the Head was a rare instance of a journeyman work for Hill, whose involvement was purely to bring the script to the screen. By the time Hill joined the production, it was already a Sylvester Stallone picture in preproduction; it was after original director Wayne Kramer departed from the project over disagreements with its star that Hill got the call. "I had worked with Wayne on *The Cooler*, so I knew him already and I liked him," Camon says, "but Wayne and Sly didn't quite see eye to eye. So, Wayne left and suddenly the movie was financed, it was ready to go. Sly had given the producers a window to make the movie, so they really needed to find a director quickly to replace Wayne. I would like to take credit for it but I think it was someone else who suggested Walter Hill, and I was super happy about that because of my old relationship with him."

"*Bullet to the Head* was one of the few times that I took a job of work," Hill admits. "I hadn't done much in a while and Stallone called me asking if I was interested. Sly and I knew each other for years and we had talked about working together. The source material is a graphic novel by Matz and he and I have since done a couple of graphic novels together. I wrote three of them that Matz adapted for me which were published in Paris. One of them is called *Tomboy*, which became *The Assignment*."

The film was also an opportunity for Hill to reunite with Hollywood heavy-hitter Joel Silver, who is credited here as executive producer and who brought with him a distribution deal with a major studio. However, the legendary powerhouse personality of the producer meant that demands were made of the script that put Camon out of place.

"Walter and I worked on the script for a while, cutting it down a bit for budgetary reasons. I would go over to his house and we would sketch out a scene and he would ask me what I think. It was just joyful working with him. Then at some stage late in the game Joel Silver came on as a producer. With Joel came a guarantee of distribution, which gave him a big voice and big authority, which he has anyway because he is Joel Silver. So the movie got set up at Warner Bros. for distribution through the deal that Joel had, which was that he would produce a certain amount of movies that they would distribute. But Joel has his own way of doing things and he replaced me with another writer that came on and changed the script fairly extensively. I never even met Joel, he just decided 'I want my own writer!' I don't think Walter had any say in that; I think he would have kept me on but it was not a possibility.

"There were maybe six people who worked on that script—that's the way it is in Hollywood! It included myself, Walter, Wayne, Sly, all of whom are writers as well, so we all worked on the script at some point, and then they had this other guy brought in. The way it works is if you don't individually rewrite a certain quota of the script you're not going to get credit; you have to individually rewrite 40 percent of the script. All these people together rewrote more than that, but this last writer didn't meet that quota, so I ended up with some credit, which you don't argue with because having some credit means residuals, it means money. When you are in the system you have no incentive to say, 'I don't want credit on that because I don't like that scene.' The reality is that there is a lot of the movie that is not my work and that kind of hurt a little bit because the movie has some great stuff in it but it's not great, in my opinion. The writer can be very powerless. The easiest way for studios to exert control is to fire the writer and change the script. It's very hard to fire the director and it is next to impossible to fire the actor. But they think they can shape the movie any way they want by throwing in writer after writer."

As ever, Hill assembles an action film with some truly dynamic and superbly choreographed fight scenes, including a massage parlor rumble between Bobo and Ronnie Earl (Brian Van Holt) that is reminiscent of the similarly shirtless opening sauna scene in *Red Heat*, while the final fire ax showdown between Bobo and Keegan can't help but recall the climactic hammer duel between Willem Dafoe and Michael Paré in *Streets of Fire*. However, given the contemporary filmmaking techniques at hand, the fight scenes of *Bullet to the Head* are far more hyper-edited than those previous films, assembled in the immediate manner of a modern action movie montage. The kinetic camerawork can be attributed to the presence of Hill's regular cameramen: cinematographer Lloyd Ahern and 2nd unit DP Bobby LaBonge. In an era in which every other film is shot on digital technology, Ahern was relieved to learn that *Bullet to the Head* would be shot on film. "I was scared to death the whole time that I would be made to shoot it on digital, but I shot it on film. Digital photography was almost standard in Hollywood when we made *Bullet to the Head*, but I really wanted it to have a specific film look. I tested a bunch of stocks at night because I knew I was going to have to force-develop the film, so I tested it on Fuji film and Kodak film, I went around and I shot the same scene with available light at night in LA with an assistant cameraman. The whole time that I was in New Orleans preparing they kept postponing the movie as they brought in different producers and the longer this went on the more I just kept thinking 'they're going to make me shoot digital.' Ultimately, they never said a word, but up until the first day of shooting I thought I was going to have a big fight on my hands, but I didn't. Though at one stage Walter said to me that they were talking about shooting the film on a Red camera and I said, 'Well, that shows you how stupid they are, because they should shoot it on anything else.' I would never have wanted to use the Red. He said, 'I just thought you should know that they are thinking about it.' But they never said anything to me, and I got to shoot it on film."

"When I got called in to do the second unit on *Bullet to the Head*, I walked onto the set and went right over to the camera, opened up the Arriflex, and smelled the film," remembers Bobby LaBonge. "I hadn't seen a film camera in a few years, as the movie and television industry had switched to digital cameras several years earlier. You can imagine what a dark room smells like, and so when I opened up the camera that smell brought me back to my youth. I was just so happy to shoot *Bullet to the Head* on film. When you are shooting on film there is more respect for the whole process. Walter was always maintaining a super-positive approach to the process of making a movie and a lot of that quality of filmmaking has gone south since the advent of the digital world. I grew up in a world where film was expensive. When you rolled camera you were chewing up money, but now in the digital world you press a button and record it to a chip and there's never a mention of what it costs to do any of that. A lot of the protocols of making a movie have changed."

"In the old days you didn't have digital intermediates," Ahern says, "so you relied on these guys who were in the business about 40 or 50 years making prints. They were really old-fashioned lab guys and your life depended on them. Whereas now, you can shoot a fairly lousy scene and it can be saved in postproduction—they can put color into it, they bring it up or bring it down—there's so much latitude with digital now that you can really feel safe. But the problem with that is you don't really learn to be a cameraman, and I feel sorry for the new cameramen because they don't get the training that we had in film where you had to be right. You could make mistakes, but they looked like mistakes. Now you can make mistakes and the DI guy can fix it and make you look good. When you learned on film and perfected that craft, then you could really go crazy and create something brilliant, because once you learn all the rules, then you know how to break them. Training is key and the guys that I really admire the most are the guys I was shooting with on very slow film and so were working with these huge lights. They had to have grips who could cut light and really knew what they were doing. A good grip is as artistic as anybody on the set. There's an artist at work when they utilize light the way they do."

"*Bullet to the Head* was an enjoyable movie to make," LaBonge says. "I can't say enough about the collaboration between Walter and Lloyd. They know each other super well and have such a wonderful rapport that they have their own language. When the sun's going down and you are really in trouble with making the day, Lloyd would just say, 'Let's shoot the shots that are going to be in the movie,' and instead of doing five setups they would do two shots, but they are the exact shots that are important to drive the movie forward."

For film fans who came of age in the 1980s, the troika of Walter Hill, Joel Silver, and Sylvester Stallone would suggest a hot box office ticket. After several years in pop-culture wilderness following a series of bombs such as *Get Carter* (2000), *Driven* (2001), *D–Tox* (2002), and *Shade* (2003), Stallone made the good commercial decision to resurrect his two most iconic characters with the franchise entries *Rocky Balboa* (2006) and *Rambo* (2008). Further cementing his status as one of Hollywood's leading men and heralding an appetite for aging action heroes of the eighties, *The Expendables* and its sequels made the kind of money that would have been expected of a Stallone picture three decades earlier at the height of his fame. *Bullet to the Head* seemed like it was the perfect vehicle at this stage in the actor's renaissance.

"Sly is very good in it," Hill applauds. "He has got that star thing, he's got the eyes and the voice and the heart and he is a great communicator with his audience. There are actors who are very, very good but stars are something else, and Sly has that and it gets through to a mass audience. And Sly would be the first to tell you, as all of us who have been around a long time have, that he has done his share of movies that he probably shouldn't have done. I liked working with him."

"Sly is still a great movie star," Camon says. "There is something about his appeal which is undeniable. He is a man of the people. His work and his charisma are universal. I could talk for an hour about how much I disagree ideologically with the *Rambo* movies that followed the first one but there is a certain populism that he expresses that sees him embraced by the masses. When we adapted it, the producers gave it to Sly at some point and he loved and wanted to do it. It wasn't written for him, but I like Sly; it was going to be different with him, but it made sense. In my take on *Bullet to the Head*, the character that Sly plays was a young man in his

Jimmy Bobo's (Sylvester Stallone) arrest history depicts a career criminal through the decades in *Bullet to the Head* (2012).

twenties, and I don't think I specified it in the script, but I always imagined him to be black. So, it was a surprise to me when the producers told me Sly wanted to do it. My initial reaction was: 'Oh, he wants to play the cop?' and they said, 'No, he wants to play the hit man.' I said, 'Okay, well, that changes quite a lot.' But I thought it could work and it could make sense, with Sly's skill, so things went in that direction."

Despite the immeasurable screen presence of their star, it wasn't enough to convince audiences that the film merited a trip to the theater, as *Bullet to the Head* ultimately proved to be one of Stallone's weakest-performing releases of his prolific career. It didn't help that much of the criticism of the film was rooted in what some critics perceived as racially insensitive material in the depiction of Bobo and Kwon's relationship. For Camon, the negative press was particularly troubling, as his initial version of the script didn't even envision a dual-race duo. Caucasian actor Thomas Jane was initially cast to play the detective opposite Stallone, but on the insistence of Joel Silver the script was reconfigured so that the character became Korean, with the role ultimately going to Sung Kang. This meant the film took on the formula of the mismatched, mixed-race, buddy-cop film, something Camon was somewhat skeptical of. But the critics whose negativity was fueled by the film's racially charged dynamic were not aware whose version of the script was being quoted in those moments; for all they knew it was the work of Camon, whose name is ascribed the screenwriting credit.

"My script had Thomas Jane and Sly Stallone, who are both white, so there was no racial dynamic whatsoever. I didn't write the version that the critics saw, but they don't know that because my name is on the screen. I know some people say, 'Oh, I

Walter Hill directs Sylvester Stallone on the set of *Bullet to the Head* (2012) (Photofest).

don't read the reviews,' but I read the reviews and they said the movie was racially insensitive or just downright racist. Manohla Dargis said something to that effect in the *New York Times* and she name-checked me and Walter. I think Manohla is a great critic, I've been reading her since she worked for the *LA Weekly*, so when I read that review it fucking hurt! I do think the movie is somewhat insensitive in the sense that the cop character is kind of the butt of the joke on a few occasions and some of those jokes are pretty lame and borderline offensive. I think that is a legitimate case to make and I think the movie would never get made that way today, so it is a valid critique. On the other hand, Sly's character has that attitude and is meant to be a dinosaur. In the end, the Asian guy gets the girl, and the girl is Sly's daughter, so the final statement is not racist at all, but I can still understand where the criticism comes from. The main reasons that the movie is problematic is because of this objectionable racial aspect to it and because it is called *Bullet to the Head*, which is quite graphic. The film has a lot of graphic violence in it, you have this very strident title, and the film comes out right after the Sandy Hook shootings, so the entire country was in the entirely wrong mood to enjoy a movie called *Bullet to the Fucking Head*. Especially if the movie was supposed to be fun. So, people reacted against the movie, and it gave me a lot to think about the pros and cons of movie violence. So, after *Bullet to the Head* came out, I was a little depressed because I love Walter, I love Sly, and I wanted the movie to be great. It was good but it was not great. I didn't recognize enough of my own work in it. I began to think about everything that didn't sit right with me about that experience. It can be heartbreaking when you lose control, but you must make your peace with it. Even when the movies don't turn out the way you want, you still make money and that allows you to continue to pay your bills. You can always write another script. Life moves on."

Hill recognizes the film's flaws and acknowledges the elements of failure inherent, though is somewhat sanguine regarding its qualities as a no-nonsense genre piece, that which is a rare journeyman picture from the distinguished auteur. "The movie just went down without a bubble over here," Hill recalls, "but it has received genre attention overseas, and that's fine; you take your chances and it was a job of work. I thought the picture had limitations and that it was overly genre-bound, but that's why they wanted to make it. I like the fight at the end and the lead-in to that, but some of the film is a bit lumpy. You can't do action sequences that are just action, they have to be set up a certain way. The moment where he shoots Sung was a good moment with the audience because it was so unexpected. And then Stallone's comeuppance in the tag of the movie all worked very nicely."

After a return to the kind of explosive spectacle one would expect for a collaboration with Joel Silver and Sylvester Stallone on *Bullet to the Head*, Walter Hill's next film would be his most low-key film in years. Independently produced and shot in just over three weeks in Vancouver, *The Assignment* would bring in some big names for a small movie. Sigourney Weaver and Michelle Rodriguez costar in this taut thriller in which Rodriguez plays Frank Kitchen, an underworld hit man who has faced the wrath of Weaver's disgraced plastic surgeon, Dr. Rachel Jane, in an act of revenge following Kitchen's murder of Jane's brother three years earlier. "I used to be a bad guy," Kitchen laments, "a real bad guy. Then things changed." Indeed they did. Kitchen was set up for abduction by gangster Honest John Baconian (Anthony LaPaglia) on behalf of the rogue doctor, who duly proceeded to mutilate and perform gender reassignment on the assassin, forcing him to live in a woman's body. It is revealed that Jane had been performing illegal, unwanted procedures on society's forgotten and impoverished, which led to the loss of her medical license and her sanity, as she ended up being institutionalized for her crimes. In a macabre twist of fate, it is she who is the recipient of an act of body horror, as Kitchen makes sure the deranged doctor can never again perform her savage surgeries.

This twisted tale of revenge, with its grotesque morality play at its core, unfolds like it was ripped straight from the haunted panels of an EC comic book. And while William Gaines's stories contemplated controversial issues of the day, it was able to do so from within the cloak of horror, which distracted horrified parents from its difficult though topical themes. "*The Assignment* was something that could have fit into *Tales from the Crypt*," Hill concurs, "and I made it very *Tales from the Crypt*-style: it was shot in 25 days in Vancouver on a very low budget. So the *Tales from the Crypt* approach was the intention but unfortunately it was not received in that spirit."

In the hyper-woke world in which the film was released, undue attention was paid to the film's theme of unwanted gender reassignment and after a premiere at the 2016 Toronto International Film Festival, the film received a limited theatrical release that was met with a largely, though not exclusively, negative response. Many articles were published that derided the film for daring to depict a trans character going through a psychological crisis of identity, perhaps too touchy a subject for the film's pulp fiction context. "The subject matter was such that it was too much of the moment to be put into a semi-satirical perspective. It was a hot-button issue," Hill admits. "The film even supports trans theory but the assumption was, given the nature of the presentation, that it was lurid and exploitive. It is lurid, there's no question about that. About a year ago somebody sent me a story, a horror movie based in the Civil War about Confederate soldiers who were zombies and vampires. And

Dr. Rachel Jane (Sigourney Weaver) remains institutionalized for her macabre misdeeds in *The Assignment* (2016).

Frank Kitchen (Michelle Rodriguez) blasts his/her way through the familiar terrain of the criminal underworld in *The Assignment* (2016).

it got me thinking about how much time goes by before you can safely do something like this. In the Civil War many Americans had their lives, fortunes, and families damaged, even though it had a good outcome. So how much time passes before you can make some dopey fucking movie like this with a serious subject matter? I mean you have *Abraham Lincoln: Vampire Hunter*, and if there is any sacred figure in America it's Abraham Lincoln, it's just a given, but I don't remember anybody saying 'This is in poor taste!' about that film. They wouldn't even let me use the original title, *Tomboy*. It should have been called *Tomboy*."

For anyone willing to look beyond the controversy, and Michelle Rodriguez's unfortunate fake beard, they will find an efficient and darkly thrilling piece of work that plays into some of Hill's erstwhile explored themes of redemption and finding one's sense of value and identity on the fringes of society. A previous production that *The Assignment* shares thematic and tonal similarities with is *Johnny Handsome*, given its depiction of a criminal who wanders the urban underworld scarred and disfigured, with few allies to find solace among. And while *The Assignment* isn't as successfully stylish as the 1989 picture, Hill does deploy some suitably dark camerawork as well as some neat comic book graphics that support the film's lurid underworld milieu and mischievous immorality.

"When it came out it was a complete critical and commercial failure," Hill admits. "We got very few good reviews and nobody really got behind it, which I felt was too bad for the actors because Michelle, and Sigourney, and Tony, and a lot of other people did good work in it. It was treated as a hot potato, but listen, you take your chances and you can only control so much. I certainly made it under sketchy conditions, so I should not be totally surprised that it had a sketchy outcome."

At the time of concluding this book, Walter Hill is in postproduction on his next film, a western entitled *Dead for a Dollar*. The picture stars Willem Dafoe, who returns to work with Hill for the first time since *Streets of Fire* in 1984 and is joined by Christoph Waltz and Rachel Brosnahan. It is heartening to know that the master is once again working in the genre that feels like home territory, with a story of bounty hunters, gamblers, and outlaws. It is also good to know that Lloyd Ahern is directing the photography and Allan Graf is on board as second unit director. It might not be a popular thing within Auteur Theory to suggest that the presence of specific crew members is just as crucial to a work of art as the approbated artist in the director's chair, but throughout this book it has been reiterated time and again that these pictures that we call "A Walter Hill Film" are indeed the work of the many collaborating to bring to the screen the ultimate vision of a master filmmaker. Walter Hill has left an indelible mark on film culture and an incalculable influence within the history and trajectory of American Cinema.

"The truest thing about making movies is you work on them until they are finally released, but what they really are is abandoned," Hill discloses. "There's always more to do. I never see my movies after I finish them and ship them, because I can't change anything and improve them anymore, they're gone. My wife will occasionally turn on a movie of mine on the television and I always yell 'Turn it off!' because, as I say, you can't change anything. I've had a chance to make films, I'm still here, and you don't get to still be here if you don't have a number of hits; it's the price of admission to the club: you better make some hits now and then."

Seven

"It's a collaboration": A Celebration of Walter Hill

Lloyd Ahern: I had a home in Malibu which was kind of an open house. Everybody came and went and Walter would often drop by out of nowhere. He knew all my close friends but he wasn't part of our group, he was kind of an honorary member; everybody liked him and was interested in him. And then Walter fell in love with the beach, so he bought a house on Broad Beach with a check that he received from one of the big movies that he wrote, and this was in a very exclusive part of Malibu—Steven Spielberg was his next-door neighbor. We were not real close at the time, but we were always close enough to keep track of each other as Walter went on to become a director and I became a camera operator. Then one day when I was working as a camera operator on the TV show *Simon & Simon*, I was packing up for the day and getting ready to leave Universal, which is where Walter was directing *Streets of Fire*. I walked by their set on my way to the parking lot to put a bunch of stuff on the camera truck but I went back to say hello to Walter. He asked me what I was doing and I told him I was wrapping up *Simon & Simon* for the season and he said, "Do you want to work on this thing?" So he tells the assistant director that I'm going to be working on it and I was there for about three weeks, but all we did was reminisce. I would go on to work with Walter again as his cinematographer and from there we made many movies together. I'm proud to say I got to work with Walter Hill. Collaborating with him gave me some of the best experiences I've had in my career. It's always a real learning experience. There is a sense of humor to his work which is not overt but it is there and is also very representative of who he is; he's a quiet guy but he is also very witty, very funny, and that informs his work on a subtle level. Just to be around Walter Hill is an honor. I'm very grateful to have him in my life.

Alessandro Camon: Walter has the ability to distill the qualities of a genre, to find the essential stylistic and narrative components. His movies are a study of the archetypal and mythical architecture that allow genres to endure for centuries. Walter is a classicist. He likes the idea of being a classicist. He told me once that he considers all of his movies to be westerns and that if he could be making only traditional westerns then he would be happy doing that. It is a form that he is comfortable with. He goes back to the classics all the time. He would say all of his characters are Greek because they go back to the traditions of Greek tragedy. That's his original inspiration. He likes to be a professional in the mold of Robert Aldrich or Howard Hawks, these guys that made movies every chance they got and which didn't always have to be this ideal pure artistic statement; it's a profession, it's a job. I don't think Walter is fully appreciated in Hollywood in the way that someone like Clint Eastwood is, though he should be. Some great artists are discovered for their importance posthumously, and I hope that is not the case here, I hope that there will be a big discovery of Walter Hill's body of work and people will say, "Oh yeah, he was one of the giants," and I hope it happens while he is still alive. Walter is a class act, a true gentleman.

William Sadler: Walter really took me under his wing, he was my introduction to Old Hollywood. He taught this farm boy from upstate New York about all these cinematic things. Each director has their own unique qualities, and Walter has tremendous integrity and humility. There's this iron in his backbone that you can't help but admire. I don't know where that came from or how he was raised, maybe he is just emulating those great old directors that he loves, but everyone around him senses it and respects it. Walter is a man of very few words and what he says he means; some people can't work that way, some people can, but there's a sort of two-fisted honesty about what he does and there's no nonsense with him. Walter said to me one time, "I feel very lucky. I keep making movies that make just enough money to let me make another movie." I thank Walter for teaching me what he did. I owe him everything, and I don't think I could ever pay back that debt. He has a very special place in my heart. I hope he continues making movies until he's 110 years old. Don't ever stop, Walter.

Maggie Greenwald: Since becoming a director myself, I have more of a retrospective insight on what makes Walter such a special filmmaker. He prides himself on being a craftsman and he is very proud of being a commercial Hollywood director with no pretensions about his films being art; he is totally unpretentious like that, he just wants to be a good, solid filmmaker. He is a really down-to-earth working director in the Old Hollywood tradition and that was his ethic. He is a wonderful leader and has tremendous respect for the people who work for him; he trusts them and leaves them alone to do their work. He steers the ship with a sure hand. Walter is a really fine man, he is uniquely real, friendly, and engaging.

Ken Friedman: There is no director that I have visited on set or observed working who has a greater command of his cast and crew than Walter Hill. And that is not achieved by yelling or screaming—it is just the authority of someone who knows exactly what they want and has ultimate respect for all the creative and technical people around him. There are a lot of directors in Hollywood who are good at their job, but they are often producers' directors, not necessarily actors' directors; they are very skilled and can get things done, but they don't have a vision. Well, Walter is a visionary, he is one of the last directors who unabashedly has a vision. If you look at a Walter Hill film, you can tell it is a Walter Hill film.

Craig Raiche: For all concerned, as film directors go, Walter Hill is very easy to work with. He is not exceedingly serious, but he gets his point across in no uncertain terms. He is not exceedingly jocular, but he has an excellent sense of humor. One of his great virtues is his capacity for patience. Better still, Walter doesn't yell at or belittle anyone, and given the amount of pressure that any director can be put under, that's really saying something. In everyday conversation, Walter's speech is absent any manner of pretense or braggadocio. But if you happen to engage him in any topical or lengthy conversation, you quickly realize that he is not just well educated, well spoken, and knowledgeable—but impressively so. He is a gentleman, but he is also, very much, a man's man. As well, Walter genuinely welcomes creative input from his key crew members. All do bear in mind, however, that he has already made known exactly what he wants and what he expects, so one's "new suggestion" had better be pretty keen. His demeanor is consistently pleasant and quite positive. Unlike the protagonists in his films, he is not prone to anger or violence. He's just a man's man.

Larry Gross: The only pejorative term that one hears Walter Hill consistently say about people he's not fond of is for him to call them bullies. When he says someone is a bully that's a big condemnation for him and obviously it's something he's witnessed a great deal. I happen to know from my tiny experience of directing that the whole business of being a director is resisting the temptation to be a bully every minute of every day. There's a mythology in Hollywood, which is that good people scream because they care. Barry Diller once said, when talking about the quarrels and difficulties he had with Warren Beatty during the making of *Reds*, that you have to show a certain amount of viciousness in order to show you care. That is a piece of bullshit that is widely disseminated in Hollywood and a lot of people believe it. The fact of the matter is when people encounter Walter and he doesn't treat them that way they're weeping tears of joy. It's not that they demand it masochistically, it's just that the minute they're treated better than that they take to it like a duck to water. Walter just doesn't believe in being abusive. He considers it subprofessional to lose your cool and lose your voice. He considers it part of his responsibility not to do that, and the result is that crews love him and actors love him. Walter very sincerely believes in having a good time and he believes very sincerely in the idea that one is fortunate and blessed to be in a position to make a film. Walter Hill has something that's all but disappeared from American society during my lifetime—he is possessed of something called "working-class values." He comes from a working-class place and family so has a tremendous amount of respect for work and the idea of work; he walks on set respecting all the people he's working with. He wouldn't have picked them to work with him if he didn't respect them and he expects them to do their job well. It's a very self-fulfilling phenomenon: he works with people he likes, he works with people he respects, they respect him, they like him, it's all mutual. It's a matter of taste and it's a matter of knowing your own mind and knowing the kind of people you want to work with; as he said to me over and over again, talent is a huge part of it but so is knowing what kind of people they are and whether you want to be in a foxhole with them or not, whether they're going to respond to the pressure of circumstance or whether they're going to become assholes.

Van Dyke Parks: I have never met a man who followed Confucius, Lao-Tze, or any of these boys—"he who governs best governs least"—and to understand what delegate strength can reveal. I know everyone was in right formation with Walter. There was no question that they understood that he was up to something in his work and that this was a chance to gain altitude. Walter brings to his films an ability to escape the rigors of dogma and nationalism and so forth, he has the ability to accept

America as she is, warts and all. I think these films are a great way for Walter to channel his anger; there is something unhesitatingly urgent about what Walter does. There is an enduring ability and a detergent awakening in his work. That's what he does and that takes a real tensile strength because of the corporatized dumbing of America. That's what is great about the authorial director, as Walter is; he brings resonance to the term "film literature." I was very grateful to be able to meet Walter, who is, as I'm sure everybody has told you, a very terrifying man because he is capable of such trust and mutual empowerment … and now, dear Wayne, you are holding the bag!

John Fusco: Walter remains a director who has influenced and inspired me. He brings a tough American rugged individualism to all of his films and I have a great appreciation for his body of work. Walter Hill is really an iconic director and in so many ways the last of a breed. It is a privilege to talk to someone like you, Wayne, someone who is going to let the world know what a wonderful filmmaker he is.

Dan Moore: Walter is such a hero to me. After I spend time with him I always think, "God, if only I could be a man like Walter I could be somebody." It was wonderful to be part of the Walter Hill family, and that's really what it is, a family. I worked with him from *The Long Riders* right up to *Last Man Standing*, so we had a pretty good understanding of each other whenever we worked together. There is a funny joke from *Hard Times* that Walter tells on the set. They were doing the costume fitting for James Coburn and Walter tells the costumer, Jack Bear, that Coburn looks too good and Coburn says, "Yeah, you are going to have that problem with me, Walt, I always look too good!" It is even funnier because he called him "Walt," which nobody does!

Gina Gershon: Walter is a very gentle man. I was really mesmerized by him. I loved him and being around him. I remember at every lunch I just wanted to sit with Walter and talk to him rather than hanging out with the other stars, and he would be like, "Are you not hanging out with the other actors?" and I'd say "I like talking to you!" I just became so enamored with him, he felt like Papa Bear. Something about him reminded me of my father. I loved the stories he would tell me; it was like going to a masterclass. I wanted to absorb everything that he had to offer. And he was so generous with his knowledge, he really gave me so much confidence to speak my mind and to trust my own instincts, and since my time working with him I have carried his wisdom throughout my career. That was a real gift that he gave me. I was such a newbie back then, but he was so encouraging and supportive, there was no question that I could ask that was dumb. He made me feel safe.

Matthew Leonetti: Walter has a certain kind of communication with actors that some directors do not have. He would always make the actors feel very comfortable and I think that always comes across on the screen. He is very loyal, he always liked working with the same people assuming those people were available, and they always did a decent job for him. One of the things that I thought was really good about working with Walter was that he would always sit underneath the camera and watch the scene. Very few directors would ever do that. He always wanted to be where the camera was so he could get exactly the same view as the camera was getting. I thought that was pretty impressive to tell you the truth.

Bobby LaBonge: Walter has a presence on set, you know immediately he is in charge. Everyone knows he is the commander in chief, and in the world I grew up in it was important to have strong leadership because we're all worker bees and we want to do great stuff, but we really need some direction to march off to war and Walter always provided that. One of the great things about Walter is that he can do any kind of film he wants, any genre. If you look at something like *48 Hrs.*, you can see it has some really great comedic elements in it, but then you have a very serious film like *Last Man Standing*, which is something completely different, but Walter does it all with ease.

Michael D. O'Shea: Walter knows how to mix things up aesthetically and still make a good movie. It isn't repetitious, he might mix things up with the style of editing or photography from one film to the next, but it is always the Walter Hill style. Even when he is doing something different from the last movie you can still feel that it is a Walter Hill film. He is a gentleman and a decent human being, and he is one hell of a filmmaker. He is the kind of guy that if you don't see him for five years and you meet him walking down the street he will remember your name. Walter brings tremendous respect to his fellow filmmakers and that brings out their best. You are not just punching a clock, you're in it to make the best possible movie that you can.

Michael Paré: Some writers write because they're not good at talking, and that would be my assessment of Walter. His strengths as a filmmaker are in his writing and storytelling, it's on the page. They are simple stories told very specifically. Walter is kind of like the general, or the captain of a boat, and if you are not clever enough to listen to every word he says, then that's your problem. Walter's a great storyteller. He has had a long and brilliant career and he has done really important films that will never be forgotten.

Larry Gordon: Walter is very well-read, he knows a lot about the movie business, and he is very much a cinephile. The biggest thing Walter brings to a movie is his skill as a writer. That is number one. Number two: he has a great eye. And number three: he has got a lot of the old guys in him, the old masters; he is the same class as John Ford, Sam Peckinpah, Howard Hawks, and George Stevens. Walter is the last one left of that kind of filmmaker, and he was like that when he was young. He didn't have to wait until he was old to be like those guys, he was already like that going back to *Hard Times*. I knew some of those guys when I was a kid but I never got to make a movie with them, but I feel like I got to work with them by working with Walter. He is the only filmmaker that I have worked with in the 60 years of my career who is genuinely like that. Walter is timeless. As a director and a writer he is absolutely timeless. Seven movies and we never had a fight. I find it interesting that his movies aren't always like he is as a person; he is a very soft-spoken and gentle man. He is wonderful director, a brilliant writer. I love the guy. We have been friends for so many years now. He greatly deserves to be honored this way with a book on his career.

Allan Graf: I've been told that when Walter and I work together it is a cinematic marriage made in heaven, that people know they are in for a great movie experience, and I couldn't put it better myself. That is the ultimate compliment because I consider myself an extension of Walter's arm. When we worked together we never storyboarded. Nowadays directors want to storyboard every shot, but not Walter. He might make a little chicken scribbling on a napkin or something, but he never storyboarded. And that's how I feel that he put a lot of trust in me. He would just say, "Get this shot; this is what I want, but you go and get some more." That's how we worked, and it is typical of the kind of belief and assurance that he had in me to grab the stuff he wanted. I always wanted him to be excited about what I shot, because there would be nothing worse to me than Walter being disappointed, that would tear me up. But he knew that and he would always play that for fun—"You better get it the way I want it, Graf!" But it was always at the back of my mind. When I think of Walter, I think of the word "loyal." Walter Hill is loyalty personified, and I've been making movies with him for 45 years now, countless productions as an actor, a stunt coordinator, and a second unit director. How awesome is that, to be blessed with the rare and unique experience to work closely with Walter Hill, the great action director.

Neil Canton: Walter Hill is one of the great directors of our lifetime.

Interviewees and Dates

Interviews

Allan Graf, Zoom, May 27, 2021
Alesandro Camon, Zoom, June 19, 2021
Bob Gale, Zoom, March 31, 2021
Bobby LaBonge, Telephone, July 11, 2021
Craig Raiche, Email, May 30, 2021
Dan Moore, Zoom, June 2, 2021
David Mansfield, Zoom, April 26, 2021
Gina Gershon, Telephone, June 25, 2021
Herschel Weingrod, Telephone, April 7, 2021
Jack Sholder, Zoom, March 30, 2021
John Fusco, Zoom, April 30, 2021
Ken Friedman, Telephone, July 10, 2021
Larry Gordon, Zoom, May 25, 2021

Larry Gross, Zoom, June 8 & 14, 2021
Lloyd Ahern, Telephone, April 30, 2021
Maggie Greenwald, Zoom, April 26, 2021
Matthew Leonetti, Zoom, March 21, 2022
Michael Paré, Zoom, June 21, 2021
Michael D. O'Shea, Zoom, November 3, 2021
Neil Canton, Zoom, April 12, 2021
Nicholas Guest, Telephone, October 28, 2021
Van Dyke Parks, Zoom, April 22, 2021
Walter Hill, Zoom, June 3, 2021
William Sadler, Zoom, September 23, 2021
William Malone, Telephone, June 4, 2021

All interviews conducted by Wayne Byrne except those with Alesandro Camon, Ken Friedman, and Larry Gross. Those interviews were conducted by Paul Farren.

Index

Alien 55, 96, 176
Aliens 96
Allen, Woody 7, 166
Anderson, Lindsay 43
Another 48 Hrs. 59, 65, 77, 96, 119–126, 129, 131, 188
The Assignment 189, 194–196
Auteur Theory 5

Babe, Thomas 161
Barr McCutcheon, George 78, 82
Battleship Potemkin 45
Becker, Harold 111
Blue City 86–87, 138
Bonnie and Clyde 7, 8, 99
Bordello of Blood 133
Bresson, Robert 61
Brewster's Millions 67–68, 77–86, 94
Broken Trail 163, 183–188
Bullet to the Head 188–194
Bullitt 7, 13, 104

Cahiers du Cinema 5
Capra, Frank 83–84
Carey, Harry, Jr. 43
Colorado Territory 11–12
Cooder, Ry 44, 91–92, 95, 112, 129, 131–132, 157, 162, 169
Coppola, Francis Ford 178–180
Crossroads 17, 67–68, 86–95, 162–163
Cutting Cards (*Tales from the Crypt* episode) 128, 132

Dead for a Dollar 196–197
Deadline (*Tales from the Crypt* episode) 128, 132
Deadwood (book) 161
Deadwood (TV show) 167
De Vorzon, Barry 30
Dexter Pete 161

The Driver 23–30, 59, 61, 80, 108, 117
The Drowning Pool 13, 15, 16

E.C. Comics 127, 135
Eisner, Michael 61–63, 66
Extreme Prejudice 96–104, 109, 111, 138, 144, 155, 169

Fasano, John 121
Fathers and Sons (play) 161
A Fistful of Dollars 168
Ford, John 5, 28, 43
Fort Apache, The Bronx 137–138
48 Hrs. 17, 38, 59–69, 84, 105, 119–120, 126, 132, 150–151, 169, 202
French New Wave 5, 17
The Fugitive 118–119

Geronimo: An American Legend 145, 150, 162–163, 169–170, 184, 186
The Getaway 9–11, 16, 17, 49, 91, 99
Giler, David 72, 86, 128, 131, 176, 181
Godard, Jean-Luc 5, 28
Godey, John 109
The Great Northfield Minnesota Raid 42
Greenwald, Maggie 87, 199
Griffith, D.W. 28

Hailey, Oliver 12
Hammett, Dashiel 168
Hard Times 17–23, 49, 59, 112, 168, 201–202
Hawks, Howard 5, 55
Hickey & Boggs 8–10, 13, 59, 62
High Sierra 11
Huston, John 13, 136, 150

Ireland 14

Johnny Handsome 109–119, 131, 196

Katzenberg, Jeffrey 63, 66
King, Rodney 148–150
Kleiner, Harry 104
Kurosawa, Akira 28, 100, 168

LA Riots 148–150
Last Man Standing 167–175, 201–202
Lethal Weapon 9, 59, 96
The Long Riders 39–49, 59, 101, 108, 170, 201

The Mackintosh Man 13, 14
Malone, William 176
The Man Who Was Death (*Tales from the Crypt* episode) 128, 129
Manning, Michelle 86
Martin Kennedy, Troy 104
Melville, Jean-Pierre 9, 26–28
Milius, John 151

New Hollywood 7
Newman, Paul 13–15

Peckinpah, Sam 7, 10–11, 45, 48–49, 97, 99, 202
Perversions of Science 133, 135
Point Blank 8, 28

Red Harvest 168
Red Heat 104–109, 111, 117, 131–132, 190
Rio Bravo 55
Ritual 133
Rustler's Rhapsody 86

Le Samourai 27–28
The Savage Skulls (*Esquire* article) 136–137
Sholder, Jack 177–180

Southern Comfort 49–59, 108, 170
Streets of Fire 56, 59, 67–78, 80, 87, 94, 101, 108, 129, 138, 151, 169, 190, 196, 198
Stuart, Jeb 121
Supernova 176–181

Take the Money and Run 7, 8
Tales from the Crypt (TV show) 121, 127–136, 138, 195
Tales from the Crypt: Demon Knight 133

Tales of Science 133
The Thief Who Came to Dinner 12
Thompson, Jim 9
The Three Worlds of Johnny Handsome 109
The Treasure of the Sierra Madre 55, 136–137
Trespass 133, 136–150, 164, 169
Truffaut, François 5

Undisputed 181–183

Von Sternberg Josef 61

Walsh, Raoul 5, 11–12, 44
The Warriors 30–39, 56, 59, 70, 150–151
Welles, Orson 36
Wild Bill 146, 160–167, 169, 184
The Wild Bunch 7, 45, 99

Yojimbo 168
Yurick, Sol 31, 35–36

www.ingramcontent.com/pod-product-compliance
Lightning Source LLC
Chambersburg PA
CBHW060343010526
44117CB00017B/2947